PRAISE FOR FIREPROOF

"Like Anthony Bourdain's *Kitchen Confidential* meets *Sons of Anarchy*."
  —Peter Blauner, *New York Times* bestselling author

"Curtis's story is one of tragedy and triumph, the art of perfection and perfecting the art, and what it means to be one of the country's best chefs. His journey is deeply personal, yet universally resonant. Readers will discover reflections of their own lives and the drive to rise."
  —Grant Achatz, Chef/Co-owner The Alinea Group

"How Chef Duffy defeated his demons and fulfilled his muse will genuinely blow your mind."
  —Joel McIver, Bestselling Author of *Justice for All: The Truth About Metallica*

"*Fireproof* is proof that the fragility of the human experience can be fortified by determination, consistency, and finding purpose in your passion. Through Jeremy Wagner's raw and honest narrative, Chef Curtis Duffy allows us to relive his own personal tragedy and triumph not for sympathy or praise, but as a shining example of what it means to never, ever give up."
  —Frankie Nasso, Film Director and Producer

"*Fireproof* is no ordinary chef's tale, it's the story of perseverance and finding salvation in the kitchen. Besides becoming a world class chef, Curtis Duffy is an inspiration and a survivor with an important story to tell."
  —Del James, Author of *The Language of Fear* and *Consensual Violence*

"Curtis Duffy knew innately that both talent and tenacity are essential for success. His refusal to surrender and his commitment to his craft and vision has given him the accolades he so deserves."

—**Paul Stanley**, *New York Times* **bestselling author and front man and rhythm guitarist of KISS**

"'When life hands you lemons, make lemonade,' goes the old saying. But a select few grab a chef's knife, a few other carefully selected ingredients, and get to work turning acidic circumstances into Michelin Stars. Chef Curtis Duffy is one of that rare breed. *Fireproof* is the deeply human tale of a young man rising from a background of poverty and hair-raising familial violence in small town Ohio, and through applied discipline and sheer force of will, turning himself into one of the most celebrated chefs in America. Co-author Jeremy Wagner conveys Duffy's life story with a deft and insightful hand, striking a balance between preserving the chef's raw voice and artfully arranging the book's narrative like a polished multi-course meal. While there's more than enough insider stories from the kitchens of world-renowned chefs to state the appetites of the Foodie Lit crowd, *Fireproof* is more than just another 'celebrity chef' memoir—it's a mediation on the universal values of resilience, mentorship, compassion, and the purpose-driven life. Alternately heartbreaking and inspiring, this story of food, fortitude, and (ultimately) forgiveness will linger in your mind like the memory of a favorite dinner with family and friends. Outstanding!"

—**D. Randall Blythe, Frontman of Lamb of God and Bestselling author of** *Just Beyond the Light: Making Peace with the Wars Inside Our Head* **and** *Dark Days: A Memoir*

"*Fireproof* shows how the power of love for food, friends, and family provided the necessary grit to build (and rebuild) a life. Chef Curtis Duffy shares how he was able to keep his flame burning without letting it consume him, even in the direst of circumstances. *Fireproof* kept me captivated from harrowing beginning to hopeful end."

— **Regina Garza Mitchell, author of** *Shadow of the Vulture*

FIREPROOF

Memoir of a Chef

CURTIS DUFFY
with JEREMY WAGNER

DEAD SKY PUBLISHING

ALSO BY JEREMY WAGNER

Fiction

The Armageddon Chord

Rabid Heart

Wretch

Nonfiction

Fireproof: Memoir of a Chef (with Curtis Duffy)

Biography & Autobiography / Memoirs

Biography & Autobiography / Culinary

Hardcover: 9781639511358 | eBook: 9781639511365

Published by Dead Sky Publishing, LLC

Miami Beach, Florida

www.deadskypublishing.com

For Mom and Dad: I love you!
Your unwavering dedication, relentless love, and ferocious strength shaped my life in ways I will always be grateful for. You faced every challenge with grit and fortitude, showing me what it means to persevere. Your passion for family, hard work, and doing what is right continues to guide me every day. Though you are no longer here, your love remains my greatest gift, a constant presence in my heart. This memoir is dedicated to you—an expression of my gratitude, my love, and the legacy you left behind.
Until we meet again ...

And for Jennifer: my amazing, incredible, gorgeous wife—my ride-or-die soulmate/best friend; for my two beautiful daughters, Ava and Eden; and for my amazing stepchildren Van and Jolie.

The most powerful weapon on earth is the human soul on fire.

—FERDINAND FOCH (1851-1929)

CONTENTS

PRELUDE: PREHEAT, 131 DEGREES
A POT OF OLD GHOSTS, STIRRED

October 1994

"Are these your parents?"

The detective pressed his index finger down on one of the dozens of crime scene photos spread out between us and pushed it toward me.

A few days before, my father had shot my mother dead after a ten-hour standoff with police, and then turned the gun on himself.

I stared at the table, still numb from the day before, unable to focus.

"*Are these your parents?*" the detective asked again.

I stared, without wanting to, at a photograph of Mom, her blue eyes wide open and her face framed by her wild, long, blonde hair. Tattoos of roses, butterflies, and feathers dotted the landscape of her cold body.

Bloodless.

Naked.

In the next image, Dad—known to all as *Bear*—was expressionless, long hair and goatee gnarly, two earrings in one ear; a single earring in the other. He still wore the gold wedding band, never able to accept that the marriage was ending.

"*Are these your parents?*"

I forced my lips to move. "Yes …"

It had never been so difficult to utter a single syllable.

He kept presenting more photos from the spread, showing me Dad's left wrist tattooed with chain links, B-E-A-R inked across the fingers above. Elsewhere, his body boasted tattoos of a moon face, a star, a snake slithering from a faux gash, a spider, a red devil.

I began to shiver, trying and failing to tear my eyes away from the pictures. "Please stop."

There was Mom again, her chest perforated by the bullet that went on to tear through her heart, esophagus, and spinal cord.

The numbness began to constrict me and I struggled to catch my breath. "Please ... stop."

"We'll *stop* once we're convinced that you've identified your parents."

"I already—"

There was Dad, his own chest displaying a terrible symmetry to Mom's ... the self-inflicted gunshot wound had cut through his heart and lungs before exiting out his back.

"Please ..."

I had made the ID, yet the photos kept coming.

These cops, who'd hated my dad and his headstrong disrespect for authority, were taking out their aggression on me.

My family was never really religious, not the church-going type. My dad, however, seemed to have found religion somewhere toward the end of his life as he name-dropped God and the good Lord in some of the letters he wrote before he died.

A most appropriate Bible line I'd picked up somewhere popped into my head: *The son shall not BEAR the iniquity of the father.*

So here I was, nineteen years old with these detectives. Too young to adequately process any of this trauma, but old enough to recognize a mind-fuck.

I exhaled, trying to loosen the constriction in my lungs before it over-whelmed me.

More photos were laid down as if from a poker deck, as though they were trying to make sure I'd draw a losing hand. It was no longer just my parents dead faces, naked bodies, bullet holes, and tattoos. Those cops made me look at the work the coroner had done to them on the slabs, both of them splayed wide from scalpels and rib-spreaders and shit.

My stomach seized into my throat. I took a breath and looked down.

Guilt floods through me—could I have done something, *anything* to keep this from happening?

Their entire ribcages were opened and stretched apart as if their chests had exploded and burst outwards. And I had to see what they looked like on their insides? No one in this world should ever have to see their parents dissected on a slab. I would never be able to un-see these images and they knew it.

"*Are … these … your … parents?*"

"Yes."

This time the word somehow made it more … *real*.

But I am in many ways my father's son, and, although my eyes burned, I refused to break down or lose my temper in front of them.

My father had been a complicated man, with a core of strength I'd admired and tried to develop in myself. He also had a fire inside that drove him to succeed, which I recognized in myself too, but in his case, that fire had ultimately consumed and destroyed him.

Was that to be my fate as well? As I looked back at the previous twenty-four hours—shit, at the full nineteen years of my life, and whatever future stretched out ahead of me—I tried to summon up strength but all I could see were endless flames.

I didn't realize it at the time, but I was becoming *fireproof*.

Winter 2020

I love fennel.

I use it often in new dishes. The fact that you can use the entire plant in different ways—bulb, stalk, fronds, blossoms, and seeds—is part of what piques my interest and part of what gives the perennial herb its value.

"Fennel was prized by the ancient Greeks and Romans who used it as medicine, food, and insect repellent," Utah State University professors Dan Drost and Ken Adams write in *Fennel in the Garden*. "A fennel tea was believed to give courage to the warriors prior to battle. According to Greek mythology, Prometheus used a giant stalk of fennel to carry fire from Olympus to earth. Emperor Charlemagne required the cultivation of fennel on all imperial farms."

That was my kind of flavor. It had power—and I knew I'd need to tap into that to give my new restaurant, Ever, a fighting chance.

I stood in Ever's remarkable, gleaming kitchen.

When was the last time I'd had my own kitchen?

How long since I had earned a Michelin star?

Or any awards, for that matter?

Years.

Too long.

That time away made my soul hungry … and my mind both restless and nervous.

Was Chicago ready for my return?

The city had served as the stage across which some of my greatest achievements had played out, yes, but also the background for betrayal, failure and heartbreak.

I glanced down at a bowl filled with a mélange of premium Ossetra caviar, king crab, cucumber, and citrus lace. Next to the bowl was a small plate showcasing a green quenelle of seven-herb butter with *fleur de sel*, resting beneath a narrow strip of white butter refined with black cypress salt.

These creations were a small part of the planned Ever Experience, a $285 per person, eight-to-ten-course tasting menu featuring seafood (Hamachi frozen with liquid nitrogen, scallops, king crab), meats (Wagyu beef with sunchoke, orange, and tatsoi; squab with guajillo, raspberry, and sorrel; lamb; rabbit), and four courses that emphasized seasonal vegetables, fruits, and grains—*all* of which would change when the seasons changed.

I felt my own season changing—and the vibe was more spring than winter.

I regarded my creations, the ingredients in their stages of transition.

I planned to weave in plenty of truffles. And fennel, of course.

~

July 2020

Ever was supposed to open months ago.

In mid-March, however, the global COVID-19 pandemic bore down, and our opening was stalled before we even had a chance to get going.

The restaurant closures devastated Chicago's dining scene; many long-thriving spots would never recover. But once the city began a cautious lifting of the indoor-dining ban—albeit with restrictions—and after endless months of rehearsing, preparing, strategizing, and promoting, Ever had finally opened. And we were booked solid for the next six weeks.

At the end of that first night, I stood alone in Ever's kitchen, hours after service ended, and indulged in a late-night treat: chartreuse sorbet over compressed pineapple, topped with bits of black licorice and a dash of raspberry powder.

I was tired, yes. But exhaustion on the verge of success just hits differently than exhaustion teetering around the edges of tragedy. And my gratitude extended far beyond the reservation bookings.

Over the past few years, I had focused on becoming a better version of myself, and I was regaining my confidence in my skills and abilities. I had married the love of my life. I had four beautiful children who owned my heart—and as we'd all grown closer, they'd helped me heal. My family had become my wings.

It hadn't been a journey without bumps and twists, though. What road ever is? But even in the most stressful moments, I had begun learning to search for and discover purpose and joy.

As I tasted my sorbet at the end of that first night and savored the alchemy of exquisite flavors, I cycled through the crises I'd endured. I made a conscious decision to maintain my focus on gratitude: each time my world had burned down to ashes, I'd been singed but not consumed.

It hadn't really been a case of *Out of the frying pan and into the fire.*

More like, *Out of the frying pan and into the abyss.*

The good news for me in those situations?

I often do my best work out on the edge.

PART ONE

Portrait of a Child as Kindling

ONE
RAISED BY WOLVES

I arrived in this world on Wednesday, July 2, 1975. Captain & Tennille's "Love Will Keep Us Together" topped the charts. A few months earlier, the last helicopter had lifted off from the U.S. embassy in Saigon, marking the end of the Vietnam War, but in Newark, Ohio, battles raged on throughout the Duffy household.

Steeped in endemic poverty and locked down in a volatile marriage with two kids, my nineteen-year-old father, Robert Duffy—more commonly known as Bear; nicknamed as such by his fellow motorcycle club initiates in honor of his six-foot, muscle-bound frame and long brown hair and beard—fought a constant war against the world.

And because the world didn't give a fuck about him, Bear's hostilities and bitterness hardened into a constant fury, which he channeled toward his wife and family.

Like many angry and frustrated young men, Bear believed he might be able to outrun the darkness. So, shortly after I was born, he got it into his head to move our family to Colorado, where his mother lived, and to join the Army. Tired of living month-to-month and wondering how he would afford our $100 a month rent and forty-four-cent-per-gallon gas, the stability of military service and a government paycheck were attractive—especially because the Vietnam War and active combat were no longer a concern.

My dad's idea quickly grew into an out-of-character ray of *hope*.

Was there a catch?

You bet your ass there was.

Bear wasn't sure whether my brother's and my biological mother, a local girl named Sue, would follow him.

Things hadn't been good between my parents for a while. They were just teenagers playing house, after all. They'd had no idea that taking on adult responsibilities would threaten every day to break them, and having children didn't bring them the kind of joy, love, and gratification with which I would one day be blessed. For them, it just intensified their resentments and conflicts.

How long Bear and Sue would've ultimately lasted in Colorado remains an open question, however.

Sue, whether consciously or otherwise, helped him make that decision for all of us.

WHEN BEAR CAME HOME one day in 1975, the muffled cries he heard didn't initially cause him much concern. After all, I was an infant and Robert Jr., was only a year-and-a-half old. Sue—who spent a lot of time in tears herself, what with Bear's constant anger issues and physical abuse —was lackadaisical about practical matters such as feeding and changing diapers, further priming the wailing chorus.

My dad, however, saw his sons were asleep in their room.

You probably see where this is going.

And maybe Bear did, too, as he pushed open the bedroom door.

Years later, he confessed to my brother and me that, in his fury, he ripped this man he'd never seen before off of Sue and then annihilated him—breaking his jaw, dislodging his teeth, attacking him with repeated blows until he crumpled, motionless, to the floor. Then he turned to Sue.

"You cheating cunt!" Bear raged, as Sue bawled hysterically, wrapping the bedding closer to her body as if a piece of fabric could somehow magically ward off my dad. "I'm leaving! And I'm taking Robert!"

"What about Curtis?"

"Too young," he snapped. "He needs his mom right now … even if she is a *fucking cheating bitch!*"

Desperate to defuse the situation, Sue reached for Bear. He back-handed her straight off the bed.

Sue tumbled across the floor, sobbing and shrinking back from Bear as he spat in her direction. He stomped into the boys' bedroom to snatch up his firstborn son, and Sue took that moment to shift her attention to her unconscious lover, who was in no shape to help her. Bear marched back into the bedroom to gather his meager belongings and then headed out the door, determined to put as much space between himself and his unfaithful, lawfully wedded … *bitch!* as possible.

I was left behind while Bear hurtled down the highway with blood on his hands.

It didn't take long for Sue to throw in the towel.

Without Bear's paycheck, paltry as it had been, she was forced to move out of the apartment we'd all shared, and she couldn't pay for diapers, baby food, or even food for herself.

Distressed and frantic, she went looking for Bear's whereabouts. In January 1976, she tracked down the address where he was living with Robert Jr. and a rumored new love interest.

Maybe she was hungry and exhausted and terrified and had run out of options.

Maybe it infuriated her that, despite it all, she'd been replaced so quickly.

Maybe she just wanted to cut off her last remaining tie to Bear.

Whatever the reason, Sue somehow managed to borrow some wheels. She planted me in the front seat—no way she could afford gas *and* a baby seat—and traced Bear's trail to Colorado.

I was all of six months old when Sue showed up on the doorstep of the home Bear shared with Jan Marlene Terpstra, a beautiful, fifteen-year-old high-schooler with straight, blonde hair and a sweet smile.

Sue didn't waste any time getting to the point when Jan answered the door.

"You want my man?" Sue said, shoving me—wearing, according to Jan's sister Judy, a days-old, dirty diaper and nothing else—into Jan's arms. "You can have both my children, too!"

And then she was gone, leaving Jan sitting on a couch in her parents house, with a bawling infant in her arms and Robert Jr. crawling around in a diaper at her feet, surely confused about how all this insanity had befallen her.

Think about it: Some older guy from Ohio lands on her doorstep, first with one kid, and then, his wife—*he's still married?!*—shows up and dumps another kid.

Meanwhile, all Jan's high school friends were going on dates and driving around without a care in the world while she was trapped at home with a surly older man and two needy babies that weren't even her own.

Still, love was blossoming. Jan wasn't surprised Bear was so cuckoo for her. Most guys in the area were attracted to her. Bear wasn't like other guys, though. He'd pursued Jan as if he had something to prove.

And Jan's parents actually liked Bear. They'd allowed him to move in with them and their daughter, after all, and her father said he'd give Bear steady work at his tire retreading shop when he'd finished his Army stint at the huge military base nearby.

Jan was developing feelings for the two of us kids as well.

She would appraise us. "You boys could be mine, huh?"

We, of course, assumed we *were* hers.

Blood is not always thicker than water. To this very day, I call my biological mother *Sue* and I refer to Jan as *Mom*.

I also refer to my dad as *Bear* often—a name I never dared call him by when he was alive, but I cite his nickname with much love and reverence. *Bear* sums him up, but also, *Bear* is as meaningful and respectful to me as saying *"Dad"*—if not more so when I refer to my father.

Unfortunately for Jan, her reward for this devotion to Bear and his boys would eventually become a nightmare.

TWO
DON'T SLAP THE FACE—THE LORD HAS PROVIDED A BETTER PLACE

B ear and Jan soon had a daughter—my sister, Trisha Ann.

Their own child cemented the connection between them with blood.

I was around five or six when I learned the truth about my own blood.

Bear and Jan sat Robert Jr. and me down in the living room and Bear, displaying his trademark tact and subtlety, told us point-blank that Jan wasn't our actual mom—that he'd caught some guy fucking our biological mother and had beaten the guy within an inch of his life.

Overwhelmed with shock and distress, my brother and I burst into tears. Jan quickly jumped in to revise that lurid framing.

She was our mom, she assured us—Dad, Robert Jr., and I had adopted *her*. She promised us that our family dynamic would never change.

It took a while for us to stop crying but relief began to converge with the panic and confusion. Sure, Bear was our father, but Jan and her family were the balance to his instability. Grandpa Terpstra was a hardworking, self-made, blue-collar guy who kept his promise to hire Bear after he got out of the Army.

I loved Grandpa's tire retreading shop. It was a safe harbor for me, one of the few places where a clear change in Bear's attitude would emerge.

I loved it so much I'd feign illness just to go there rather than school—which for me, at that time, was the worst place in the world.

"You're not fucking sick, Curtis," Bear would say. "And don't worry; I have plenty of menial shit to keep your scrawny ass busy for the next ten hours."

Those tasks felt less like punishments and more like bonding rituals, and that shop is where I learned, from watching Bear, what it means to be a self-starter, to develop a strong work ethic, and to take pride in managing your own business.

But none of this meant that Bear was going soft. He possessed zero tolerance for any bullshit Robert Jr. or I would think up. Jan wasn't much more forgiving: ass whippings were doled out for the slightest infraction. For all their disagreements, Bear and Jan found common ground in their partiality to a wooden-handled, ten-inch leather strap embossed with the words:

"DON'T SLAP THE FACE ... THE LORD HAS PROVIDED A BETTER PLACE."

Of all the things to choose to bolster parental harmony, it was the strap that brought them together—even if they never fully gave up on fists, open-hand slaps, shoes, belts, shit from a toolbox, or simply whatever was close at hand as blow-delivering devices.

Different times ...

At the Colorado house, Robert Jr. and I shared a bedroom on the second floor, and that fucking strap hung on display at the bottom of the stairs, positioned there as an ongoing deterrent.

Practically speaking, however, it didn't matter how well behaved we were—proper thrashings were dispensed daily. I'm surprised my ass wasn't permanently stamped with that strap's catch phrase.

Even so, these early Colorado days—surrounded by grade school friends and Jan's family, who treated us as something akin to true blood—would prove to be the happiest times of my childhood.

BEAR WAS RUMORED to have been a member of the Hell's Angels in Colorado.

As a kid, I'd hoped it was true. The Hell's Angels, after all, were the ultimate bikers, the kings of the outlaws. It seemed right and proper that Bear—a true fucking outlaw, to give credit where credit is due—would matriculate with the *créme de la créme* of the worst of the worst—*le plus mauvais*, motherfucker.

Later it became clear Bear wasn't actually a Hell's Angel. For one thing, he didn't wear the required regalia. But there *were* always bikers at the house. It was common for me to be on the back of some dude's Harley. I fell head over heels for that lifestyle.

Bear encouraged this love for two-cycle engines and speed. He'd gotten Robert Jr. and me dirt bikes and he'd take us to an ATV property in the desert that offered endless trails and a dirt track where motocross riders could race, do jumps, and tear things up. The three of us would pull up in a pickup truck, unload the bikes, and wild out all day.

One afternoon, however, Bear flew over a jump just as another motocross rider hit the same jump from the opposite side, going the wrong way, and they collided in midair. Bear crashed into a broken and bleeding heap on the hardpan. Back fractured, he was unable to get up. Robert Jr. and I flagged down a couple of nearby riders to load the dirt bikes into the pickup. They got Bear into the front seat and Robert Jr.— still a child—drove us all to a nearby hospital.

Bear's convalescence took a year, and that marked the end of the Duffy boys' dirt bike riding club.

Another nail in the coffin where good times went to die came soon after my dad healed: Grandpa Terpstra decided to sell the tire retreading business. And Bear, never one to miss an opportunity to take something personally, felt as if he'd been stabbed in the back after years of running Grandpa's business almost single-handedly ...pouring his blood, sweat, and tears into it.

He exploded. "All right, it's over," he shouted at all of us, shortly after hearing the news, cursing his father-in-law and the entire town. "We're moving the fuck on!"

That night, our Duffy clan packed up and set out for central Ohio, back to where most of my dad's family lived—his father, Grandpa

Temple; his cruel, head case, cop brother, Bill; his rarely seen brother, Randy; and his piece-of-work sister, Penny.

A dark age was dawning for the Duffy family. I would soon learn how deep some of our roots stretched into rotted soil.

Bad news again? Abso-fucking-lutely.

THREE
SKELETONS (AND ME) IN THE CLOSET

R obert Jr. did *not* want to go to Ohio.

I remember how he threw an epic fit and begged our parents to let him stay in Colorado with our paternal grandmother Duffy, with whom he was very close. Our parents finally acquiesced.

We had lived fairly well back in Colorado. We'd had a decent, five-bedroom house with plenty of room and a backyard. We didn't worry about food or clothes. I'd had a nice bedroom. My dad had owned a drag car, motorcycles, and assorted other grown-up toys, and had room to store them.

We had a bit of that currency of modern American life—*stuff*.

The Duffy's packed up what things we could fit into our vehicle with my dad's drag car in tow. The day our clan landed in Johnstown, Ohio, my dad gave the locals a Bear-styled Welcome Wagon as he brutally beat the fuck out of a guy who got cocky and too close to his drag car as it sat on a trailer outside an apartment building.

It was that same first day in Johnstown that I learned the apartment building we'd pulled up to was our new home. We downgraded from a house straight into a minuscule two-bedroom apartment.

Culture shock would be an understatement.

It was two kids and two adults at first. Two years later, when our grandmother passed away, Robert Jr. moved back in with us, and the population of that tiny apartment swelled to five. Our grandmother's death was incredibly difficult for Robert Jr.—as was the move back to our family. He had never gotten along with Jan. They fought nonstop.

Under this new arrangement, Robert Jr. shared the second bedroom with Trisha, and I ended up moving to the only remaining, unoccupied space in the house: my parents bedroom closet. I didn't have a mattress, but the spare, cramped quarters were nothing compared to the vicious, circular arguments, the blaring TV, the passed-out snoring, the explosive, cacophonous fights, and the threatening demands for silence. I dwelled on the other side of the closet door from that perdition every night *for years*.

But I discovered I could customize my own microscopic universe, taking advantage of the way the ceiling rose at an angle, plastering it with posters of KISS and other rock and metal bands above my parents hanging clothes.

Maybe in a less chaotic family I would've resented my older brother and younger sister for their separate room and bunk beds.

Maybe being forgotten and ignored is a nightmare for kids that grow up in pleasant, affluent suburbs, relying on stable parents.

For me?

To be pushed aside was a dream come true. Being out of sight, out of mind kept me clear of beatings from my parents and my pain-in-the-ass brother.

The closet sucked, but it was often also my salvation.

THE ATMOSPHERE in the Duffy apartment became more erratic whenever Robert Jr. entered the mix. As time went on, he fought more and more with Jan, which added gasoline to the continuously stoked fires of Bear's rage. Robert Jr. wasn't enamored of Trisha or me, either. He got into it often with us, too.

By the age of fourteen, Robert Jr. was living on the streets, sometimes crashing with friends, girlfriends, whomever. Our parents just couldn't corral him. As a student, he was always getting suspended for fighting until he finally bailed on the whole high school trip. He just left one day, got a job somewhere, and never returned home.

My brother's permanent departure meant I got my own bedroom space back, sharing it with my sister as Robert Jr. had done. I had the top bunk and I remember lying on that mattress and telling myself that there was no way I was going to live like this for long. I vowed that the moment I reached the legal age to get a real job, I would work my ass off and save enough cash to escape this disaster of a family situation and the black hole of Johnstown.

Money was the root cause of so much misery at home that, even as a kid, the importance of earning it always loomed large in my mind. One time I asked my parents why they couldn't just write a check for the things we needed. They answered with a strap across my ass and a reply that I never forgot: "What the fuck do you think we're gonna write it against?"

The whippings continued, of course. And Robert Jr. got the usual clobbering whenever he popped in. Trisha never really got beatings, though—at least, not physically. Instead, Bear would use words as weapons.

You wench …

You heifer …

You fucking little pig …

The grass, we were learning, was not greener in Ohio.

FOUR
YOU CAN'T TALK TO A MAN
WITH A SHOTGUN IN HIS HAND

My father's bloodline is an artery clogged with fury and darkness.

Before the "Duffy" family name, there was an original family surname, "Temple." My father's father was named, William Temple. According to paternal family lore, my Grandpa Temple was a twisted psychopath who never spared the rod when it came to his wife or children.

In my experience, the apples didn't fall far from Grandpa's tree.

When Grandpa Temple's battered wife divorced him, she fled to Colorado with their kids—my dad being one of those apples. She soon remarried and took her new husband's last name for herself and her kids: *Duffy*.

But the Temple darkness wasn't going to let a minor rebranding shake its power or legacy. Child abuse and heavy-handed domestic violence would continue to run through the family.

Robert Jr., later nicknamed *Tig*—short for Tiger—grew into a muscled teenage delinquent. Like our father, Tig lived to brawl anyone in his path —especially me.

The sibling rivalry between us was as endless as it was aggressive.

In Colorado, Tig sucker punched me in the face one day. In tears and consumed by a blind rage, I hurled a heavy clawhammer at my brother, missing his head by inches.

"You two little bastards!" Bear lifted us off the ground by our hair. "You wanna fucking fight? Put on boxing gloves!"

From then on, we'd don those knuckle pads and beat the crap out of each other at the drop of a hat. Bear got a kick out of watching his two small boys awkwardly throwing punches and curse words in our grade-school voices. My dad had legit boxing skills, not just street-fighting skills. He had been an undefeated Golden Gloves boxer during his very short time in the Army—and he relished his time in and outside the ring, beating other men silly.

Dad's intense approach to child-rearing wasn't limited to exhibition matches, alas, and it continued after we arrived in Ohio.

One day he drove me out of town and into the woods beyond to shoot guns. I was thrilled until he thrust a 12-gauge into my hands rather than the usual .22 rifle.

I was terrified of firing a larger firearm. I could barely carry it, never mind handle the kick.

"Now, shoot."

"I don't want to, Dad. I'm scared."

"Shoot, Curt."

"I'll get hurt."

"Shoot, goddamn it!"

"No! Please, Dad!"

Shaking, I began to cry.

At first my father's silence was a relief … and then I turned around.

My father stood shouldering his own shotgun. He had chambered a round of buckshot, stepped forward, and pushed the barrel of his 12-gauge into my forehead.

I shit you not.

"You're going to shoot that fucking shotgun like a man *right now*. Or I swear to God, I *will* kill you!"

I spun away from my dad's gun, my bladder let go, warm piss running down my leg as I closed my eyes and pulled the trigger.

As anticipated, the recoil knocked me on my back.

Bear lowered his shotgun with an expression that rested somewhere between disgust and disappointment.

It was as if father and son went out in those woods hunting pride and empathy and love—and fumbled all three.

Remember that TV show about the outlaw motorcycle club, *Sons of Anarchy?* Bear would've easily eaten all of those wannabe biker sons for breakfast. And maybe Bear would've eaten his own sons, too—just like the Greek god, Cronus, who devoured his own children to prevent some fucked-up prophecy.

Me, I was simply happy to be alive.

FIVE
LIFE AMONG THE BERSERKERS

O ne day at home, a biker acquaintance came into our house uninvited, broke out a gram-sized rock of cocaine and started chopping up rails of powder on the Duffy kitchen counter.
Big mistake.

"Hey! What the fuck you doing in here?" Bear roared. "Don't even think of doing that shit in my house!"

Bear had joined a new biker club after he moved our family back to Ohio. Despite his brutal motocross accident, he still loved motorcycles, particularly Harley Davidsons, and he was always riding, trading, selling, or building them. His gang had a clubhouse somewhere, but I never saw it. Members only—no kids or wives allowed. My parents hosted biker rallies on their property as well, which was how this cocaine cowboy had stumbled into my dad's line of sight.

Now, raising hell was fine on our property, even *encouraged* at these gutter soirees—but only tolerated *outside*. When it came to drugs or alcohol, Bear enjoyed a drink or a joint. In fact, I probably got contact highs as a kid from all the secondhand marijuana smoke and, though I don't partake, the smell of pot brings back childhood memories to this day. That, however, was where the elder Duffy drew the line.

Unfortunately for the pencil-thin piece of scooter trash in the kitchen, someone had failed to post the rules at the entrance to Duffy Manor and now, having ignored his one courtesy warning, he found himself with Bear's massive hand wrapped around his throat and his feet dangling in the air. My father carried the dude to our porch and tossed him into the air. The landing was hard … but not as hard as it could've been.

"You're lucky that's all you got, motherfucker," Bear pointed out as the biker got up and limped away.

My dad walked back into our house. "Jan! Goddammit, where are you?!"

Bear was on a tear—beating the dogshit out of surly acquaintances was a hobby he indulged in regularly that always fueled his ire but when Mom appeared in front of him, visibly angry, with one hand on her hip and a nickel-plated .44 magnum revolver dangling from the other, it gave him pause.

"I found the boys in our bedroom playing with the fucking thing." Jan waved the gun at my dad, her voice charged with rage. "They were pointing it at each other. I beat their asses and I should beat yours, too, for leaving it lying around."

Bear took the revolver from Jan and looked it over. He had every type of rifle, shotgun, and handgun you can imagine stuffed under his bed, in closets, in cupboards, in the garage, under the bathroom sink, everywhere. But he knew his inventory intimately and this revolver wasn't on the list.

He thought that one of the drunk bastards outside must've dropped it somewhere; they'd arrived the day before and had been target shooting ever since. Jan had been livid about that, too. She hadn't slept much the previous night thanks to the raucous crowd outside our windows who'd whooped it up with their shooting and fighting, blasting music and loudly banging their chicks throughout the night.

The Duffy clan always was generous when it came to providing our neighbors reasons to hate us.

Bear tucked the revolver into the back of his jeans. "Where are the boys?"

"They're in their rooms, sulking after I whooped them."

"Send 'em in here."

"Get 'em yourself. I'm leaving."

Bear grabbed Jan with a large, paw-like hand.

"What the fuck do you mean you're leaving?"

Jan glared at him and tried to shake his hand off her arm.

"I *mean* that I'm leaving for the damn store, okay? I'm picking up groceries and some smokes. I need to get away from this madhouse for a while."

Bear pushed her away. "Good. There's nothing to eat here."

He watched Jan grab her purse and keys on the way out the door then turned his attention to Robert Jr. and me. "Tig! Curt! Get your asses in here, *now!*"

We came out of hiding. Bear looked down at our faces, which were no doubt pale and fearful. We dreaded his wrath.

Bear held the handgun before our faces.

"Mom says you guys were playing with a damn gun. True?"

We nodded, penitent gazes turned to the floor.

"I taught you both to always respect guns, didn't I? They're not toys."

We nodded again.

"Guess it's my turn to pick up where Mom left off."

With that, Bear took turns grabbing Robert Jr. and me by our hair, nailing our asses with hard wallops, ignoring all our sobs and apologies. After a few agonizing minutes, he was done.

"Go outside and get outta my goddamn sight."

My brother and I ran out into the backyard and mingled amongst the motley crew. A couple of asshats fired guns in the air while a drunken biker smashed another man's face into the engine block of a Harley Sportster.

A few of the bikers' old ladies flashed their tits at us.

Others were using the driveway as a makeshift latrine.

This was our playground.

Bear never looked for us after he set us loose. When Jan came home, she found Robert Jr. and me hanging with the bikers, grabbed us by our ears, and marched us inside, where we were confined to the dinner table the rest of the night.

As we ate, someone outside fired a shotgun at the stars.

The blast was met with drunken cheers, but my overdeveloped nerves were rattled.

MOST WEEKENDS, Robert Jr. and I would travel with Bear to any race track within a hundred-mile radius that would have him so he could drag race. We took in the rowdy crowds, fights, loud engines, and the smell of fuel as if it represented the highest peak of human joy and evolution.

When I was sixteen, my dad approached me. "I know you love my drag car. Would you like to take it to prom?"

Bear was talking about his blue Oldsmobile 442. Just a beautiful, stunning car. And that bitch was *fast*.

I couldn't believe it. "Are you kidding? Hell, yeah!"

"Okay, I'll put street tires on. I'll put the headers back on so it's street legal and you can take it."

"*No way!*" my girlfriend shrieked. Like me, she also couldn't believe it.

It was such a … *nice* gesture and, as you may have gathered, thoughtfulness wasn't exactly Bear's forte.

However, a couple of weeks before prom, Bear traded his drag car for a motorcycle frame and I was out of a dream ride.

Don't count your fucking chickens …

"Dad! How can you trade a car for a … a … fucking *frame?*"

It's a testament to how upset I was that I dared question Bear so aggressively.

"Someday you'll understand."

There are not many instances of Bear in the *Father Knows Best* role, but here, he was actually right. That frame was for a 1942 Knucklehead—a rare and extraordinary skeleton he eventually built into a gorgeous custom ride.

Back then, though, all I cared about was showing off that car at prom and impressing my girlfriend.

Now, I get it … I get that young love is fleeting.

And that love for a 1942 Knucklehead is forever.

I wish I had that bike today.

BEAR TOOK his biker lifestyle very seriously and took great pains to indoctrinate me into that ideology.

He consistently lectured me about One Percenters ... about colors and brotherhood ... about what it means to be part of a motorcycle club.

To my dad, it was a mystical catechism.

Still, I never felt the desire to join a club.

Maybe if Bear were still alive, it might be different—especially now that I have my own Harley and some other bikes. Not that I'd join a gang, but my dad and I could bond over motorcycles and ride together now ... we could build a bike together or something, y'know?

I wish he were here to do that.

I really do ...

I still have Bear's leather jacket, which was given to me after he died. I don't have the *colors*—the patches which were sewn onto it—because one of the specific wishes my dad wrote in his suicide notes was for our family to make sure specific things went with him.

Bear took his badass religion to the grave.

TATTOOING WAS another of Bear's obsessions. One of the Duffy bedrooms in Colorado was a dedicated tattoo parlor. Bear did tattoos nearly every night—on others and even on himself.

When I was a kid, I'd roll into my dad's tattoo room in the evenings to watch him work and listen to the banter. I would always overstay my welcome, of course, running in and out, asking a million kid questions while he worked—shit that got under Bear's skin like so much ink.

Jan knew how desperately I wanted a tattoo back then, but she was adamant that I reach at least the age of fifteen before I got one.

I couldn't wait for that day to come. Years later in Ohio, fourteen was barely in the rearview mirror and I was chasing down Bear.

"Let's go, Dad! Tattoo time!"

When Bear finished a tattoo, he'd clean it and put Neosporin on it, and whether you were a biker dude, a woman, or a young punk like me, he would smack your new tattoo as hard as he could—on purpose—because he wanted to make it *really* hurt.

That was Bear Duffy for you.

I treasure the fact that my dad gave me my first tattoo. If I close my eyes, I can still feel the slap. And I treasure that, too.

Over the years, he gave me a few more tats. One remains bright and sharp on my shoulder to this day: *Love, Dad.*

After Bear died, I got my hands on his tattoo equipment and, despite not really knowing what I was doing, I gave friends permanent skin etchings. We were in college and back then, leaning into questionable decisions was the rule, not the exception—including the eventual choice I made to give Dad's tattoo gear to Robert Jr.

Thankfully, I still have reams of Bear's tattoo sketches and books, which keep me connected to his calmer, artistic side. In one self-portrait, Bear rises out of a genie bottle fully bearded, powerful, eternal.

I've got that framed and preserved under glass.

Music was a big deal for Bear, too; and for me, it was another connection to his creative side. His nickname in high school was "Ringo" and, truth in advertising, he was an awesome drummer. I remember him rocking the fuck out of his drums when he played Iron Butterfly's "In-A-Gadda-Da-Vida." It blew me away every time.

"Don't go near my drum set," Bear must've said to Robert Jr. and me a thousand times. "I'll break your fucking hands. Understand me? Don't touch it. Don't even look at it!"

Naturally, we banged the shit out of that drum set when Bear wasn't there. The temptation was too great. In fairness to my brother and me, though, my dad had trained us kids in the ways of the outlaw. Sometimes that comes home to roost.

Still, Bear was always one step ahead of us. He always had his drumsticks set down in a certain position on the snare to catch us, like a spy hanging a piece of thread over a door.

Spoiler alert: Bear *always* found out—and when he did it was assbeating time all over again.

∾

"Your dad's just a soft teddy bear inside."

Jan would say this as if it gave Bear a pass for his all-grizzly, all-the-time exterior.

Bear was so rough around the edges that getting a hug or kiss good-night from him just wasn't going to happen. My dad didn't show affection—and he didn't want it from anyone else, either. If you tried to make that connection with him—to feel any normal parental-offspring warmth —it became awkward for everyone involved.

Eventually, I just gave up trying to *give*.

And when you abstain from being warm and affectionate with someone you love, a small piece of you deep inside withers away.

SIX
THEY'RE COMING TO TAKE HIM AWAY, HA-HA

M y daily after-school ritual was to get in and out of my house as fast as possible, ditch my school books, and leave the family abode in a cloud of skateboard dust.

What was I supposed to stick around for?

The beatings?

The empty fridge?

My parents wild fights?

The hazing, courtesy of Robert Jr., who had abandoned a friend's couch to return and exile me back to the closet?

Even Trisha seemed to have internalized the lesson that everyone's job in the household was to make my life miserable.

Three quarrelsome kids and two volatile parents all up in each other's grills inside a super-tiny, two-bedroom apartment would drive anyone insane, I figure. But as I got older and my hormones revved up, the lack of privacy—the absolute impossibility of ever bringing a girl back to our apartment—was completely uncool and made a terrible situation worse for me.

Things were, however, about to change.

∽

25

ONE DAY, sometime around my eighth grade year of school, I opened the door to our apartment in Johnstown and overheard a summit in progress: Dad, Jan, and Trisha were all in the living room, talking. Tig wasn't there.

"Curt." Bear motioned for me to sit down. "'Bout time you got your ass home. We got some news you kids need to hear." This was bad, I instantly knew. My parents never came home early from work for anything. "It's about Grandpa Temple."

Like what? I thought.

Was Grandpa Temple headed back to prison? Between his convictions for money laundering and tax evasion, it sometimes seemed like that prison was his second home. His most recent stunt then was when he'd gone and lost his mind, pulling a gun on his girlfriend and holding her hostage in his house in St. Louisville, Ohio.

Grandpa Temple had eventually let his girl go … but taking a hostage and the impasse he created with the cops surrounding his house got him charged with kidnapping and attempted murder.

Years later, I'd see this *same scenario* play out firsthand in the *same house* like some fucked up Duffy version of *Groundhog Day* times ten— and with a much, much different ending.

"The judge finally made his call today." Bear frowned and shook his head. "Grandpa got the maximum prison sentence. He's going away forever … and things are about to change for us all."

"Kids," Jan interjected, "we're all going to move into your grandpa's house. There was a huge fight with Aunt Penny and Aunt Nell over it, but your dad convinced your grandpa that we should take over his place and keep the mortgage paid while he's in prison."

Bear looked agitated. "I'll tell you this, I'll kill myself before I ever go to fuckin' prison."

Jan paused and gave Bear a *look* before returning to stay on topic with Trisha and me, trying to lighten the mood with us kids. "This means we'll all have a house again. Great, right? You'll all be switching schools, too."

I was in shock.

Another new fucking school?

Then again, St. Louisville couldn't be worse than Johnstown, right?

And … no more sleeping in a closet! Maybe my parents would chill out in a less cramped environment.

Hope springs eternal.

~

"IF YOU CAN GET A RIDING MOWER to run," Bear told me, "you can have it."

I was twelve years old at the time, back in Johnstown, and I was making money selling cinnamon-flavored toothpicks. I'd buy cinnamon oil for two bucks at the drugstore, a pack of a thousand toothpicks for another two bucks, put it all in a container with all the toothpicks and shake it up. The next day I'd sell the toothpicks for ten cents apiece. Kids would buy them like crazy.

That's how I—future restaurateur, chef Curtis Duffy—was able to buy lunch for myself at school every day.

When you're raised by wolves—when you never have lunch money; when you never go shopping for even school-mandated supplies—the hustler spirit becomes such a fundamental part of your worldview it might as well be encoded into your DNA.

Point is, though the cinnamon-flavored toothpick biz had been very good to me, by my thirteenth birthday, grass cutting had the potential to be *even better*.

I had put together a riding lawnmower from assorted mower corpses and cast off parts my dad had lying around at a small-engine shop he worked at. My new business was called "Morrison Lawn Service," because I was in love with Jim Morrison of the Doors. I couldn't afford business cards, so I went with homemade advertising signs.

I started making money right away, but I soon found myself up against a huge obstacle: the rogue cop of Johnstown, Ohio, a.k.a. my uncle, Bill Duffy. He'd pull up behind my mower as I traveled between jobs, hit the cherries and the sirens, and this mountain of a tough-guy would then roar and berate me on the side of the road. He gave zero fucks that I was his little nephew. He'd threaten to write me up for some bullshit infraction like "driving a lawnmower across a paved road," or not having a "slow-moving vehicle" sign on my ride.

"If I see you on the road with that lawnmower again," he'd say, "I'll beat you stupid and fucking impound this thing!"

27

Nice guy, right?

Bill has three kids of his own. And, while I don't know if he was abusive to them, my own experiences with him suggested it's likely.

Uncle Bill lived in the same Johnstown apartment building as my family did—his apartment was situated on the same floor as ours and he had a unique vantage point with full view of our place from his windows. One time in my grade school years, my brother Tig and I were mooning people from our apartment window and Uncle Bill grabbed a pellet gun and sniped Tig, nailing him in a butt cheek. Tig went down screaming in pain, rolling on the floor with his pants wrapped around his knees and blood flowing from the pellet embedded in his ass.

When Uncle Bill wasn't trying to be the next Vasily Zaytsev, he'd lie in wait to assault me in our apartment building. He'd hide his hulking frame behind doors, and then as I'd come or go from home, he'd pop out and zap me with his cop-issued stun gun. Once he accomplished his mission, he'd just walk away and leave this kid writhing in misery on the floor.

This one time when I was in eighth grade—before we packed up to move into Grandpa Temple's house—my parents took a trip to Colorado and left Trisha and I in the "care" of Uncle Bill and Aunt Nell—both of whom kept us locked down in their apartment.

One day during this temporary stay while Uncle Bill and Aunt Nell were out, a buddy of mine came by and asked me to help him drag some lady's car out of a ditch down the road. I was happy to lend a hand, but I didn't realize that I had committed a major transgression by not asking Uncle Bill for permission first. The fucker wasn't even home to ask, so I just went.

Well, when I came back to the apartment, Uncle Bill was there waiting for me. I was just a kid who came up to Uncle Bill's knee, but bullies don't care, the smaller, the better, right? I tried to explain what happened and the good deed I'd done, but he didn't care. He beat me so badly that I was knocked out cold. When I woke up, my body and head were killing me and blood was gushing out of my nose.

No good deed goes unpunished.

My motor skills were off; my thinking fuzzy and my world was a spinning sphere of pure agony. Somehow, in some unsupervised window of opportunity, Trisha helped me to my feet and walked with me as I staggered over to our family apartment next door.

"I ... wanna call ... call Mom and Dad ... in Colorado ... tell 'em what Uncle Bill did to me."

Trisha looked both concerned and horrified. "Curtis. You *did* call Mom and Dad. You just hung up the phone with them."

Not that it mattered. Though I certainly suffered *at least* a concussion, my parents didn't do a damn thing about any of it. In fact, they acted as though I probably deserved it.

Lucky for me, however, I was about to discover an unlikely vehicle that would take me far and away from the vicious clutches of Uncle Bill, my parents, and all of my tormentors—*Home Economics.*

PART TWO

At one with the
(Culinary) Misfits

SEVEN
BOOK OF RUTH

"**G**ood job here, Curtis."

Ruth Snider smiled as she inspected the backpack I had made.

"This is better than that pillow you made last year," she continued. "You know how I often tell you about the importance of sewing, cooking, keeping a house, making a table, etiquette? These are all things you'll want to know how to do when you're an adult. And who knows? Maybe there's something you like so much you'll want to do it when you grow up. Imagine being the inventor of a new line of skateboard clothing!"

I beamed. At the time, I skateboarded a lot and thought maybe I wanted to be a professional skateboarder. And though I hadn't taken Home Ec in seventh grade, and then again in eighth grade, in search of safe harbor—who would've—that's exactly what this class was becoming.

"That sounds cool." I mustered a smile. I felt ... *happy*. It had been a while.

Mrs. Snider looked around, then bent down and whispered in my ear: "Things better at home, Curtis?"

"Nah."

"Well, don't forget you can always talk to me about your problems or anything. I'm here for you."

I knew this already. Mrs. Snider had been the one to buy the materials for me to make the backpack when she found out my parents didn't have the money for it. I'd gotten an A on the assignment, but just as importantly, I used that backpack to carry my skateboard for years afterward.

My high school principal has said that he couldn't figure out how I got so interested in culinary arts because there's nothing in St. Louisville or Johnstown that offers anything relevant to that world.

But as I've come to realize, it's not so much about the town, it's about people *inside* the town—such as Ruth Snider—who care enough to awaken the spirit and drive *inside* the individual.

Now, I won't try to tell you I had some divine revelation in eighth grade about becoming a great chef, or even a line cook. No, my evolution as a chef was more organic—but it all goes back to that Home Ec class. Ruth's kindness and sincere interest in what would connect to *my* interests broadened my horizons and gave me a new lease on life.

If anyone says angels don't walk among us, I've got a two-word rebuttal:

Ruth. Snider.

I ATTENDED WILLIS C. Adams Junior High and then Johnstown-Monroe High School for two years before I went over to the vocational school—the JVS (Joint Vocational School)—to continue a culinary program for the last two years of high school.

It was the first time I didn't look at a school building as the fortress of the enemy.

We were actually *making* shit! Learning how to do practical things and gaining actual *skills*. And that was something I enjoyed more than anything. I iron my own shirts to this day because of those classes.

I've had girlfriends in the past who needed clothing repairs done.

"Oh, I'll fix that for you."

"You can do that?"

Indeed, I can.

I fucking loved JVS. It got me out of sitting in regular classrooms, which always felt like the longest eight hours of my goddamn life, and—bonus!—we never had homework!

The people in my kitchen class were all misfits. I felt like the system just filtered them in there because … well, what else are they going to do with these guys? This mishmash of unpopular students ended up in the food service world. I saw all these guys as deadbeats who didn't take the kitchen seriously, and, as a young, pissed-off and driven punk, I resented them. Looking back now, I cringe, because I never want to be a dick. But my attitude then was, *You have problems and aren't one of the cool kids? I have problems that'll make your head spin—but I'm here to master this cooking shit!*

I learned later that the kitchen is *exactly* where the misfits belong! It's the clubhouse, the haven … the one place for the unpopular kids to let loose and do it through food.

I don't remember much of the cooking. Ruth says I was always doing this weird stuff to the food—experimenting with ingredients, approaching simple foods in a different way by adding things. I'd want to add unusual vegetables to a pizza and then bake it all with more mozzarella cheese.

My vibe was already *out there*, evidently.

I think if more schools' current curriculum did more to teach the things that I learned, the world would be a much brighter place—showing them how to do the things that actually excite you. Make a backpack for carrying a skateboard. Make a pillow that's better than any pillow you sleep on at home. Want a sick guitar case? Let's make it!

That's the type of liberty that we need to have in the school system. Empower people to do what they want to do at a young age. Don't say *No!* to kids all the fucking time. Instead, encourage their imagination and help them bring their ideas to life. And if your own kids are at a school that does this—support that in every way you can.

Ruth sometimes had a substitute teacher who would come down from the high school to fill in for her. Her name was Kathy Zay. When I went on to high school, Kathy was the culinary teacher there—a blessing atop a blessing. Kathy had great contacts in the professional chef world and eventually helped me get my foot in the door of an exclusive golf club's kitchen.

At the JVS, we ran a restaurant in the school, which was open to the public for two hours every Tuesday and Thursday. Teachers could come and eat, along with anybody from the outside world. Your parents could come.

The one day I skipped JVS to hang with a pal and fuck off all day, Jan and her friend actually came to the JVS restaurant to eat. Jan had bragged to her friend that her son Curtis was a hell of a chef. When Jan found out that I wasn't there, she was super-pissed. When I got home later, Jan asked me if I had a good time in the kitchen at JVS that day. I nervously blurted out, "JVS was great today! Worked my ass off!" As you can imagine, I was immediately busted—and immediately grounded for months by Jan.

I've since learned that it's best to tell the truth, even if it hurts.

Cooking, creating, tasting, smelling, being free, and being in that refuge of the school kitchen with all the misfits—it was my first love, a true obsession.

At fourteen, I got a job washing dishes after school from four to eight. Everybody called the place the Greeks' Diner, but I think the real name was Main Street Diner. It was owned by a husband and wife, Tina and Bill. The gig paid fifteen dollars a day. That place is still operating today as Dashing Diner Uptown. Ironically, a friend of mine bought it and now runs it. She joked that I could come back to work anytime. Who knows? I might surprise her one day and step through the back door!

I took my work at the diner very seriously. I was a teenager and wanted to buy a car. It wasn't a lot of money, but it was still much more than I'd ever made mowing lawns or selling flavored toothpicks! I put my cash in a sock drawer and kept going.

The owners let me do other kitchen tasks as time went on. I learned how to chop and peel vegetables there, for example—not at a professional level, just for chunky soup. I was always trying to peel the skin off boiled potatoes in one big piece.

Seeing the guests enjoying their meals, I felt like a part of something larger than myself—something good. I learned how important doing my part and taking direction and following through on the smallest details truly was.

Oh, and I got *paid* for it, too?

Wild!

Also, the restaurant owners would let me make a free meal every night. If I wanted a burger, I could cook it myself along with the fries and other sides and garnishes. I wasn't eating this well at home.

Soon they moved me on to being a short order cook. I was making simple diner food: Burgers and fries and fish sandwiches and the like.

Back at the JVS restaurant, my history teacher, John Saunders—a true foodie who was extremely knowledgeable about cuisine—would come in every Tuesday and Thursday. "This is good, Curtis," he'd say as he savored a dish. "Aromatic and delicious." Or he'd be critical in a helpful way, like, "You could do this dish better, my man. I think you could have added more ..."

Really, Saunders should've taught at a culinary school or had his own restaurant. He worked as a waiter at one of the best restaurants in Columbus a couple of nights a week just because he loved being in the world of food and wine. We became good friends. He actually gave me my very first bottle of wine.

"I want you to have this," he'd said. "It's amazing. I'm not telling you to drink it, but I want you to have this."

And I *still* have it. It's an '83 Morgon from Beaujolais. I've never opened it. I probably *won't* ever open it because it means so much to me.

"I know you don't want to sit in my history class," John would say with a smile. "'Cause who the hell wants to talk about history when there's a kitchen calling your name?"

Perhaps to make up for my mandatory time in history, John would give me special, personalized homework. "Okay, Curtis. Tomorrow, I expect you to tell me what a *béchamel* sauce is. And this week, you should learn the origins of sauces. Then you're going to tell me what the five classic French mother sauces are. Also, find a recipe for *this* by Monday."

Food history?

Fuck, yes!

I took it all in like a sponge. I wanted to absorb it all; I was craving it so much.

I was also learning that I could fine-tune tastes in a recipe. Blandness was the enemy ... and I fought that war on every front.

Are the tastes and aromas too murky or too bright?

I discovered that I could make flavors come through and glow by using salt or other briny items such as salted butter, fish sauce, soy sauce,

37

miso, pickled vegetables, hard cheeses, cured meats, olives, capers, and canned fish such as anchovies, spreading them on meat and mixing them into marinades and sauces to boost the flavor profiles of dishes from dark and bitter to mild and sweet.

Does a root vegetable like a parsnip have an astringent taste?

Does a gourd such as winter squash have a sweet and/or savory taste?

What can be done to correct those profiles?

Yes, I was thinking about these concepts even as a teenager.

I was already obsessed with flavor.

I'd add cold water or a potato to cut too much saltiness in a broth as I brought it up to a simmer. Or maybe I'd utilize acids like vinegar or lemon juice as a flavor mask to balance overpowering salt, or add starch to remedy a fiery, curry-based soup, or use heavy cream to mollify a too-intense chicken dish—which in turn helped make the chicken richer and more succulent.

I also enjoyed experimenting with, of course, garlic, thyme, and tarragon as it suited me. I learned that foods such as Brussels sprouts and broccoli have a pinch of bitterness that could help to balance certain dishes. I worked with mustard and anise, even beer and sugar.

I learned early that scientists have identified seven basic tastes in food: salty, sour, bitter, sweet, astringent, pungent, and that wonderful umami, baby.

Umami is the Japanese word for "pleasant, savory taste." Foods rich with umami include cooked meat, broth, gravy, soup, fish, shellfish, tomatoes, soy sauce, cheeses, dried shiitake, yeast and meat extracts, miso, mustard, hydrolyzed vegetable protein, and many more. The elements of umami harmonize with the flavor of glutamates. People perceive umami through the taste receptors that usually react to glutamates—found in fermented items and meat broths, or in foods that contain monosodium glutamate (more commonly recognized as MSG).

Umami is unique, with its own distinct taste, and it plays a precious role in food pairings, so it's probably clear to you by now why this would appeal to me on more than one level.

People taste with more than the sides and dorsal surfaces of the tongue. The soft palate—the roof of the mouth—directly locks in the sense of taste. Perhaps because of this, *palate* is also used as a term to define flavor. I grasped its importance as I learned to use ingredients across all the flavor profiles, which were broken down into notes—Low, Middle, and High.

Low notes strike the palate at the back of the mouth. These are the warm, homey, rooted, and heavy flavors—cinnamon, beans, smoky spices, mushrooms, nutmeg, and the seared red meats that make you totally salivate at the slightest whiff or sound of the sizzle. They create the foundation for other flavors to come.

The Middle notes strike the palate at the middle of the mouth. They are blander and more neutral, serving as padding between food items and offering a quieter dimension to flavors. They don't linger the way Low notes or High notes do. Fish and chicken, raw vegetables, tofu, and unseasoned grains fit into this category.

Finally, the High notes come in and strike the palate at the top of the mouth. These are ebullient flavors: hot peppers, fresh herbs, and citrusy fruits. They explode in the mouth with pizzazz.

The more I began to understand the complexities of taste and smell, the better I was able to layer the flavor profiles of my dishes.

JOHN C. Saunders passed away at age sixty-nine on Monday, July 10, 2023.

I learned of his passing the day after he died. Overwhelmed with shock and grief, I had difficulty processing the information.

My first thought was that we lost an incredible man … an incredible soul.

My second thought was that it really sucked that John never made it to Grace or Ever.

John's daughter, Natalie, was the one who contacted me about John's death. She told me how he'd passed away unexpectedly at home, and while she was going through his things, she found a card from me to John with my number on it. Natalie said she thought John ended up not reaching out to me because of how shy and introverted he had become the past few years of his life. But she did tell me how, over the years, he had told Natalie and her siblings that I was one of his favorite students—and he really *did* want to dine at one of my restaurants and bring his family.

I rode my motorcycle to Westerville, Ohio for John's funeral on Friday, July 14, 2023. It was a long drive, but when you're on a motorcycle, it's nice to be able to zone out and not have to talk to anybody, so it felt therapeutic.

I'm so happy that I made the trip. John's service was beautiful, just friends and family celebrating his life with Champagne! It did my heart good to be there to pay my respects in person and to honor John with his people—all of whom he'd touched in wonderful ways.

I learned a lot, too. John was the youngest of four children and he'd attended Ohio State University, where he was awarded several advanced degrees. He'd taught American Government at C-TEC Career and Technology Education Center of Licking County for more than thirty years. In his forty years as a part-time server at the Refectory Restaurant, he was always excited to share his passion for and knowledge about pairing wine and food with those lucky enough to be seated in his section. And with his "Einstein" hair and mustache, he was easily spotted on the restaurant floor, often taking in the aromas of a new wine pour.

John enjoyed retirement, reading classic American literature, birdwatching, and re-living his Kanku Dai competition days. He was an avid gardener who took pride in his rose and basil plants. He ended each night with his beloved cat Tora and a FaceTime with his grandson, KJ. His family and friends could always count on lengthy conversations over bottomless fine wine. He enjoyed political discussions and traveling to see and critique new restaurants. You could always catch him at a wine tasting, talking about all things "Provence."

John loved his family and friends with all his heart and he will be deeply missed every time a magnum of Champagne is popped—especially by me.

I know that John witnessed my three Michelin stars, my James Beard awards, my Grace ascension, the innovations I developed for Ever and After—and where I've gone since. And I want him to know that my deep appreciation for finer food, wine, and a high level of culinary art exists all because of *him*.

I'd never been able to tell John these things in person. Really, it's a debt beyond words. I've always just wanted to give back to him in the language I speak best …

John, can I just cook for you? Let me show you my love for something that you've been a part of in a way you may not have realized.

When you're a kid who keeps getting pushed to the edge of the abyss, you can only dream that some adult might glide in and be a hero. I'm lucky that that happened for me when it did, because, man, in so many ways, that saved my life.

EIGHT
OUT OF THE FRYING PAN, INTO THE OVEN

On one hand, it was weird living in the house Grandpa Temple had to leave behind when he went to prison for armed kidnapping.

On the other, I finally had my own bedroom.

Nothing extravagant—essentially, the unfinished basement of the house—but a major upgrade from the tiny closet I'd been living in for years.

Though still in high school, I was by this time working as a cook every night at the Buxton Inn in Granville, some twenty minutes away from our house. It had been a stagecoach stop back in the day and was supposedly haunted. They used to have a tavern underneath the kitchen in this dingy, subterranean space that was super-creepy. You had to walk down these ancient, creaky wooden stairs to get down there and everybody would say they'd seen ghosts. I never saw anything but always kept my eyes open.

I would get out of school at two-thirty, get to the Inn by three-thirty at the latest, work until about eleven o'clock at night, get home by midnight, do my schoolwork, go to bed … and be up early the next morning and do it all over again.

The mission for me never wavered: work, save, get the hell out of that town.

~

PART of my kitchen job involved learning to work with different types of people.

Specifically, I quickly learned about dealing with different *personalities*.

It was often trying.

I, of course, brought my own cutlery to work with me. A knife should be an extension of your hand—and your style. Slash or Keith Richards or your favorite guitarist isn't gonna borrow a different random guitar every night and hope it works out, right? Same with cooks and knives. When you pick up someone else's blade, it's not the same. The weight is different. You feel slightly out of tune.

Anyway, I'd bought a set of knives and one night I left one of them in the kitchen—and when I went to use it, it wasn't there anymore. A few days later, I saw a coworker in her forties wielding it.

"I didn't steal your knife, you little bastard!" she snarled when I confronted her.

Well, you see, my dad had engraved my name on the plastic handles of *every* one of my knives when I'd bought them, so that I could identify them if they were ever to go missing. So, when this woman eventually walked away for something, I picked up the knife to inspect it and the spot where my dad had engraved my name had been melted off! I was furious. When I called her out, we really got into it, but she refused to admit anything. I finally just let it go.

"Let me tell you something, Curtis," a Buxton Inn chef told me that day, "you're going to have shitty people pop up throughout your career that you're going to have to learn to work with—even if you don't trust them. Even if you can't stand them. Adapt, work, shine. And fuck 'em."

I took the lesson to heart and it helped me become better and stronger when dealing with people in the kitchen and in life.

Speaking of better and stronger, while still at Buxton Inn, I upgraded to a more expensive Henckels chef's knife. My dad couldn't understand why I elevated my cutlery. "Why would you spend a hundred bucks on a fucking knife?"

The irony here was that Bear was just as mystified and as incredulous as I was when he traded in that Oldsmobile 442 for a 1942 Knucklehead frame.

He didn't realize this superior knife was going to last me a lifetime.

I still have it.

~

I SOON GOT my first "big break" in a kitchen.

I was in eleventh grade when Kathy Zay introduced me to John Souza at Muirfield Village Golf Club in Dublin, Ohio. The club, owned by Jack Nicklaus, attracted an extremely affluent class of people—the polar opposite of my home crowd. In the club kitchen, Souza reigned. He was one of the best chefs in all of central Ohio. He was a legend. I never imagined I'd be under his tutelage.

Kathy's class was given the opportunity to work the Annual PGA Tournament at Muirfield every Memorial Day. The school would allow us the week to prepare and attend. I fell in love with the club and the kitchen and what they were doing there. Afterwards, I stayed in contact with Souza.

If he's the best, then I want to be around him.

Eventually Souza let me work in Muirfield's kitchen three days a week.

Muirfield was an hour's drive from my house in St. Louisville. I'd go there right after school and work until midnight or so. Then I'd be up again at six in the morning for classes. Why did I take on this crazy schedule—one step crazier than the Buxton Inn—for the small hourly wage Souza offered me? Because that crazy step was a step *up*—and closer to my goal of maybe forever getting out of my house.

There was a chef at Muirfield, Regan Koivisto, who remains a good friend of mine to this day. He was the banquet chef and I would marvel as I watched him make huge batches of penne all'arrabbiata for the guests. It's a very classic Italian dish and very simple—noodles, garlic, oregano, red chili flakes, Kalamata olives, olive oil, basil, tomato, a little bit of salt, if needed. I mean, it's not fresh tomatoes; it's canned tomato pulp. It's dried oregano. It's dried chili flakes. The only thing fresh in that whole dish is the basil and the garlic, but the taste is freaking beautiful. I used to just love that dish.

One day, I went to a grocery store to search for the right ingredients to make penne all'arrabbiata at home. It wasn't as easy as you'd think. For starters, I couldn't find the right olives. I used green ones, thinking they'd be the same as the ones Regan used. Spoiler alert: they weren't. What I needed were Kalamatas, but I don't think you could get them back then at a grocery store—at least not where I lived in 1993. Hell, I don't even think you could get fresh basil. Anyway, the first time I made penne all'arrabbiata was also the very first time I cooked for my parents at home.

They pretended to like it.

I think they were trying to be nice.

In high school, I'd always loved cooking, and the thrill of being on the line and under pressure. The chaos—sometimes controlled, others … not so much.

When I got to Muirfield, however, I experienced things at a different level. Even for a cheeseburger, every ingredient was the *best* of the best. We'd grind up the whole shoulder of the cow to make the patty. Add the most appetizing varieties of lettuce, tomato, and onion. The kitchen wasn't going to Kroger to buy generic white hamburger buns. We sourced gourmet rolls from a small bakery. Everything was done right— always from scratch.

I was able to work with food I'd never seen before.

I remember the epic walk-ins: a meat cooler, a seafood cooler, an all-produce cooler. One entire cooler was full of nothing but *cheese*: Crazy-ass blue cheeses, specialty cheeses, aged this and that, and all kinds of stuff that I didn't even know existed: Brie, L'Edel de Cleron, Sainte Maure French goat cheese, Normandy Camembert, Pave d'Affinois, Reblochon Mountain cheese, Morbier, Manchego, Stilton Blue, Taleggio, Italian Gorgonzola, cheeses selected from Spain, France, Italy, and Napa Valley.

Today, those cheeses are normal for me to see and use, but back then, it was a wonderland playground. Souza let me explore the inventory of the cheese cooler.

Are you fucking kidding me? Whoa!

One day I told Souza I wanted to go to culinary school. He told me I'd be wasting my time. I did want to continue that part of my education, though. I had been offered scholarships to some prestigious schools around the country due to winning some cooking awards through Future Homemakers of America and national, regional, and state competitions, which featured preparations that showcased proper handling and minimized food waste or for carvings that turned fruits into beautiful displays. Despite these offers, though, I ultimately decided to go to a local college and pay for it myself.

Considering that I had always dreamed of escaping from Ohio, that probably sounds funny, right? But I really wanted to also invest in what I saw as an incredible opportunity to work for John Souza at the country club. So, I said, "Fuck it. I'm going to go to college and stay here and work with the best."

When the time came, Souza agreed to take me on as a *stagiaire*, or a *stage*, working a brief time for free in the kitchen before moving into a paid apprenticeship.

That alone was worth the change of plans.

$\sim$

In 1994, I graduated from high school.

Hallelujah!

I immediately started at Columbus State/Ohio State in Columbus, studying for a degree in Culinary Arts and Applied Science. It was a three-year program, a four-year degree, and the school required you to find a restaurant and a chef who would take you on through an apprenticeship program for three years. No bouncing from job to job; they wanted you to stay put with one chef and learn. The pressure was on to work with and learn from a good chef. The competition among students to land these positions was fierce and I felt lucky and grateful that I was already aligned with Souza.

I set about learning basic tasks and the workings of the restaurant business.

Though I had picked up basic culinary skills, knife skills, and general knowledge of ingredients from my time at Buxton Inn and the vocational kitchen, I realized there was much more to learn: dishes I'd be expected to cook, kitchen procedures, and the use of commercial equipment such as mixers, choppers, fryers, toasters, steamers, stoves, and ovens.

In Souza's kitchen, I worked long, hard hours on my feet—but that was nothing new. I was right in there with the executive chef and the *sous* chefs, prepping and cleaning up in a crowded and hectic professional kitchen with its hot ovens, slippery floors, sharp knives, and cranky chefs.

Young and desperate not to get in anyone's way, I did my best to become competent at such basic, yet crucial, tasks as managing stock rotation, advising food inventory levels, ensuring that ingredients and leftover food were stored correctly and used judiciously, inspecting food deliveries to ensure that both accuracy in quantity and level of quality, and cleaning and serving food as required. I also learned, under each chef's tutelage, to set up all the food stations, and correctly prepare each day's ingredients and recipes while adhering to portion control, cooking time, and presentation requirements. Underlying the tasks were the required standards, which included maintaining an organized and sanitary work environment, making sure food arrangement aesthetics were consistent with the restaurant's firm instructions, and ensuring protocols for the best, most ethically sound food practices were followed precisely.

As I mastered the tasks, I was soon promoted, assisting Chef Souza directly with developing menus and the preparation and cooking of dishes, assisting chefs by co-managing tasks and providing logical suggestions for substitute ingredients for spices, entrees, sauces and more.

There wasn't a scholarship from Ohio State for me, so I took out a loan for six grand to pay for my first year. By this time, I had an actual bank account and was managing my money properly. No more stuffing cash into a sock drawer. I was finally living on my own for the first time, too. Right after I finished high school, in June of '94, I moved into a one-bedroom apartment, paying two-eighty-five a month.

I wish I paid that now!

I really thought I was some big-timer.

Fast forward a few months. My parents died. Lost in a dark place, I stopped college cold and defaulted on my student loan. My loan was a deferred payback—once you graduated or dropped out, you had to start paying it back. I needed to take on another job to pay the loan and make rent.

But I was surviving, proud to be on my own. I managed two full-time jobs and eventually started college again. I only had to be at school one day a week. My classes were on Mondays for a full day from 7 a.m. to 10 p.m. The apprenticeship deal with Souza stayed the same. But paying for my school was a bitch, man. I wasn't able to apply for another loan because I'd defaulted on the first one.

And man, I hated college too. *Hated* it.

I felt I'd been ripped off. I was already learning so much in the field, working under a pro chef at a killer restaurant. Then I'd go to school and be treated like an amateur.

I had a moment where I thought Souza was right about wasting my time at culinary school, but I was determined to get a college degree.

"The cooks in the school kitchen are trying to teach me how to make meringue, right?" I'd vent to coworkers. "Dude, I've been making meringues for five fucking years already!"

But I had to do it to get that college degree, right?

Right?

Honestly, when applicants walk through the door of my restaurant, I don't even look to see if they graduated high school, much less college. To me, experience and passion are paramount. I tell the kids I meet who want to go to culinary school to *really* think about it. They can learn so much working in the culinary business that they usually don't need that degree. My advice is always to dedicate yourself to the craft for ten, fifteen years and then figure out what you want to do. Go work for a butcher for a year. Go work at a fishmonger for a year. Work at things that will make you better at what you do day to day. And if you want that college education to augment your experience, consider an MBA or a financial accounting degree, something to teach you the *business side* of a restaurant. Learning where the money goes in this industry is vital.

Learn how to create a spreadsheet; how to read a Profit and Loss statement. Learn all the skills you'll be required to perform as a chef, including preparing and balancing budgets, scheduling and managing staff, creating and maintaining your social media presence.

You might hate that shit and only want to cook. Too bad. That ain't the world we're living in now. You have to do it *all*.

Now, I realize that not everyone walks into this cooking world as early as I did, and for those whose culinary education and connections into restaurants didn't begin in junior high or high school, there can sometimes be value in pursuing experience through the channels offered in higher education.

I serve on the board of the Auguste Escoffier School of Culinary Arts and I do a lot of cooking videos and demonstrations for them. I also enjoy visiting their campuses in Boulder and Austin—I'm all about getting the kids interested. And I'm honored that there's a $25,000 scholarship in my name that will help students to pursue their dreams. (And I have to say also that I'm honored there is a whole kitchen named after me.) But that doesn't mean I think it's right for everyone.

Whether it's someone considering college or learning primarily through hands-on work in the industry, I always give the same advice because it's something I believe in: Put your head down and learn the craft. Learn everything you possibly can about what you're doing in this business. Try to be the best at it but also, follow what you want to do in life from within and not from a monetary standpoint. I've always believed that when you do that, the money will come. It will come full circle, so be patient.

Don't push to be the *sous* chef as soon as you get out of school, because there's still so much to learn. When you start putting yourself in those roles, you're in a position where you're supposed to be educating the staff. They're expecting to learn from *you*. If you can't properly butcher a chicken or filet a fish and demonstrate all the other basic skills and protocols, how are you going to teach somebody else?

AT MUIRFIELD, I was cooking and learning non-stop.

The dishes being created in John Souza's kitchen were like nothing I'd ever seen.

In the beginning of my stint at Murifield, I worked in an area downstairs called the "mixed grill" where I was cooking burgers, making chicken sandwiches, and wraps—traditional restaurant food, basically. Then I moved upstairs to the main kitchen where fine-dining cooking was happening and I was exposed to so many new ingredients for the first time: truffles, lobsters, sushi, raw oysters. I soon ran one of the stations there, serving the high-end dishes.

That's where I spent all my time. I didn't want to go anywhere else.

Chef Souza was always one to encourage learning and growth, and I had so much curiosity, so with his approval, I began to marry things up. I might make a truffle mayonnaise, top it with Gruyère and a relish made of celery, spread that on a dish that melts in your mouth. Maybe I'd make Chilean sea bass guacamole tacos utilizing the fat in the avocado to help push flavors in the sweet meat of the fish—and then add a salsa with a lime juice and chipotle base. Or baked Asian mushroom pasta; or chorizo and cheese-stuffed, grilled bell peppers. Or blackened Brussels sprouts with a briny anchovy butter. Or coconut chicken nuggets in peri-peri sauce with raspberries. Or broccoli in fish sauce and pickled chili.

With some appetizers, I'd kick it up a notch. I'm allergic to shrimp, so I couldn't touch it. But there are other means, right? I'd take a basic tilapia fillet, pour dry white wine into a sauté pan with bay leaves and peppercorns and kosher salt, squeeze lemon halves over all the liquid in the pan, drop in the lemon halves. I'd simmer for ten minutes or so and add the tilapia, cover it all up, and poach it for four minutes. I'd chill the tilapia for a day, cut it into pieces, and serve it cold with a jalapeño and red onion cocktail sauce like one might do with shrimp.

Wagyu beef tenderloin wasn't available to us back then, but I'd use the next best thing when making a Japanese-style beef carpaccio—USDA grade beef or even a local, grass-fed beef tenderloin—and freeze it. Later I'd *brunoise*—finely dice—cucumber and shallot, leave half of those ingredients raw and put the other half in vinegar to pickle for half an hour. I'd remove the tenderloin from the freezer and slice it super thin across the grain. The meat was always really tender; I didn't need to pound the hell out of it. Instead, I'd lay out the thin slices on a cutting board and, using my fingers, press the portion of meat down and outward like a pizza, making it even thinner and larger. Then I'd arrange those slices on plates, drizzle them with olive oil, spread on the raw and pickled cucumber and shallots, add pepper and bits of potato chips, and serve.

It was amazing—and, most importantly, no one else was doing that.

I learned how to handle my precious $100 Henckels knife in creative ways. I used it to chiffonade herbs into thin strips for garnishes and to cut carrots and potatoes and squash using an oblong, *tournée* cutting style. I'd *brunoise* and *batonnet* and implement various other knife techniques to clean and chop, dice, peel, and julienne. As I mastered the work, I saw how my efforts enhanced my dishes.

I was always changing things up. And Souza would *almost* never say "no" to anything—so long as it wasn't a lark. Whatever we bought had better be made into a worthwhile creation.

"Chef, I've never used black truffles. Might be interesting?"

As long as we didn't buy fifty pounds of truffles and not use them, all good. Truffles were expensive then—hell, they're still expensive. The black truffle—a species which is reportedly threatened today by climate change—sells for around six hundred bucks a pound. But even back then, truffles weren't easy to get. Souza was able to source them from distributors who bought them from suppliers in Europe. We used black truffles, burgundy truffles, white truffles. Truffles are both edible spores and a spice. So, I'd flavor dishes with them. I'd use the truffle-slicer to shave them over certain dishes or cut them up with my knife and put them in sauces and spreads and vinaigrettes and oils. I used them to flavor meat, rice, pasta, you name it.

I also created several recipes under Souza's guidance: white truffle risotto, seafoods in truffle sauce, roasted quail with truffle-infused salsa pronta ... the ideas went on. And if I didn't use all the truffles in one night, I was able to keep them for a couple of weeks in a fridge.

Imagine getting something that high-end and crazy to play around with in the early nineties! Sure, you can get truffle mayonnaise in a bottle from Amazon and anywhere else now, but not back then. I was *making* this stuff.

The principles of cooking and teaching were everything to John Souza. He wanted me to learn as much as possible and felt that experimentation was an important part of the process. My ideas aren't so crazy in today's cuisine culture, although you'll still occasionally see things on a menu that might sound like science fiction to some. Back then, though? My ideas could seem totally off the wall. Yet, those ideas were nevertheless given serious consideration by Souza.

That level of trust allowed me to blossom and to be creative without fear. "Chef. I've never worked with lobsters. Can we do something with lobsters for Friday night's service?"

"Okay." Souza would nod and consider. "Let's get a dozen lobsters in for the dinner menu and create a dish around them."

Next thing you know we'd have stuffed Maine lobster; pan-fried lobster ravioli with scallops; lobster gnocchi; lobster with a caviar glaze;

Thai pomelo and lobster salad; baked lobster and noodles with aioli and crab; butter-poached lobster in an emulsified *beurre monté* butter sauce ...

Souza sometimes had me pump the brakes. He'd say, "Don't get too far ahead of yourself there, cowboy." But on the rare occasions he denied me, there would be a good reason behind it.

My "experiments" continued after hours. Alone in the kitchen, the joint locked up, I'd transform into Doctor Duffystein, mad scientist. Banquet chef Regan Koivisto was my main guinea pig, but anyone who lingered in the kitchen might suffer the same fate. One time, I dabbled in ice cream and ran around to everyone the next day. "Taste this! Taste this! It's smoked cherry ice cream!"

Smoked cherry ice cream?

My coworkers were maybe a little baffled. But in my mind, I loved ice cream and cherries as well as all the smoked foods out there—cheese, fish, meat, vegetables, and even some beverages. So why not more of a good thing?

I had taken these juicy, delicious cherries and laid them out on a sheet placed directly on a grill grate in a smoker over hickory chips. I smoked the cherries for a couple hours then simmered them in a saucepan until the liquid was reduced and syrupy. I added high-fat milk, heavy cream for density and richness, sugar, salt, and egg yolks all into a saucepan and simmered it while whisking away until it was a thick sauce that I strained into a bowl and chilled. This was my ice cream base. I churned it until it was a real creamy homemade vanilla ice cream that was ready to be married with my smoked cherries. I put the finished product into an airtight container and then into a freezer for twenty-four hours.

Voila!

I developed an infatuation with making ice cream—three or four different types, every single day. It started to bring out my creative side. The possibilities were limitless. I think that's when I fell deeper in love with food. Because it was about creating. I had made it—not from some-body's recipe, but by combining my own skill and knowledge. The crazier, the better. The floodgates opened in a big way.

Around this time, Souza brought in a *sous* chef to be my boss. "I gotta work for him? Get the fuck outta here! I can out-cook this guy already."

It was always the way. I knew I could work circles around anyone new who outranked me. But I wasn't ready to run a kitchen yet and Souza knew it.

Still, I was already confident about such things as meat preparation. If you handed me a chicken back then, I could break it down into the eight traditional pieces without even thinking about it, and I still can. But these days, you might be surprised at how few chefs have that skill. If you asked fifteen chefs to break down a chicken, I'd say maybe three would be able to do it properly.

It wasn't all cooking and Kitchen 101. When you have the keys to the kingdom, anything can happen after-hours—and often did.

That my roommate at the time happened to also be the overnight security guy didn't curb that potential at all. (Don't worry, for his discretion he was rewarded with a constant supply of killer food.)

On any given Friday or Saturday night at three in the morning, you'd find me and a couple of chicks in the club's hot tub, chilling. Some shenanigans that I'll leave up to your imagination might occur, and then I'd head to the kitchen and make food for everyone.

"What do you girls want to eat? Filet mignon and lobster tail? No problem, ladies!"

I probably—by which I mean, *definitely*— should've lost my job multiple times.

If Souza knew, he turned a blind eye.

And I wasn't the only one.

Kitchen partying conjures up Anthony Bourdain-esque tales of sex, drugs, and rock 'n' roll. Maybe it seemed like hyperbole to the uninitiated, but Bourdain told the truth.

I witnessed all kinds of nonsense firsthand—and heard about plenty more: drinking and drugging on the job, banging coworkers, even banging patrons! I had guys telling me they'd gotten a blowjob in the walk-in, not three feet from the dining room.

Look, you get some staff hot for each other and you also have access to free alcohol twenty-four hours a day?

It's a mix that trumps inhibitions and professionalism.

It might manifest as sex.

Or it might spill out as a fistfight in the middle of the kitchen.

I remember one *sous* chef who had keys to the banquet department, which he ran—his own little private kitchen and dining room area—a space completely separate from everybody else. He'd brag about banging the shit out of chicks on a workbench or on top of the cooking table in the back kitchen after everybody else on staff had left. That's gross, just thinking about anyone exchanging bodily fluids on the surface of a table where food is prepared.

Then he'd go home to his wife …

Yeah, the dark underbelly of the culinary world is real.

I'D BEEN WORKING for John Souza for close to six years when my friend Regan Koivisto left to open a brand-new kitchen at another golf-course clubhouse about two miles down the road from Muirfield called Tartan Fields.

Would I like to join him as the *chef de cuisine*?

Absolutely!

In fact, I worked at both restaurants for a while. I was transparent about it. Souza knew what I was doing but didn't seem to care so long as he still had me in his kitchen. In the morning, I would set up the menu at Tartan Fields and then I'd come back to Muirfield for dinner service. I was working seven days a week and getting pretty burnt out. I finally asked Regan if he could pay me more so I could just be full-time at Tartan Fields. He agreed.

It felt like a straightforward decision to me—business, not personal. But I didn't foresee the complications it would unleash.

NINE
TAKE YOUR STINKING PAWS OFF ME, YOU DAMNED DIRTY APE!

With college almost behind me and the promise of a full-time job ahead, I was focused on my future. Throughout high school, I had worked hard and won cooking awards. I had also escaped the daily physical abuse I'd endured as a child. I had persevered and kept moving forward.

Now I was on my way to Muirfield to give Chef John Souza my notice. I'd spent six years there and was extremely grateful for the opportunity and the experience. It had been invaluable.

It was a beautiful day at Muirfield. Golfers milled about. A few guests and coworkers greeted me.

Souza won't be happy about this, I thought, taking a deep breath and walking into the kitchen. *But he'll be cool. I've always been respectful and thankful. He'll understand what I need to do next …*

And then there Souza was, bent over a station table, reviewing some papers—most likely the menu ideas for the night. A dishwasher and a server chatted near the ovens.

I cleared my throat. "Chef? A word?"

Souza didn't look happy at all. He tugged on his chef's uniform as he stood and straightened. He was a really big dude—nearly the same size as Bear had been at his most imposing. If my dad was a grizzly bear, Souza was a great ape.

On this day, Souza seemed even bigger, more intimidating. Like a gorilla in a chef's outfit.

"What is it, Curtis?"

I paused. "I wanted to give you my one month's notice." I then handed Souza my typed and signed resignation.

Souza took the notice in his large hand, read it. When he finished, he crumpled it up and threw it in my face. "You ungrateful little shit."

Immediately the dishwasher and server hurried out of the kitchen. I was jolted. I had expected a negative reaction from Souza, but not this. "Chef, I appreciate all you've done for me. I'm getting my degree now. I graduated culinary school and I—"

"I don't care what you want! I told you college was a fucking waste of time and money. This *is* culinary school, you stupid shit!"

It seemed I had a knack for facing off against huge and intimidating dudes in my young life, be it Bear, Uncle Bill, John Souza—and others who came into my orbit later.

I felt my emotions change from uneasy to angry. I was twenty-one by then and had suffered bulldozer toughs and had survived so much already; I wasn't that scared little kid people could kick around anymore.

"Don't talk to me like that."

"I groomed you to take over!" Souza roared back. "What did you think these last six years of apprenticeship were for? So you could just leave me after wasting time at some shit school? And to what end? So you can run an Applebee's?"

"It's *my* life. My future," I said. "I have plans."

"*Plans*? How's this? I *plan* to kick your ass!"

Souza stepped forward and reached out to grab me by my shirt.

I leaned back, away from his reach, but stood my ground.

"Don't touch me, John. I won't go down so easy, asshole."

"What did you call me? I'm gonna kick your ass all over this country club." He shifted his weight forward, pulling his fists into a boxer's stance.

"Do it and see what happens when you beat up a kid in front of everyone. You'll get fired and thrown in jail."

Souza's arms dropped to his sides as he glared at me. "Get the fuck outta my kitchen!"

I flipped up a middle finger. "Fuck you, Souza."

I walked briskly through Muirfield and past the befuddled expressions of guests and staff who were probably wondering what the hell had just happened in the kitchen. If Souza was reprimanded by any higher-ups for that confrontation, I never knew. I only hoped I'd never have to see Souza again because he was so fucking hostile. I was really bummed out.

I *never* wanted to leave on bad terms with Souza, but he made any other option impossible.

Still, I'd spent *six years* with Souza, and I now kind of get the unhappiness and anger: It's a very personal thing for a head chef to lose a protégé. When somebody I've mentored gives *me* notice, I want to scream, "Fuck!" You've spent so much time with someone; teaching, nurturing, making them greater. It's a two-way street. When that relationship ends, it blows. Even if you go into it knowing it's going to end, it's never easy.

But I'd never threaten to kick anyone's ass over a career choice.

A couple years later, I needed Souza to sign off on a book that detailed the work I'd done as an apprentice, a *stagiaire*, which my college required for me to graduate.

Souza ignored my calls and messages. I ended up taking the book to him directly at his restaurant office. I politely asked him to sign off. He refused.

"What gives, man?" I asked, starting to get hot. "I need this to graduate college. You're really screwing with my life."

"You want a signature? How 'bout I beat your ass instead?"

Again with the threats?

"Fuck you, Souza!"

We went back and forth, spewing threats and curses. It escalated. Souza—a grown-ass man in his forties with a few kids of his own—got up from his desk and chased me outside.

In the end, he didn't touch me. He must've come to his senses (again) and realized it wasn't worth risking his job.

Despite all this unfortunate and unnecessary bullshit, I actually think fondly of Souza today. He had given me a platform from which to soar, high and free. Not to mention he took me into his own home for a short period of time right after my parents died, during which time I'd gotten to know his wife and children very well, and to observe his relationships with them. He had a heart.

Since Souza refused to sign the paperwork I needed to graduate, I had to explain the insanity to the folks in charge at the college. The higher-ups kind of shrugged and essentially said, "We get it. Here's your degree."

Whimper, not a bang.

I had finally wrapped my time at Columbus State/Ohio State and graduated with a degree in Culinary Arts and Applied Science.

Three years later, I sent Souza a heartfelt handwritten letter telling him how sorry I was for the way we ended—and how grateful I was for what he'd taught me.

My letter went unanswered. As did a similar emailed overture another few years down the road.

Shortly after my restaurant Grace opened, I was invited to Ohio to receive a chef's award at my former college. I was surprised to see John Souza's wife, Diane, at the ceremony.

"Diane … you know, I … um …"

She pulled me in for a big hug. "John has followed your entire career." She smiled. "We both know everything you've accomplished and he's so proud of you."

A year later, I went back to Ohio *again* as a guest to speak at *another* college about my culinary career and about how I'd built Grace and how well it had done. I thought this was a great opportunity for me to thank everyone who'd changed the course of my life up to that point. As I stood in front of five hundred people, I was so happy to see many of the great teachers and good friends from Ohio who had helped me as a young person. Ruth Snider was there. Kathy Zay and Regan Koivisto were there. My sister Trisha showed up. John Saunders wasn't there. And, to my disappointment, neither was John Souza.

I reached out to Souza again via email in February 2016 when my team and I were planning a special event in Chicago to celebrate five years of Grace and the three Michelin stars I'd been awarded in 2015. I wanted to bring all the amazing chefs who had mentored me together and make them a multiple-course dinner—you know, show them all that I never forgot where I came from.

The invitations went out and almost everybody was on board. I'd given them an entire year's notice, after all. Not Souza ... but he *did* respond for once.

Sorry, I have a commitment in Boston. Can't do it.

I was happy, though, to be able to honor most of my mentors as we celebrated this milestone in my career.

It was a peak, but, as I soon would learn the hard way, not the pinnacle.

PART THREE

Darkest Days

TEN
WHERE THE END BEGINS

W hen I left Tartan Fields, I was making sixty-five grand a
year.
I moved to Chicago in 2000 to earn ... *sixteen* grand a
year.

That's how much I wanted to work for the great Charlie Trotter.

In Chicago, I would pursue my dream of becoming a world-class
chef. I was going to finally escape from Ohio—but Ohio's scars would
remain. I'd always be haunted by my past—especially my parents
terrible fate, which will weigh on my heart and mind forever.

⌒

When I was in sixth grade, my dad "stepped out" of his marriage to Jan
for an eighteen-year-old girl, Amy.

She was in high school and my dad was in the middle of a stint as a
Johnstown police officer, thanks to bad cop Uncle Bill getting him the job.
The gig, predictably, didn't suit Bear's outlaw soul whatsoever. He had
hated cops his entire life—and the local cops and detectives sure hated
him. Plus, he got assigned the overnight shift, which in Johnstown was
super boring. Trust me, I rode along in his cruiser sometimes, so I can
attest.

I don't know how Bear and Amy met. What I do know is that I was in sixth grade, sleeping in my parents closet—which was bad enough—when my dad suddenly left our family and moved in with a teenager who lived a minute's walk from our door.

Shortly thereafter, my parents sat me down and asked which of them I wanted to live with.

I stayed put with Jan. Sometimes I'd go over to Bear's apartment to hang out, but it was really fucking weird.

While he was shacked up with Amy, Bear's attitude was a magnified version of what it had always been: You could live life his way or hit the goddamn highway—proverbial or otherwise. I was so confused and uneasy about this whole situation.

As I lay in the closet at night, I'd hear Jan cry herself to sleep.

That hurt me deeply.

Once, on my way to school, I saw Bear kissing Amy in the parking lot.

A girl not much older than me.

And Jan not more than fifty yards away with her heart breaking.

I just acted like I didn't see them and kept moving.

What else was there to do?

I got out of the cold and into the warmth of school that morning, stashed my winter coat in my locker, and went to class. There were Christmas decorations everywhere, most of them made by fellow students. I'd been taught that Christmas was supposed to be a time when family came together and made memories, but I had never experienced that spirit of the season.

What did I have to be thankful for except not being beaten to death?

Or my father leaving our family for a teenage fuck buddy?

Hark!

Nah, those angels could go sing at some other asshole's house.

In class, my teacher gave us an assignment before the Christmas break. Each student was to write about their biggest Christmas wish.

I wrote a few paragraphs about how I wished for my father to end things with this high school chick. I wrote how I wanted him to come back to Jan and tell her that he loved her and *only* her. For him to say that he wanted us all to be together again as a family. I wrote that I loved him and needed him.

When I turned in my Christmas wish, the school immediately reached out to my parents.

Years later, Aunt Penny gave me some of Bear's stuff, including his old wallet. I opened it up and inside was my Christmas wish letter. I began to cry as soon as I saw it.

"You know, your Christmas wish letter made your dad decide to come back home to you all," Penny said. "He kept it in his wallet until the day he died. You really got to his heart."

Bear was hard as granite, but apparently even he could be cracked.

From then on, *everything* was all about Jan. Bear was still cruel, but dedicated.

He really *did* love Jan in his own fucked up way.

In the end, of course, Bear would literally love her to death.

WHEN TRISHA'S first baby was born, my parents were ecstatic.

Hey, who doesn't love a baby?

Of course, the Duffys often show love in a different way than normies: At the time of my niece's birth, the father was completely missing from the picture. So, Bear put a bounty on the dude's head and went hunting for him.

As one does.

During this time of good baby vibes, however, dark clouds were gathering. At this point, Mom, Dad, Trisha, and I were all living in Grandpa Temple's old house. One day I happened to notice a strange wire hanging from the ceiling over a little sectioned off area of my basement lair where there were screws, nails, and all kinds of my grandfather's shit stockpiled. I followed the wire to its terminus: a cassette player.

What the fuck …?

I popped the cassette into my Walkman and pressed play. I heard recordings of phone conversations. I heard my mom talking to her friends. I heard *myself* talking to my girlfriend!

Turns out Bear had taken some phone tap gear from a box of surveillance equipment as a souvenir of his short stint with the police department. He tapped the phone because he thought my mom was cheating on him. He'd made many accusations before—and their domestic skirmishes escalated. Whether she was cheating or not, I don't really know. But there was definitely a new level of vehemence added to the usual, on-brand bad vibe in the Duffy house.

It wasn't long after I discovered the phone tap that my mom got her own apartment and moved out with Trisha and the baby.

History repeats itself: Jan was only fifteen when she first met my dad, my brother and I landing in her lap. And now my sister, at fifteen, had just had her first child.

I was working as much as possible. I hadn't graduated high school yet. I was still living at home, but always coming in late when everybody was already in bed for the night. I also got up before everyone else to go to school and work again. Even on days off at home I was riding on the lawn mower cutting our acres of grass, jamming to cassettes on my Walkman with my headphones on, tuning everyone out. We had this big, country yard and I always had hours of work to do out there on the weekend.

Which is to say, I was too busy busting my ass to notice the marital problems.

When I found out my dad admitted himself to a psychiatric hospital as his marriage fell apart, it *crushed* me. I had this idea that if someone goes in, they're never coming out again.

I remember crying like a baby for him.

But the therapy seemed to work: Bear was suddenly friendly and kind—the nicest I'd *ever* seen him.

"Your father is on antidepressants," Mom eventually confided. "He's taking pills to cope."

"Please … give Dad the whole bottle of pills!" I said, thrilled at what appeared to be an immediate miracle cure. "This is awesome!"

I was in my late teens at this time with no knowledge of what depression really was, or how wild mood swings could get on or off medication. I was naïve as fuck about prescription drugs. In my mind, a kinder, gentler version of the man who used to beat me and put a shotgun to my head seemed like one hell of a positive development.

But I didn't understand yet that the dark side, while being masked, was far from being overcome.

I kept working and became a newly minted high school graduate. It wasn't long before I moved out of the Duffy house and into my first apartment. I'd see Bear maybe once a week. He was living alone.

What did I know about his true state of mind?

What did any of us *really* know?

Depression and suicide are twin demons that have ravaged my family, friends, and, yes, myself later in life. From my middle-aged perspective, I can discern things about the situation that previously flew over my younger self's head: I'm sure that as things got worse with Jan and then spiraled into her filing for divorce, even Bear came to understand that despite the tough-guy loner front he put up, he feared abandonment and isolation more than anything else.

Bear kept trying to see Jan. He'd call me and try and convince me to make the impossible happen.

"Hey, Curt ... have your mother come over for dinner tonight. Tell her you want her to have dinner with you and me at my house."

It was sad and desperate and uncomfortably close to begging.

Bear was legitimately, deeply in love with Jan. But it was just too late —too much damage had been done over the years. Emotional distance and physical abuse are a tough combo to overcome. I later saw the police reports and documents from the Domestic Relations Court for my dad's DUI and domestic violence convictions. The police had real problems with Bear. They had taken all his guns away—well, only the ones they knew about, that is.

Through her divorce attorney, Jan took out a civil protection order against my dad and resisted all attempts at reconciliation. She was just over it and wanted to move on as painlessly as possible. One of her sisters told me that Jan would call her in Colorado to tell her about Bear's harassment and her plans to run away.

Unfortunately for all of us, though, the dark thoughts tumbling around Bear's mind were gaining power over him like a tsunami.

ELEVEN
OVER AND OUT

"It's good to see you, Curt." Jan sat across from me in the booth of a small diner, smoking a cigarette over a cup of coffee. "How's school?"

We were ignoring the elephant in the room, but who could blame us?

"Same as always. Getting through it. College is way better than high school."

"Well, you're the one and only Duffy kid who made it this far. You always shine."

"Thanks, Mom."

Jan seemed happy. I noticed how she'd grown a bit nicer since leaving Dad. It was becoming a strange world to me.

"You and Trisha doing well? The baby?"

Jan nodded. "We're all good. Listen, I wanted to get a few things out, so you understand why I left your dad."

"I think I have a pretty good idea."

I may have blurted my words out a little too fast.

"You say that, but you don't. Not really. I didn't do this to hurt your dad or you or Trisha. I had to do it for *me*. Or else … I don't know what would have happened." Jan paused and stared out the diner window. I could see this was painful for her. "You gotta understand something, I haven't had a chance to live my life." She stubbed out her cigarette. "That's not meant to be harsh, Curt. You know I love you and your brother—shithead that he is—with all my heart, as well as your sister."

"Do you love Dad?"

Jan slumped back in her seat. "I'm not what you'd call 'in love' with him." She tried to smile. "That might sound funny, but it's you kids I really love … know what I mean? Bear was part of the package. I had to *learn* to love him for your sake because I was *stuck* with him. You understand?"

I nodded.

"Curt, I needed my life back. I sacrificed *everything*. I gave up my prime teenage years, my twenties, and almost all of my thirties for your dad. Even when he stepped out of our marriage for that teenager, I stayed on."

Again, I just nodded.

"Your dad has always been cruel to me. And I know we weren't good parents to you and your sister and brother. Your father hurt all of us in many ways—he hurt me in ways you don't even know. And there's no excuse for any of that, even though I tried making excuses all these years."

Jan began to cry.

"Just so you know, I *never* cheated on your dad, despite what he claims. I don't know if he's getting unstable because he's on or off his meds or what. But … it's just been too much." Jan wiped away her tears, lit a fresh cigarette. "Fighting every single day, all these years … screaming and worse. Goddammit, I deserve a break. I deserve to have my own life now."

I believed her. I understood her. Even if I hadn't, I would've pretended I did out of respect for the life she lived and what her loyalty to my brother and me had cost her.

Jan was the definition of unconditional love and sacrifice.

I reached for Jan's hand across the table and gave it a squeeze. "I know you deserve all of that, Mom. I really do."

Jan smiled and sniffled. She squeezed my hand back. "You've always been the sweet one, Curt."

We chatted for a while longer and then parted ways with a hug and promises to make time to get together again soon. I went off to work, thinking about everything Jan and I had discussed, and about how drastically and quickly things were changing—especially for Bear.

***

YOU'VE HEARD people say that hindsight is 20/20 and that "red flags" are what they are—you see warning signs ... but what do you do about them?

In some of the letters my dad wrote in 1994, you could see he was in a bad place and that his prescriptions weren't helping him cope with anything. There were notes he'd leave for me when I'd swing by his house for a visit and they concerned me greatly. I tried to comfort him and talk to him at these times. He'd tell me not to worry ... he just missed Jan is all, he was lonely, and his heart hurt.

But I learned later that that Bear was just *telling* me benign things while unbeknownst to me, he was separately *writing* down what was *really* raging on in his distraught head and heart.

I didn't realize at the time how off the rails my dad really was, but I know now that he was better at telling the truth of how he felt through writing. He had learned to do that in the psychiatric hospital, so he wrote the family and me letters to get his emotions and thoughts out via pen and paper.

Unfortunately, I never got those letters at the time.

Then there were other Bear letters with much more serious and foreboding tones and warnings in his words that Aunt Penny got her hands on—but she didn't share them with my family or me until the worst had already happened.

You can't throw someone a life preserver if you don't see them or hear them screaming for help. You can't rescue or warn anyone if you're told things are sunny and fine, yet you shoulda got the memo that a fierce hurricane is coming so you can batten down the hatches and at least try and save everyone in its oncoming path.

MARCH 1, 1994

To my loved ones,

I love you all.

This letter is to let everybody know how I feel inside and how hurt and lost one can get.

My world has given up on me. I am dead on the inside and just haven't laid down to let the rest go. I will never give up on my marriage because I know God made Jan for me, to be with me the rest of my life—how ever long it may be!

I know I haven't been a very good father or husband, but the Lord has told me what to do to make it work and I will try my hardest until my last breath.

I'm laying here on my wife's and my bed and holding her pillow in my arms because I can smell her on it and it makes me feel good. I know in my heart that you love me, honey (Jan). I just pray you would open your heart to me, with all that I have to give you, how could you not, for I love you more than anyone could ever ...

— Robert "Bear" Duffy

TWELVE
RED FLAGS WAVING

Circa 1994

Curt,

I'm real sick and don't know what is wrong. I'm sorry for bringing this on you. This is your most important time in life. But when I come home to this house, I can't deal with it. No one here … I miss all of you so very much it hurts. I've tried to talk to your mom but she won't talk to me. Maybe you can. There is no way we can make it here, we don't have enough money for bills or anything. You need your mom here, your sister, your niece. I see it in your face every day. I see the hurt and paint and ask God to give me your hurt and pain so you don't feel it. But I still see it. I'm sorry your mom and I put that there.

This is supposed to be a happy time for you. You are about to graduate and go to college, but I know you're not happy. This should be a happy time for our family, our son is almost grown and making a father _very proud_. I am so happy for you making something of yourself.

I'm sitting here so very tired. My head hurts. I'm so very cold, my stomach is killing me and my heart is smashed.

I don't remember when I ate last other than coffee. I quit taking my medication a couple of days ago. I guess I'm not supposed to, but I give it all to God to take care of it.

I'm tired now. When you get home, call your sister and see if she will come ... or call your mom or Angie. I need someone. Your Uncle Bill has to work

All my love, Dad.

*Tell your mom I love her.

*Wake me up when you get home for a hug.

*Call your mom…

∼

"DAD?" I called out as I entered the house.

There was no response.

As I set my keys on the countertop, I discovered a prescription bottle on its side with dozens of pills spilling out.

It had been a busy night at the restaurant. I had promised Dad that I'd stay with him that night and we'd do breakfast together in the morning. I was looking forward to a hot shower and bed.

Now this.

Please, Dad, tell me you didn't OD on this shit …

I entered my father's bedroom and turned on the light. There Bear lay, facedown, splayed across the mattress. I checked for a pulse. It was there. He was alive and breathing evenly, but seeing him in that condition, it struck me how gaunt he'd become—no longer the imposing guy he'd once been. I shut the light off and turned to leave.

"Jan?" Bear whispered. "That you, Jan?"

I hesitated, not wanting him to know I'd heard this vulnerability. "No, Dad. It's Curt. Just got in."

"There's only Jan. Only Jan, Curt … only her."

I stepped out of the room.

"I don't want to ever wake up again …" my dad mumbled in the darkness.

∼

THAT NIGHT SHOOK ME.

A couple of weeks later, I stopped by to check in on Dad.

"Curt, come here." Bear waved me over to the living room.

I looked around. The house appeared to have been emptied out. Something was off. It was odd as fuck.

"Where's all of your stuff?"

Bear shrugged. "I got rid of a bunch of shit I don't need anymore. Gave Penny some furniture. Gave some of the guys in my MC all my bike parts and cleared out the rest of the junk."

Drained. That's how I remember my dad looking. I almost said something, but I was still trying to process the fact that Bear would clean house in such a profound way. Like a lot of people who experienced true poverty, my father had always held on to *everything*, no matter how worthless it may have appeared to the outside world.

I'll wait. Maybe I'll talk to him later, I thought.

Bear waved a hand at the nearby stereo system. "I want you to have this."

"What? No way."

The massive, high-end, Pioneer stereo had a turntable, equalizer, tape deck, and a 185-watt-per-channel receiver that weighed around eighty pounds. A pair of enormous speakers flanked the rack of components. I had grown up with this stereo. It had been taller than me for a long spell. Bear *treasured* this system. He never considered selling it even when the pantry was extremely fucking light in the way of food. He loved it; loved cranking his favorite albums through it.

"I can't believe you're just giving this to me. This is, like, one of your favorite things. Don't you wanna listen to your music?"

"Nah." Bear stared blankly. "You can have all my albums, too. I'm simplifying shit. You always liked this stereo, so it's yours."

"Well, hell, yeah!" I exclaimed, visions of my favorite heavy metal records shaking the foundations of my new apartment building dancing in my head.

Concern was replaced by enthusiasm in my teenaged brain. If only Id've just *really* looked around. If only …

Hindsight, right?

We loaded the stereo into my car and shared a half-hug. I drove back to my place with Bear following to help set it up.

"Fuck it." Bear said, more to himself than me. "Can't take it with you."

Funny how what sounds like enlightenment can in truth be nihilism —the appearance of a ghost that will haunt you forever, even though you don't know it yet.

THIRTEEN
DEATH TRAP

"Happy anniversary!"

Bear was outside Jan's apartment, roses and card in hand.

From the window, Jan told him to go away or she'd call the cops.

"This is the last time I'm ever going to try," Bear said.

The last time ...

~

I FOUND out later that my father had written letters to the Duffy family just a few weeks before he did the unimaginable in 1994.

He wrote numerous letters telling us how lost he was, how he couldn't handle life anymore, how doomed our family was, apologizing for all the bad he'd done to us all, how God told him what to do to make everything right, and how Jan was on his mind 24/7 and he didn't want to live without her at his side anymore.

He had given his letters to my Aunt Penny who shared them with the family and I *after* my father had set out and completed his mission.

I wish Id've seen all this *before* Bear completed his mission because all of our lives maybe could've turned out so much better—and my parents might still be alive.

◃≈

AUGUST 20, 1994

To My Dearest Family ,

This is my last request I will ever make of anyone. Myself and my wife—and she is still my wife—Jan Marlene Duffy are both to me cremated together and our ashes to be spread on the mountains of Colorado overlooking Colorado Springs.

This is my last dying request.

Penny, you are to see to this before Jan's family gets involved. Please. If this cannot be fulfilled, we are to be buried side-by-side no matter what anyone says. She is not to be taken to Colorado without me.

Please Penny see to this.

Jan and my children are here and here's where we should be. I'm sorry this has happened, but I know no one understands how deeply in love with Jan I am.

Family, I do love my wife and have for almost 20 years. I know she was put on this earth for me. It is in my heart of mine and could never go away. NEVER. I have fought for and cried for her and will die for her.

I know what I've done is the unforgivable sin, but our GOD will forgive all sins and so must you all.

I just can't go on seeing my wife out drinking and partying without me ... with the people she hangs out with ... it kills me more and more every day.

I've tried the drugs, the nut house, and my family and friends, but nothing seems to ease the pain. It just gets worse ... what I have to deal with every day. Please try to understand but I pray you can all forgive me.

All My Love To You All,

Robert Earl Duffy

*Penny take care of my family for me.

— Robert "Bear" Duffy

◃≈

MY FATHER PULLED into the Kroger parking lot that September day in 1994 behind the wheel of no ordinary car. He had traded some shit for a cheap heap and had gotten right to work on the last build he'd ever make.

Bear had ditched the antidepressants, antipsychotics, and non-benzodiazepine hypnotics cold turkey—he couldn't have pulled anything off on all of those pills. He'd taken that car, stripped it down, rigged it to the max, and created a true deathtrap.

Bear built a "Death Proof" car akin to the stunt car in the Quentin Tarantino movie of the same name—and made with eerily similar intentions.

No one was going to ever get in that car and roll down the windows or unlock it—only Bear could do that from the driver's side.

No way his passenger would get out unless someone did so from the outside—no door handles. He had removed the backseat and left only the two front seats.

Bear lay in wait until Jan and her coworker Angie appeared, then floored his car toward the pair as they walked toward McDonald's golden arches on their lunch break.

I wonder what was going on in Bear's head at that moment. Was he upset that Jan's friends, such as Angie, provided support, happy that Jan had gotten away from Bear? Maybe he was convinced he'd catch her with a new flame. I'm sure the presence of Angie didn't de-escalate those feelings. Whatever the case, it's impossible to retroactively read my father's mind.

Here's what I do know:

When Bear reached Jan and Angie, he jumped out of that customized car with his every step carefully calculated. And despite a court order barring him from possessing firearms, Bear still had a few tucked away and on his person—like the sawed-off shotgun he now pointed at his soon-to-be-ex-wife, for example.

Jan's eyes were wide. "Bear? What the hell are you doing?"

Bear grabbed a fistful of Jan's blonde hair and pulled her head toward the barrel of the shotgun. "You're coming home with me. *Forever!*"

Jan screamed and struggled as Bear pushed her into the car and slammed the door shut. She pounded on the passenger window and door. Useless.

Angie grabbed Bear as he walked around to the driver's side. "Are you insane? You can't do this!"

Bear whirled and turned the shotgun on her. "Get away from me, bitch, or I'll blow your fucking head off!"

Angie put her hands up and backed away, then ran for help as Bear peeled out of the parking lot.

My parents were going home again.

~

HERE'S a report from the *Associated Press* that gives an overview of the events that followed:

TEN-HOUR STANDOFF **at Home Results in Homicide-Suicide**
Man Shoots Wife, then Kills Himself
September 14, 1994
ST. LOUISVILLE, Ohio. A man took his estranged wife hostage at a store, then held police at bay outside his home for ten hours before shooting the woman and himself to death, authorities said Tuesday. Newark Police stormed the house at about 10 p.m. Monday [September 12, 1994] and found that Robert E. Duffy, 39, and Jan M. Duffy, 37, had been shot in the chest. Duffy was pronounced dead at the house. Mrs. Duffy, of Johnstown, was taken to Licking County Memorial Hospital in Newark, where she died, said Vicky Walbright, a nursing supervisor. Both had been shot with a 9mm assault weapon similar to a rifle, said sheriff's Capt. Ray Back. He said the shootings were being investigated as a homicide-suicide.

The Duffys were separated and were getting a divorce, Back said. Authorities said Duffy abducted his wife from a grocery store in Johnstown Monday afternoon and drove to his home near this Licking County village. Sheriff's deputies and police surrounded the house and began negotiating for Duffy's surrender. Police decided to force their way into the house after hearing one gunshot from inside at about 10 p.m., the sheriff's department said. Duffy told a negotiator by phone that he had accidentally fired the gun and was about to surrender. But after waiting a few minutes, the negotiator called back and got only an answering machine. Police then tossed tear gas canisters through several windows and entered the house. Back said Duffy's sister, Penny R. Peterson, 34, who lived with her brother, was charged with obstructing justice during the negotiations. A bond hearing was held Tuesday in Licking County Municipal Court, and she was released on her own recognizance.

As is so often the case, what's printed in the papers isn't always quite accurate and only tells a fraction of this story.

FOURTEEN
UNDER SIEGE

B ear wrote specific suicide letters to me, my siblings, and Aunt
Penny—along with letters and notes he'd written from March
through August 1994. He provided detailed instructions on the
disposition of his intentionally meager estate, his debts, his body, and the
people he owed money to—even the details of how he wanted to be laid
to rest. He packaged up all of these letters and instructions in a five-by-
seven-inch tan envelope and sealed it shut on the morning of September
12, 1994.

With his suicide package in hand, Bear drove the approximately ten
miles from his house to the Kelsey Hayes Company in Mt. Vernon where
Penny was a clerk. My dad had worked at Kelsey Hayes for a short time.
His employment ended because of his psychological and physical issues.

Penny's daughter, Shawna, called her mom at 10:30 a.m. to say she
was sick and needed to leave school early. Penny couldn't leave work to
pick her up, so she told Shawna to walk to Kelsey Hayes and sleep in
Penny's gray Ford Taurus until she could take her home after work.

Bear arrived at around 11 a.m. and chatted with his sister for awhile.
When she (allegedly) asked him if he would take Shawna home, he
demurred.

"No ... no, he couldn't!" Penny reportedly exclaimed as she watched

CURTIS DUFFY & JEREMY WAGNER

her brother walk across the parking lot to his car. "He's going to kill himself today. Oh, my God. He said today is the day."

But she didn't run out after him … maybe Penny had to think about the situation some more. Let it *really* sink in despite all the warnings. Hell, she'd known Bear's intentions for some time before this day … but she had a lunch break coming up, so …

Penny had allegedly been telling her coworkers for three weeks that she was worried that my dad would commit murder and kill himself. She had kept all those family letters Bear wrote the month before that pretty much showed the writing on the wall. The Friday before the standoff, Penny let slip that she was going to see my dad that day to give him some money; that she believed the *murder-suicide would occur over that weekend or on my parents wedding anniversary on the following Monday and that she hoped he wouldn't hurt anyone else.*

Just so matter of fact. Like a weekend barbecue or a day at the races.

How this didn't lead to someone, anyone, dropping a dime to the cops and have a SWAT team descending on my father's house before he went too far, I'll never understand.

Bear spotted Shawna in the backseat of Penny's car en route to his own and passed off the suicide package with a warning that sounded menacing to her. "Don't you dare open this," he said, glaring at her. "It's for your mom. You give it to her later when she's away from work."

Penny got Bear's package an hour or so after he'd driven off to abduct Jan. Police reports have indicated that he left Kelsey Hayes at approximately 12:05 p.m. Around the same time, Penny left the office to go to lunch with a coworker-boyfriend named Steve. Later, a little after one, Penny and Steve returned from lunch. Penny went to check on Shawna. Penny opened the envelope, gasped, and bolted from her car. She rushed into her office, distraught, and immediately began making phone calls to try to locate Bear. Coworkers watched as she raced around the office, shaking and frantically calling numbers over and over with no success.

As Penny desperately tried to reach Bear, he actually called *her* at the office. Coworkers overheard her begging my father not to do anything until she saw him in person.

She asked if Jan was with him and if Jan was okay. She also asked if Jan was *tied up*—a disturbing question for those who heard it.

Penny hung up, extremely agitated, telling her stunned coworkers she had to leave immediately because her brother had kidnapped his wife and she had to stop him from hurting her. Penny's boyfriend Steve wanted to go with her, but she refused.

"I don't want anyone else to get hurt."

Penny left at 1:20 p.m.

≈

BEAR FORCED Jan out of the death trap car and into his house, which had undergone a sinister redesign.

What furniture was left had been turned into barricades in front of doors and boarded up windows. He'd made sure if—*when?*—his place was surrounded, no one could locate him. Bear also made sure there was only one way in and out of the house—through a side door. Anyone who breached his makeshift fortress would be easily shot dead.

Bear had found an effective yet horrifying way to employ the tactical training he'd received courtesy of the state police academy.

≈

IT WAS a rare day off from work and school but, other than that, unremarkable. I woke up, ate, did homework in my living room—all while a metaphorical wrecking ball began its descent toward my life.

Two o'clock rolled around. My girlfriend Nikki arrived at my place after school, per usual, but rather than come up, she laid on the horn. I stuck my head out the second story window.

"Did you hear what happened?" Nikki yelled up to me.

"No. What?"

"Oh my god, *Curtis!* Cops came and took Trisha out of school today. Your dad took your mom hostage at gunpoint!"

As I ran downstairs to try to clarify what Nikki was saying, a Johnstown police officer—a townie asshole who'd always hated Bear and my family—arrived at my door.

"Your father is at his house," he said to me. "He's barricaded himself in with your mom as a hostage and we can't get to him. You need to come with me—now!"

I told Nikki I'd call her when I knew more and jumped in the back seat of the squad car. We took off and raced to St. Louisville, siren and lights blaring. We arrived at the scene, along with sheriff's department squad cars, SWAT vans, TV crews, ambulances and other emergency vehicles.

I was then brought down the road to some kind of safe house/command post. My sister was there, my older brother, a bunch of cops, and Uncle Bill, who had driven from Johnstown—where he was still a police officer—to St. Louisville, way the fuck out of his jurisdiction. He was clearly out of his element among all the *real* cops.

Phone negotiations had taken place between Uncle Bill and my dad, but Bear didn't care what Bill had to say ... leaving Bill to trip over his dick as he tried to act important. The next day, for some reason, Uncle Bill would attempt to gain entry into Jan's apartment, but thankfully the detectives wouldn't let him in. I still wonder what the fuck he tried to do that for ...

Oh, and there was also a priest on site of the siege and that instantly struck me as a bad omen.

I found out later that my dad had allowed Jan to make her final phone calls before the cops showed up. She called her family in Colorado and told them what was happening, triggering the police response. Angie, Jan's coworker, had obviously been in touch with the cops, but that was in Johnstown. They didn't realize that he'd taken Jan back to the house in St. Louisville, some thirty miles away.

My mom, weeping, told her family she loved them and said her goodbyes.

Jan also spoke with my sister Trisha one last time.

Bear asked to speak with me, but because he refused to cooperate, the cops wouldn't let him talk to me.

I'll go to my own grave wondering what my dad would've said—and whether I perhaps could've convinced him to peacefully abandon this madness.

FIFTEEN
LOADED FOR BEAR

"Robert. Please ... you don't have to do this. Think of the kids. Don't."

Perhaps Jan thought there was reason for hope: This was, after all, the same house in which Bear's own father—my Grandpa Temple—had kidnapped a girlfriend and held her hostage at gunpoint. That girl *lived*, although Grandpa went to prison for life. Jan must've prayed that history would repeat itself at 8146 Horns Hill Road—with her leaving that house alive and Bear behind bars, getting the help he needed.

But as Bear continued to menace her—with a scoped 9mm, semi-automatic, carbine-rifle that he wielded in place of the sawed-off shotgun, no less—it became clear the point of no return was fast approaching.

Cops with rifles, shotguns, and other tactical gear were positioned around the property and every nearby outbuilding.

They were loaded for bear—and for *Bear*.

One person not helping matters was my Aunt Penny, who, having fought off police attempts to drag her away, stationed herself at the side door to constantly serve as Robert's eyes and ears to the outside world.

"GI Joes out in the field, Robert!" Penny screamed when she saw a pair of officers in green camouflage tactical uniform creeping up from a nearby soybean field.

Penny had put those cops' lives in peril—Bear is, after all, armed with a semi-automatic carbine-rifle—but fortunately, Bear stood down and, as it grew darker outside, the officers crawled away.

It went on this way for ten hours—the back and forth negotiations, Penny pacing around the outside of the house as Bear's spotter.

Night had fallen and the entire house and property had so many spotlights on it, it was lit up like the brightest Christmas tree I'd ever seen.

I have the cassette tapes of all the attempts at communication between law enforcement officials and my dad, but I can't bring myself to listen to them. It's too intense for me to take in.

In most hostage situations, police do everything in their power to negotiate for a death-free outcome.

"You give us something, Bear, we'll give you something," the negotiator said. "Let Jan go, come out with your hands up. We'll work it all out."

But Bear had dug in like an Alabama tick, not giving a centimeter. The negotiators had delivered a pack of cigarettes to the side door and Penny handed it to Bear ... but he gave nothing back to anyone.

The cops shut off power to the house. They also cut the telephone lines so there was only one line open—direct to the command center. Anticipating things getting uglier, the sheriff called in the Special Operations Group (S.O.G.), whose primary mission is to reduce the risk of injury or death to everyone involved—hostages, innocent bystanders, law enforcement officers, and the perps themselves.

Numerous times during the standoff, Bear announced that he would give himself up in ten minutes.

It never happened.

At some point, snipers showed up. There was one on a huge, forested hill behind the house, one planted across the road in a corn field that faced the front of the house. Others covered the house, already surrounded by an army of cops.

The cops had a big surveillance microphone and captured some of what my dad and Penny were discussing. They also heard Bear tell Jan that he wouldn't let the cops put him in prison like his father—or shoot him—he'd do it himself.

At around 9:30 p.m. or so, Bear's agitation suddenly escalated. He lifted Jan up and shoved her into the master bedroom. He sat down next to her, the gun pointed at her head. Then her chest. A shot rang out.

Penny banged on the door frame from her position outside the house. "Robert! What was that?"

"Nothing! Just an accident!"

The police dialed in from the direct line. "That was just a fucking accident!" Bear sounded frantic. "I'm coming out. I'm gonna surrender."

He hung up.

The cops attempted to call again, but my dad stopped answering.

Officers smashed through the front door.

Tear gas rounds and flash bangs were blasted into the master bedroom.

Bear shot himself.

Right in the chest.

Just like he'd done to my mom.

A couple doors down, Robert and Trisha and I heard the call come over the radio: "*Shots fired! Shots fired!*"

"*What just happened?*"

Everybody at the safe house was on hold. Eventually, someone arrived to matter-of-factly give my brother and sister and me the news that my dad was dead and medics were transporting my mom to the hospital.

She's still alive.

I sank to the floor, shivering and sobbing. Someone—it may have been a pastor; I know there was one there—put their hand on my shoulder, but I barely even felt it. I could hear Robert Jr. (Tig) pounding a table and Trisha crying but the sounds barely registered. In that moment, I was an inconsolable wreck, alone, outside of time and space.

Finally, I was placed in the back of a police car next to Uncle Bill while two cops rode up front. I thought of the cops picking up the chatter between my dad and Jan with their big surveillance microphone and how my dad had told Jan that he wouldn't let the cops put him in prison like his father and that he'd do himself in. I remembered Bear had said this before—and not just aloud to my immediate family. I looked over at Uncle Bill and I suddenly remembered that my dad had also once actually told Bill the same thing—that Bear would kill himself before he'd ever go to prison. My dad and uncle were just bullshitting about Grandpa Temple going to prison himself at the time, but it made me wonder if my dad could've ever predicted this day would come.

Robert Jr. and Trisha left separately for the hospital, but I had wanted to grab my car and pick up Nikki first. They dropped me off at my apartment, where Nikki was waiting.

Nikki said she'd drive me to the hospital, but insisted we make a quick stop to check in with her parents on the way.

"No, I need to get to the hospital right away," I told her. "They told me at the scene she's still alive."

Oh, god … you have no idea how badly I wanted it to be true.

I was holding onto hope that the EMTs had saved her. Surely doctors were working on her at that very moment.

But Nikki insisted. I strode in the door of her parents house, too agitated and impatient to read the room. "Nikki said we had to come see you quick, but I have to go to my mother now." I said to Nikki's parents, who had stood up and were looking at each other and then to me. "I need to see how she's doing. She's alive."

Nikki's mom swallowed, hard, a stricken look washing across her face. I know it couldn't have been easy for her, but she told me straight: "Your mother's dead, Curtis. She didn't survive. I'm sorry."

"What? No! No! No! No! *Fuck no!*"

My world was ending. I screamed myself raw.

I HAD DATED Nikki for three years and I'm grateful she and her family were there for me. They loved me and took me in for a bit—just the way John Souza and his wife had done.

Despite that support, however, I was tormented. I was terrified to be alone *anywhere*. My traumatized, nineteen-year-old mind kept telling me that evil was all around me. I was afraid to close my eyes out of fear that when I opened them my father or my mother would be standing there, reaching for me with their dead hands.

It took a long time to feel normal and healthy again. I was haunted and pissed and wound up with all kinds of bad feelings in my heart.

Eventually, I would get to the place where I could see the light and goodness of life and in this world once again.

Nikki and her family and I are still friends. She's married and has three amazing kids. I last saw her at a film screening in Ohio. To this day, I feel like I'll never be able to thank them enough for being there for me during the most horrific episode of my life.

SIXTEEN
SO MUCH FOR LAST WISHES

U
ncle Bill called a family meeting at his house to discuss my
dad's estate shortly after the murder-suicide.

Aunt Penny, sprung after a few days in jail on obstruction
charges for interfering during the standoff, showed up along with her
kids. My sister Trisha, my brother, Robert Jr., and Bill's wife, Nell were
there as well.

Penny pulled out Bear's suicide package and, one by one, began
reading the letters my father had written to us. We were all crying.
Maybe the others, like me, were distressed by the signs they'd perhaps
missed; the alternate histories that might've been if a different choice had
been made at this or that moment.

Most of Bear's scant possessions had been ruined by the tear gas and
police activity, but Nikki's parents had pushed me to go in and get
anything personal as fast as possible. I'm so grateful for that nudge
because I soon learned that Penny had her own plans for Bear's house.
By the time I'd retrieved half my mementos, she'd changed the locks and
she wouldn't allow me in again.

One item I did manage to find in the house that Penny hadn't appro-
priated was a blue notebook the staff at the psychiatric hospital had
given Bear to write his thoughts in, as well as several personal letters,

including a letter he'd written to me more than six months before he died:

March 1, 1994

Curt,

This is Dad. I'm telling you from my heart that you're a very special young man and I wish I could tell you how proud of you I am …You'll be a great chef, no doubt in my mind, you'll be one of the best in the world someday …

Your life is just beginning. Try to do all the right things in it. Make sure if you ever get married and have children that you show them and your wife all the love in the world. Always take time to be with them and show them love. Your wife should be shown the most love of all. Always take the time to talk to her and hear what she has to say because she'll be the most important person in your life …

I ask you, Curt, to look back and see how many wrong things you have seen me do and please don't walk in my footsteps because you'll be in a world of pain, hate, and sure won't be loved and won't be able to show love. So please be a better person than I was. I know you can …

Remember I love you, son, and always will.

My love,

Your dad

YOU HAVE no idea how much it haunts me that I had to wait until he died to receive such love and affirmation from him.

THE GATHERING at Bill's place also turned out to be the opening shot in a Duffy family World War III. The fighting stretched on for months and months. My two aunts—Penny and Nell—began fighting over who should get the house, just as they'd done back when Grandpa Temple went to prison.

Penny claimed she'd paid the mortgage when my father couldn't afford it. As Bear planned the murder-suicide, he had apparently signed his house and other things over to Penny's name. So, in the end, Penny ended up getting the house.

One thing that contradicts Penny's claim?

The suicide letters Bear left behind.

There's one that was very specific about wanting my family to sell the house and use the proceeds to "pay for Curtis's college."

If Dad thought Penny would execute his wishes and take care of me and my siblings, his trust was misplaced: Penny fixed the place up, sold it, and kept all the money.

On the other side, things weren't much better. All my mom's memorial contributions were to go to the "Terpstra Family for the Duffy Children's Education Fund," but my siblings and I were screwed out of that as well.

So much for last wishes.

WHAT WOULD it be like if my mom and dad were still here?

Maybe I wouldn't have developed as much drive to be successful if they were still here.

To be clear: I absolutely do wish more than anything that my parents were still around and that they could have everything that I have right now—all the happiness, a family.

I don't know how to make sense of the world sometimes; I'm just trying to navigate it. But I am a true believer when it comes to things happening for a reason.

I believe it even when it's impossible to fathom what that reason could possibly be.

I HAVE a photo that's very special to me.

In the photo, I'm in a sharp chef's uniform and large chef's hat with my mom and dad on either side of me as I hold a prize-winning culinary *pièce de résistance* of assorted fruits presented in an artful way on a platter. I had just won a high school competition that earned me a scholarship for a college I didn't go to.

It took a while for my parents to realize how serious I was about cooking. But as they saw the amount of time I devoted to working and my passion for the kitchen, they began to acknowledge that I was doing something with my life.

My parents were already separated when the picture was taken. Jan absolutely did *not* want to be anywhere near Dad. But she steeled herself and showed up to support me.

That is love.

~

WAS THERE MORE TO ROBERT "BEAR" Duffy than the cold, abusive individual who lived and died so violently?

Yeah, of course.

Bear put on a hard, rough 'n' tough, take-no-shit persona twenty-four/seven. That badass façade with the big beard, biker tattoos. He fought men of every size—bikers, cops, and sheriffs. He fought the world, and the world fought back, which hardened him even more. He'd had a rough life growing up and inherited a toxic cycle of cold-bloodedness and violence. All that physical, mental, and biological damage from the Temple family line added misery to his already piss-poor life of constant hardship. It trickled down and poisoned his soul. He was as dark and cold as they come, always with a grim outlook. Anger was his go-to emotion.

I don't remember happiness ever existing in our house. I wish it had. I want to tell everyone funny stories that happened, but, goddamn, it's so hard to remember funny stories about my dad. They just don't exist.

I could easily hate Bear.

I don't.

And when I refer to Bear's "badass façade." that's not a diss. He was capable of love but was perhaps too scared to show it without chemistry.

Know what I mean?

I do believe that beneath the intimidating veneer was a vulnerable man with an actual *heart*. His brutal nature was always his dominant side. But he was also an artist and a musician. He loved riding in the wind. He loved to build things. He loved drag cars.

You're not a creative without a heart. You don't feel passion for things if you don't have a heart.

And I know that my dad loved me. He admired my path in life, wanted to speak to me before he died, wanted to look out for my education and pay it off. Under those terrible final circumstances, he was still thinking of me, y'know? In that sense, I believe that Bear was really a caring person.

In some fucked-up way, I believe his heart may have been too big for this world.

My love for him is unconditional to this day.

Average people judged my dad for the long hair, the earrings, the tattoos, the holes in the jeans, the chain hanging from his belt to his wallet, the leather jacket—all that stuff. And sure, he was scary as fuck. Hardly anyone ever tried to have an actual conversation with him, unfortunately. Those who *did* found out that he was smart; that he'd soften a little if there was a common thread. Often as not, they'd walk away from that conversation liking the guy.

It's a shame that so few people could see his other side. Even Bear's own father, William Temple—a.k.a. Grandpa Temple—who was alive when my dad killed Jan and himself never saw it or cared to see it.

I visited my Grandpa Temple in prison one last time after my father and Jan died.

No grief, no comments from Grandpa Temple.

He really didn't give a fuck.

That should tell you all you need to know.

How deep do you really want to dig in the family plot?

I have a cousin, it turns out: Charles "Chuck" Duffy. He was from Mount Vernon, Ohio. It's in Knox County, Ohio, where both my biological parents are from and where my dad spent his childhood. It's about forty minutes from Licking County, the location of Johnstown and St. Louisville, where we lived after the move back from Colorado.

If you Google Mount Vernon, you might find that American pioneer and folkloric figure Johnny Appleseed once owned two plots there. Or that it's the hometown of actor and comedian, Paul Lynde.

But Knox County is toxic, haunted like some town in a Stephen King story. If you Google "murder-suicide in Mount Vernon," you'll find reports of many, many such incidents, including one particular item about a forty-one-year-old man who took his forty-nine-year-old girl-friend hostage inside their Mount Vernon-area home on Monday, August 5, 2013 and shot her before he turned the gun on himself. Their names were Charles Duffy and Christy Robinson.

History has a fucked-up way of repeating itself in my family and in those counties down in Ohio.

I'm so grateful that I got out and broke that violent cycle.

I never take it for granted that I had the determination and strength to drop the axe on that harmful succession.

There but for the grace of God go I … maybe Bear would've said that.

As I PLOWED FORWARD and upward from the trauma of my parents murder-suicide, I tried therapy.

I couldn't afford a professional therapist as I was paying for school and living on my own. My school offered a counselor for free.

How do you think the school counselor wanted to help me?

Antidepressants!

Like father, like son?

No, thank you.

I politely said goodbye and got on track all on my own.

SEVENTEEN
DEATH AFTER LIFE

How do you say a last goodbye to two parents at the same time?

First there was a Bear and Jan memorial deal at a church in Newark, Ohio, put together by some sympathetic family members, a few close friends, and me. Jan's family didn't want her memorialized in Ohio, but I felt compelled to do something locally to honor them both.

LATER, my father had his own funeral service, an open casket affair. All his biker club buddies came out to say goodbye. As I shook their hands, I kept looking over at Bear, laid there before me, resting peacefully, his hair down, in his blue jeans, biker vest, earrings, all his jewelry. I just couldn't believe he was actually gone.

Aunt Penny kept Dad's ashes and took them to Colorado. My father wanted to be spread on the top of Pikes Peak Mountain, overlooking Colorado Springs. I don't know why. It must have meant something to him and Mom.

My dad's wishes never happened.

Penny eventually let Bear's ashes go on some mountain—but she did it all by herself. She never asked me or my siblings to participate. So, I don't know where Dad's final resting place actually is. I've been on the mountain many, many times and created my own moments up there in his memory. I made a cross and put it in a place that overlooks Pikes Peak, where I thought his ashes might've been spread. That's the spot where I honor my father.

Another way I honored my father a few years ago was to grow my hair long for the first time. I actually rocked a ponytail for a moment. My dad had always had long hair, aside from his short stint as a cop. During that time, it was the weirdest experience for me to see my father with short hair—and no beard, just a cop mustache. His hair was so amazing, I couldn't wait for him to grow it back after he quit that job with the Johnstown PD. I thought then, and I still think now: long-haired guys are badass.

I NEEDED to say goodbye to Jan—but her family in Colorado had taken custody of her body and insisted she would have neither a funeral nor a cremation in Ohio.

They wanted her home in Colorado, immediately, and had swiftly put things in motion.

Why won't they let me say goodbye?

Trisha also needs to say goodbye to her mother.

Why are they doing this?

With some wrangling, I was able to block the transit of Jan's body. The hearse actually made a U-turn on the way to the airport. After the logistics were hammered out, I was told that a funeral home in another Ohio town would accommodate Trisha and me, allowing us to view our mother's body, briefly, before it continued to Colorado.

We made it to the funeral home and were asked to wait in the empty lobby. It was quiet until the squeaking wheels of a gurney sounded through the building. My heart began to pound.

She's here. Mom is here.

A man appeared and ushered my sister and me into a large room. It smelled of disinfectant.

Jan lay beneath a sheet on top of a gurney in the middle of the room.

I immediately began weeping. I only vaguely remember Trisha even being in the room but I'm sure she was crying, too.

The attendant looked at his watch, frowned. "You have thirty minutes," he said and walked out of the room.

I slowly approached. I had a million memories in my head and a million things I wanted to say as I stared at her lifeless body. She'd been embalmed for transport so the only color on her flesh was the bruised areas near the coroner's massive, stitched-up Y-cut.

"Mom … I … I don't …"

The last time I'd seen Jan, she was lively and excited about her next chapter in life.

Young enough to start over.

Now she was gone.

I blinked away tears and hesitantly caressed Jan's face. Her skin was cold to my touch.

I would've given *anything* to have those eyes open again.

I would've given anything to have my father back again, too.

I'm so proud of you, Curtis. My dad's voice echoed in my head, loud enough to be heard over Trisha's sobs.

"Goodbye, Mom," I said, then we watched the man take her body away.

~

I COULDN'T GO to Mom's service.

She was cremated in Colorado and her family took the ashes.

I try to summon up every good memory of her and how the light of her soul was channeled through her body. But memory is my nemesis sometimes. In my mind's eye, I envision her body lifeless, no makeup, skin white and bloodless, bruised, stitched up, with needle marks on her arms and neck where the Franklin County morgue had drawn blood.

And there's memories of those insensitive detectives who made me look at my parents autopsy photos.

Are these your parents?

As I I try and purge horrible images from my mind, I wouldn't trade that opportunity to say goodbye to Jan for anything, but I paid a price for it.

103

There's a columbarium for Jan's urn inside a mausoleum in Colorado Springs. Every time I go back, I visit her there. She has a nice little plaque. I bring family photos of my daughters and me and place them on it.

~

MY EX-WIFE KIM and I have two daughters, and I wanted them to know the truth about the grandparents they've never met.

As you might imagine, I struggled about how to explain it.

Years ago, when Ava and Eden first asked about their grandparents, I told them that when they got older, I'd share the story—I couldn't find the courage to do it then. I'd always say, "Oh, your grandparents aren't living. They were in an accident and passed away." I left it at that because Kim and I both felt they were too young to understand the magnitude of what happened. Why put my girls through that?

I also wanted to have the confidence in myself to be able to tell them without breaking down, because whenever I'd think about my parents murder-suicide, I'd just lose it. My oldest daughter Ava is in college now but she was always a very emotional girl, empathetic in the extreme. I never wanted her or her sister to take on this burden that I've felt so heavy on my heart for all these years.

But kids are intuitive. They know.

"Mom, I feel … I feel something bad about Dad's parents," Ava said to Kim one day when she was around twelve years old, seemingly out of nowhere. "What happened?"

Kim answered as we always had, saying that my parents simply died in an accident.

"But I feel … I feel it had something to do," Ava continued, "with a *gunshot*."

Gunshot?

Where Ava got that idea from is anyone's guess. I know that the violent details of my parents deaths had never even been discussed among adults in my house, much less in front of my girls or with them.

But around the time she entered sixth grade, *For Grace* was streaming on Netflix and I became concerned that one of her friends would see it and ask her or tease her about it—or that someone would say something to Eden, who's three years younger. That would've been devastating to me: It was *my* story to tell, period.

The time had come.

I was incredibly nervous. I didn't want my girls to hate my father. And I was doing this alone because by this point, Kim and I had long been divorced.

After dinner that night, we all climbed in my bed. I made things super-comfortable for them. I turned the TV off and eliminated all the nonsense noise so I could have their attention. I told them stories about themselves first—fun stories from when they were little girls. I shared nice stories about myself when I was their age. Then bit by bit, I slowly told them what happened to their grandparents. I didn't go into the graphic descriptions, but I was one-hundred percent truthful. I explained that wherever my parents were at that moment—in heaven or another beautiful place—they were happy and always watching over them.

"They're super proud of you," I said. "They see where you are and that you're getting straight A's in school. They love you both and they love being your grandparents."

Both the girls cried. It took everything inside of me to not cry, too, as I felt their emotion. I kept my composure, faking a cough or sneeze when necessary. We hugged for a while. I told them that I want them to always ask questions; that they should never feel that they can't ask about my parents. I explained how I'd had to process my parents deaths by myself since I was just a teenager … and I never wanted them to feel like that, ever.

I THINK of my parents being somewhere in the great beyond, but they are always close.

I take comfort in believing they're somewhere better.

PART FOUR

Second City, Second Chances

EIGHTEEN
HOT TO TROTTER

The shadow cast by the violent deaths of my parents was long.
Too long.

It motivated me even more strongly to get out of Ohio.

And I already knew the storied city I would set my sights on.

As I became more captivated with being a chef in my teen years in the mid-nineties, I devoured the Charlie Trotter cookbooks I'd found in an Ohio bookstore, falling in love with his style of food and philosophy. Then, after I got my first computer, I would scour the internet for new information on this guy and his restaurant.

I was obsessed.

He was my food hero.

One day, perhaps tired of hearing about my unrequited Trotter love, Regan Koivisto—the Muirfield banquet chef who later invited me to join him at Tartan Fields—grabbed me, picked up the phone, and dialed Trotter's restaurant. How, Regan inquired, might a young man such as his friend here get his foot in the door?

The voice on the other end kindly walked us through the process of sending in a résumé with a cover letter. Next thing I knew, the Trotter team had invited me up to work as a *stagiaire*.

If everyone had a friend like Regan, the world would be a better place.

Most high-end restaurants will invite somebody who's looking for a job to "stage," which is essentially a short-term stint as a trainee, an unpaid apprentice. It works well for everyone because the chef gets to interview and observe while the potential hire gets to see if this is something that he or she really wants to do before either side commits too much time or effort.

I couldn't believe I was actually going to work in Charlie fuckin' Trotter's kitchen. I staged for two weeks. To this day, it was one of the greatest restaurants I've *ever* worked in. The learning curve was off the charts: groundbreaking menus, pristine produce coming in the back door every single day, the caliber of people working there, the attention to detail. The custom stoves and next-level kitchen accessories blew me away. I'd never seen anything like it.

And on my third day … Trotter himself offered me a full-time job! I was floored.

Unfortunately, I couldn't take the position because I was still in college back in Columbus—as I explained to the *chef de cuisine*, Matthias Merges. But Matthias and I kept in close contact. I definitely didn't want an *out of sight, out of mind* situation to develop.

I made the move to Chicago in 2000 solely to work for Charlie.

The pay wasn't great. In fact, back in Ohio I was then making *three times* the salary I was offered. That was fine. It wasn't about the money for me—the opportunity and experience would be priceless.

However, by this time, my new girlfriend Kim and I had gotten married and she proved a harder sell on the pay cut. We were going to have to rely on her ability to become the primary breadwinner if we relocated. Still, she had faith in my desire to follow my dreams and I was—and remain—immensely grateful to her.

I met Kim while working at Muirfield. It's common wisdom that one should never date a coworker. For me, however, the situation seemed ideal, especially as Kim's role at Muirfield had her working during the same hours, though fewer than mine. When Kim and I hooked up, we were both finishing college at Ohio State in Columbus. Kim's career goals weren't culinary, they were music-related. She taught voice and violin and sang opera. She was working as a part-time banquet server, and I was one of the chefs.

Kim and I moved in together pretty quickly and had been dating for a few years by the time we moved to Chicago. Regan Koivisto's sister had worked for a jeweler and got me a discount on an engagement ring. I had the ring with me when Kim and I went to visit my family in Colorado Springs, and that's where I asked her to marry me.

During our trip, Kim and I went up to Pikes Peak together to the spot where I thought my father's remains were dispersed. From there, I drove us up the mountain—it takes a couple of hours to get to the very top. Once you're there, it's beautiful and the view is incredible.

About halfway up the north side of the mountain, we pulled over at the Crystal Creek Reservoir, a beautiful, 136-acre lake. I had the ring and I was so damn nervous about proposing that I just wanted to get it over with. I jumped out of the car and ran down into the woods across the road, waving at her to come and join me. She was a little confused because she thought I was going into the woods to take a piss. But she did follow me down and that's where I asked her to marry me.

Kim said, "Yes."

Newly engaged, we traveled back to Ohio—we hadn't moved to Chicago yet—and we finally tied the knot a couple years later in Marion, Ohio, where Kim was from. We had a traditional reception dinner and I catered it. I hired a couple of my cooks from Tartan Fields to help and we prepared all the food ourselves. Regan's wife was a cake decorator and she made individual cakes for each table. We had about a hundred people total, all friends and family.

By then, we'd been living in the Windy City for two years or so, and thankfully, since I had taken such a pay cut, Kim—who'd decided against pursuing a musician's career, despite her talent—had landed a great job at the Chicago Symphony Orchestra as a project manager and fundraiser. She's raised millions of dollars for them.

Working for Charlie was like physically living inside one of his books. I was relentlessly pushed to perform at a first-class level of excellence, learning directly from the master himself about innovations in restaurant and kitchen management.

It was the hardest job I've ever had.

We provided an *impeccable* dining experience. Charlie gave me a world-class education in the nuanced, sophisticated love affair between ambience, service, cuisine, and wine—a "four pillars" approach I use to this day.

The restaurant was beautiful from top to bottom. Charlie invested in the best, most modern kitchen equipment: custom-made French Bonnet stoves, made-to-order freezers, and a stainless-steel ceiling that ate vented smoke. The wine cellar was a gorgeous room, well stocked with the best wines available. The small, intimate dining rooms featured lush, cushy carpet and heavy, draped linens. There were beautiful sconces on the walls and every chair was fabricated by an artist. The china came from Bernadotte and Limoges and the serving ware from Christofle. Every detail was designed to exude luxury and add to the guest's dining experience.

Then there was the cuisine ... Charlie was on an entirely different, transcendent level. It wasn't just about being fancy with beluga caviar and truffles. At that time, other restaurants didn't respect vegetables the way they do now, and it was Charlie's uncommon approach to them that won my heart. He would elevate and showcase vegetarian dishes and sauces in new and thoughtful ways, in the presentation, and in the overall sensory experience of tasting and touching food, be it seeds, legumes, vegetables or fruits. He could take the simplest ingredients and make them into something mind-blowing and extravagant. He would offer guests a huge, multi-course menu featuring vegetable degustation. And there was a cool chef's table in the kitchen where lucky diners could observe the kitchen staff doing their thing.

I recall some of Charlie's memorable dishes: citrus-cured salmon and sorrel; Muscovy duck with smoked coconut, spring onion, and Venezuelan chocolate; candied buddha's hand with a yummy cardamom-scented ricotta soufflé; pan-roasted squab breasts done with birch, devil's club root, and black trumpet mushrooms; baby carrot terrine with shiitake mushroom salad; and arugula noodles with smoked yellow tomato sauce, in which the tomatoes were smoked over hickory chips burning from the flame of a propane torch.

Charlie would make a dish pairing fifty-five-plus-year-old balsamic vinegar with marinated Portobello mushrooms, then mix that up with garlic, ginger, jalapeno, cilantro, and soy. There was an Asian-style haggis, where he took the internal organs of a sheep—lungs, liver, and heart, etc.—and mixed them up with lemongrass, star anise, and ginger, along with traditional suet and stock, and stuffed it all into some type of animal casing.

Charlie loved to experiment—we were kindred spirits in that way.

He definitely brought out my inner mad scientist.

Charlie also used unorthodox methods to motivate the staff. We might be asked to give a speech on a certain topic or write a book report or even engage in role-playing to better ourselves and the restaurant. He was an unconventional mentor who instilled in everyone a passion for excellence—and then helped them develop the skillset to obtain it.

How Charlie did that is a story worthy of its own chapter.

NINETEEN
THE EXCELLENCE PROGRAM

C harlie called it *The Excellence Program*.
Three days a week, Charlie would bring in a group—we might host underprivileged children or academic scholars one day, firefighters and police officers the next—to be fed *gratis* from the menu we would serve that night while we, the cooks, would explain the courses to the guests.

The twist?

We would have to describe the present course, but *not* the *actual course* we were *making*. So, if I were, say, working the meat station, I might be pulled up to describe the dessert. If you were the reservationist upstairs, Charlie might grab you and say, "Joanne, please come here! We'd love you to tell the students how we pursue excellence in the kitchen every day!"

I was twenty-three and terrified to speak in front of sixty people at a time. But that was what was great about it: You were *never* in a comfort zone under Charlie Trotter's roof. And he made sure you weren't just *cooking* but *thinking*—that was invaluable. It helped us to internalize a mentality of ... well, excellence. That's infectious. You start thinking that way, everyone around you is thinking the same way, and it's this beautiful culture of people wanting nothing more than to just get better every day.

~

MISE-EN-PLACE IS a French phrase that translates to "putting in place" or "everything in its place." In professional kitchens it refers to the required first step of organizing and arranging the ingredients—all the cuts of meat, sauces, spices, relishes, chopped vegetables, and more—that a cook will need for the menu items to be prepared during a shift. Having everything organized ahead of time is crucial to the success of your shift. But preparation doesn't always guarantee it will still be there when you need it.

Say you leave on a Friday night and all of the push-through service was outstanding and you're feeling amazing, right? You have a decent amount of *mise-en-place* leftovers and Saturday looks promising because it might be a little bit easier with all those wonderful ingredients waiting in place for the next day. Usually, on Saturdays you're not preparing a lot of things because by the end of that night you're throwing everything out to start fresh on Tuesday. Having a little bit more *mise-en-place* on a Friday night to carry over into Saturday was a great thing. But *not* guaranteed. You could come in on Saturday morning thinking that you're prepared, only to discover that your *mise-en-place* has been thrown out the fucking window.

Why?

Well, maybe the chef came through when no one was around and rifled through your coolers and grabbed a few of your things.

Maybe something popped up when you were out, or they had an event they forgot to mention to you.

Now, suddenly, the *mise-en-place* that you were counting on to make it through the Saturday night service is gone and you're scrambling like crazy to get your shit together. Those things were always happening, so you could never have any sense of comfort. In my time, the culprits who ransacked my *mise-en-place* were mostly the *sous* chefs or the *chef de cuisine*.

The late, great Anthony Bourdain mentions in *Kitchen Confidential* that *mise-en-place* was the "religion of all good line cooks" and you "do NOT fuck with a line cook's *meez*."

And Bourdain was right on the money.

If you're a cook making risotto, you have your shallots and garlic and white wine and cheese and rice and everything ready to go—and *then* you start. So, when you have some of those things built up over the week and anticipate it all being on hand on Saturday—but it's not—you'll be yelling, "Fuck my life!"

Mark my words.

You've also gotta have a team around you in a kitchen.

Picture yourself in the kitchen and—trust me, this should not tax your imagination all that much—you're in deep shit. Something's missing or is soon running out.

What do you do?

You tap the *brigade de cuisine*—the "kitchen brigade."

The *brigade de cuisine* system was conceived by French chef Georges Auguste Escoffier, popularly known as "the king of chefs and the chef of kings." Escoffier was matchless in the culinary world of 1900, renowned for his innovative streamlining of *haute cuisine*, which was applied across many of the world's distinguished restaurants and hotels during the early part of the twentieth century.

Common in restaurants employing a sizable staff, the brigade system is vital for any modern kitchen to operate smoothly. It's structured so that itemized responsibilities are assigned to staff members who are skilled in specified kitchen tasks, with all team members maximizing the potential of their roles and collaborating with the other staff to create the best food and service possible.

The hierarchy begins with the executive chef, who oversees everything. He or she is the most senior member of the kitchen staff. They also fulfill a business-based role, often involving marketing and PR.

The executive chef's right-hand is the *chef de cuisine*, the head chef. He or she is responsible for daily kitchen management and usually answers only to the executive chef and/or the restaurant owner or manager. In addition to covering kitchen staff, the *chef de cuisine* is responsible for preparing recipes and creating dishes, helping the chef create the menu. They also manage the maintenance of kitchen and restaurant equipment and make sure that the kitchen adheres to all state and federal safety and health codes.

Under the *chef de cuisine* you have either an *executive sous* chef or a *sous* chef. If you have multiple *sous* chefs, one will usually be more senior-level than the other, so that's where you have the executive sous.

A *sous* chef is primarily the *chef de cuisine's* second-in-command, performing as the liaison between him and members of the kitchen team working at their various stations. A *sous* chef usually possesses serious culinary skills and a strong aptitude for management.

Along those same lines there's the pastry chef, responsible for creating all the desserts. A kitchen might have a pastry *sous*.

Directly below the *sous* chef is a roundsman—a person you can put to work anywhere in the kitchen. A roundsman has been with a kitchen long enough that if the chefs need someone to work the fish station that night, they can jump right in. If the meat station needs someone, they can do it. Wherever you need a body to be, the roundsman's your person. They can butcher. They can filet fish. He or she is *the guy*. The roundsman is usually the one who moves up into the *sous* chef position.

After the roundsman come the people in charge of their own stations, the *chefs de partie*. They're not the creative minds behind these dishes but are responsible for the actual execution as well as the daily ordering—for the *mise-en-place*—to put it all together, start to finish. In a larger kitchen, this can include a *rotisseur* (roasting), a *grillardin* (grilling and broiling), a *friturier* (deep-fried dishes), *poissonier* (seafood and fish), *saucier* (sauces and sauteed dishes), *entremetier* (soups, vegetable dishes, egg dishes), *garde manger* (cold appetizers, salads, charcuterie) and the *pâtissier* (pastry and dessert chef).

There is serious responsibility here: Every dish that leaves the station —and there may be hundreds over the course of an evening—must be identical to what the *chef de cuisine* created and, of course, of the highest quality. And the timing must be coordinated with other dishes for that table coming from other stations.

After *chef de partie,* you have *commis* chefs who answer to each *chef de partie.* Then come the dishwashers and busboys and food runners.

But *none* of them are expected to guard your *mise-en-place.*

Joke's on me.

"I FUCKING *LOVE* CHEESE, MAN."

My meeting with Anthony Bourdain was off to a stellar start.

As I said, Charlie Trotter used to make someone from the kitchen go out and do a dish presentation to a guest. As fate would have it, on the night Anthony Bourdain was a guest in 2002, Charlie called on me to discuss the cheeses—which comprised the final course.

We'd been told Bourdain was coming. His book, *Kitchen Confidential*, had come out in 2000—the same year I started working at Charlie Trotter's. His follow-up book, *A Cook's Tour*, published in 2001, and his TV series of the same name began airing in 2002. He was already quite well-known. Yet when he arrived that night, Bourdain was alone, no cameras, totally unassuming.

The course consisted of various cheeses, which Charlie always paired with wines. The combos created exciting flavors that guests never forgot.

Bourdain's eyes lit up as I described everything in great detail. There was a triple-cream, soft-textured, Explorateur cheese with warm crepes placed on top of a wicked almond sauce, topped with a dollop of red wine-dates, currants, and cherries cooked in a red wine reduction.

Next in line was a wedge of peppercorn-crusted cashew cheese arranged on a plate with pieces of honeycomb, smoked almonds, and dried apricots. That was followed by goat cheese terrine with leeks. Bourdain mentioned how much he enjoyed the sweetness of the leeks colliding with the salty flavor of the milky cheese. I told Bourdain that Charlie really loved using goat's cheese in other dishes such as cheesecake and a delectable eggplant puree with fig.

I then presented a creamy, soft Squacquerone di Romagna cheese wrapped with nori and umeboshi. Bourdain said he'd been to Japan a couple of times for his TV show and was a big fan of sushi and Japanese food. He loved the unique way the ingredients were combined. The salty nori seaweed and the sweet and tart pickled Japanese plum—the umeboshi—really appealed to him. It all hit his palate in a unique way; the slight acidity of the cheese reduced the sweetness of the umeboshi and provided herbaceous notes.

Bourdain remarked that he could see mixing this same dish up with some uni or raw *yagi-shashi*—which is a goat meat sashimi—and some ginger to make it even more unusual and memorable.

I joked that maybe he should give Charlie some new ideas.

"I'm not worthy of advising the master," Bourdain replied.

The last part of the course was a new wine paired with Charlie's recipe of a Maytag Blue cheese tart with Sauterne jelly and apricots, paired with a quince jam, which is a perfect match for marbled cheeses. Their robust taste complements the fragrant sweetness of the jam to make a preparation that's savory, sweet, and pungent.

I distinctly recall this tart eliciting a wonderful reaction from Bourdain, who told me that he loved a legit Blue Stilton from England, and he thought Charlie's Maytag Blue had a similar smell and taste and visual aesthetic, down to the distinct blue veins from saprotrophic fungi used in the process.

"Look man, simple pleasures like a charcuterie board with cured meats like prosciutto, sausage, terrines, galantines, ballotines, pâtés, and confit—plus cheeses and fruit?" Bourdain said when I finished my presentation. "*That* is the stuff that makes this existence tolerable."

He also told me he loved offal and organ meats, and stinky, runny and soft cheeses.

Charlie expected me to conclude my presentation by describing my role at the restaurant. I could've talked with Bourdain for hours but honestly, I would assume by the end of his dining experience with us—a fifteen-course dinner—he was probably tired of hearing fifteen different people's descriptions of each course, supplemented by what they thought was great and fresh in their pursuit of excellence. And really, what could I tell him about myself?

But Bourdain was generous with his time and he made it easy for me. "Where you from, man?" he asked.

I told him I'd come from Ohio to work for Charlie Trotter. Bourdain said I had made the right move; that Chicago was then just becoming known as an international food destination. He observed that Chicago had balls and never apologized; that it had more to offer on a culinary scale than almost any other place in America. He also advised me to travel as much as possible and experience new foods and cultures.

Then he said, "Thank you," and left it at that.

I'll never forget that night. It means even more now that he's no longer with us.

I REMEMBER READING *Kitchen Confidential* when it first came out and thinking, "Jesus Christ, he's not afraid to say anything." Bourdain was the first guy to tell you the nitty-gritty bullshit that went on in the back of the kitchens and I loved that he wasn't sugarcoating anything.

At the time Bourdain's book hit, I'd seen some crazy things that went down in kitchens I'd worked in before coming to Chicago—but it was all kinda tame compared to Bourdain's experiences.

I was young and skeptical about some of the madness Bourdain shared at the time, but as I worked throughout different restaurants and kitchens, I discovered over time how honest Bourdain had been ... how true his experiences had been.

From the good to the ugly inside peek of the cooking trade, I could relate to Bourdain's raw, behind-the-scenes testament of it all as I experienced similar things on various levels myself.

Now that Bourdain's gone, his impact is heavier, right? He became an incredible, powerful voice for the food world. He extended himself way above and beyond being an advocate for cooks. He truly touched people from *every* walk of life.

There's a special magic in Bourdain's genius because you know—and he knew—*everything* is related to food. Food is the common denominator of every culture in the world. Everybody has to eat.

The kitchen is the place you begin to chat and hang in when you arrive at someone's house. We always seem to migrate there. It's universal among cultures—gathering and warming up to each other over food. There's good feelings there. And I gotta say, Anthony Bourdain opened our eyes to those good feelings around food all over the world. He was such a great voice, and he touched so many people in that way.

IN THE THREE-AND-A-HALF years I spent at Charlie Trotter's, I learned a great deal about discipline, skill, service, and curiosity. Charlie felt a chef should be not just happy and fulfilled in his career, but also be *philosophically* satisfied.

I'LL ATTEMPT to distill the Trotter path in some small way:

- **Embrace Change**

THE FIRST YEAR I was at Charlie's, the restaurant closed for two weeks in late July and August.

Why?

Restaurants at the level of Charlie's rely on everybody to be there *every single day*. When you give people time off here and there throughout the year, it screws with the system. So, the idea is to give everybody time off all at once.

But that didn't mean there wasn't any homework.

Before that first break, Charlie pulled me into his office and gave me a copy of *The Fountainhead* by Ayn Rand. He was in love with that book. Every cook in his kitchen had read it—some, a few times over. It's one of those books that has you questioning lifelong assumptions. It's a great story about not getting comfortable doing everything someone else's way. The idea is to be not just different and creative, but also flexible, malleable, open to change.

That's what makes cuisine so beautiful—there are no rules.

Anyone who tells you otherwise is either asleep at the wheel or a liar.

Charlie Trotter was such an iconoclast. He kicked the door in on the steak-and-pizza-laden Chicago culinary scene with his European approach to foods that paired well with wine, and he meticulously prepared and presented it all with an attitude of Asian minimalism, even though neither Europe nor Asia was identifiable in his menus.

The term *haute cuisine* gets thrown around a lot, but you couldn't quite label his cooking that way. Whatever anyone decided had to be the status quo, you can bet your ass that Charlie was going to do the exact opposite.

Before Charlie, I'm pretty sure Chicago had never seen courses consisting of, say, unagi terrine with ruby red grapefruit and grilled duck heart, followed by bobwhite quail in a coriander crust served with chicken liver and watermelon radish, and a sea urchin ice cream with white chocolate and guava for dessert.

All of the above paired with a vintage Dom Perignon, by the way.

A lot of the food I created during my more than three years of experience at Charlie Trotter's emanated from Matthias Merges, the *chef de cuisine*. Matthias had been there for fourteen years; maybe even a little longer than that. He was Charlie's right-hand man. When I later became a *chef de cuisine* myself, I would create menus and invite a few of my right-hand chefs to sit down with me and collaborate on some menu dishes. I never saw Charlie sit with Matthias, though, or discuss menu ideas anywhere. Which is to say, the creativity I saw was mostly coming from Matthias—and maybe a few of the *sous* chefs.

• Don't Hold Hands—Hand Off Tools

CHARLIE WASN'T PUSHY. He'd gently encourage, but it wasn't like, "It's my responsibility to make sure Curtis isn't being complacent. I must motivate him to be creative!" He believed his job was to provide the tools to help a chef to innovate and find their own way.

An inspired chef could aspire to someday gain the opportunity to share ideas about the Charlie Trotter's menu.

Truth is, like anything great in life, no one can do it for you. You have to be motivated and make things with the tools you've been given—and do it all on your own.

I've carried that DIY attitude forward into my own career.

As part of our Ever restaurant hiring/interview process, we bring people in for a *stage* to see which ones are motivated. You give them one task to see how they do certain things. When they're done, are they looking to move on to the next one or are they going to stand there and wait for somebody to give them something else to do?

People who always ask, "What's next?" are the ones who're going to push hard all day long, tackle a list fifty things deep, and cut it down to zero.

Get as many of those driven employees as you can.

Did any of my ideas ever make it on to the menu at Charlie's? Maybe one. I remember a scallop and caviar dish that Matthias and I created together. It was very simple but good.

It wasn't my job to be creating stuff for Charlie Trotter's restaurant, anyway. My main responsibility was to make sure that the food that I cooked was the absolute *best* every single time each night—and if I could make it better the next night, that's what I'd do.

- **Excellence, from Here to Eternity**

THE MOST IMPORTANT message I absorbed from Charlie Trotter's restaurant was the aforementioned credo: *pursue excellence every day.* And that came from Charlie himself.

Most of us found the experience gratifying and life-changing.

When I think of the people I met during my Trotter days, I'm amazed by how many went on to become culinary superstars.

Look at Matthias Merges. He owns four, five restaurants now, beginning with Yusho and A10 Steak. He also has a couple of projects in Las Vegas.

Graham Elliot has become very popular in the food TV world, serving several seasons as a judge on *Master Chef* and *Top Chef,* along with owning several acclaimed and very successful restaurants.

Then there's the late Homaro Cantu, who helmed Moto.

Giuseppe Tentori has GT Prime and GT Oyster & Fish.

David LeFevre now has three restaurants in L.A., all very successful.

I can't forget Grant Achatz of Alinea. He was at Charlie's a few years before I was.

The list of greats who came out of Trotter's goes on and on—it's quite a legacy.

Matthias Merges and I are friends to this day. If anyone asks me what I'd do if I didn't open another restaurant, I tell them I'd be working for Matthias. He's an incredible person with badass skills who creates dishes that span American, Japanese, and Mediterranean cuisine, and more, from pig's tail ramen to sweetbreads to fish collar to burrata to sea urchin to king crab to lamb gyro meatballs. There's nothing he can't do—and he does it all to delicious perfection. Look around, there aren't many chefs who have been able to do everything Charlie Trotter did as a restaurateur, best-selling author, cooking TV show host, philanthropist with charitable foundations, philosopher, mentor, and pioneer—constantly pushing even at the top of his game; always being number one in Chicago and maybe number two in the U.S., perfecting concepts that no one else had yet tried, such as bringing chefs from all over the globe in to host dinners in his restaurant. And he had earned the James Beard Award, Michelin Stars, the Five Diamond from AAA—every top award you can imagine.

I wanted to be *that* guy. I did dream of achieving recognition like that —not so much for the awards, but for the *recognition* alone. I knew the opportunities that awards could bring. Charlie inspired me to aspire to become the best, and he gave me the confidence to set out to do so.

Charlie did this by investing in the best of everything so that his staff could perform at the highest level. He believed that to succeed you had to be surrounded by the finest people, the finest equipment, and the finest ingredients in the world.

Above all, you need staff to "buy in" to that Mission of Excellence.

Buy-ins possess the highest respect for this epic restaurant in which they're privileged to work.

Buy-ins have a stake in it all.

Buy-ins are proud and take it seriously.

And you can taste that in the food.

It's easy enough to *just* be a chef. If you want to make your mark, you need to be more than a chef—and Charlie Trotter was.

WHEN CHARLIE TROTTER'S would close for those two weeks in summer, my idea of a vacation was to go off and work somewhere else. I continued that all through the five years I was running Grace, and it's still my idea of time well spent.

Anyway, during this one break, I went off to The French Laundry, Thomas Keller's celebrated restaurant in Napa Valley, to experience a new environment. At the time, Charlie Trotter's and The French Laundry were considered the two best restaurants in the country—and remained so for many, many years.

"The French Laundry is the next restaurant I'm going to work at!" I declared upon my return home to my wife Kim at the time.

"I'm *not* moving to California," Kim replied. "I'm not leaving Chicago now that we're settled and you're with Charlie Trotter. Your dream job is here."

Smitten as I was with The French Laundry, I understood Kim's logic and gave up on the idea.

Enter Grant Achatz.

As I mentioned, Grant had worked at Charlie Trotter's a few years before I did. He then went to work as a *sous* chef at The French Laundry. He came back to Chicago in 2001 to become the Executive Chef at Trio in Evanston, Illinois. I was working at Charlie Trotter's when I heard about this interesting new chef. And the more I heard, the more I wanted to work for him. Evanston was just north of Chicago; it sounded like serendipity—the next best thing landing right in my backyard.

I immediately applied for the job *and* … was promptly denied.

"You're fucking crazy," Grant said. "Your credentials are too good for the positions I've got open and I can't pay you anything worthwhile."

Fuck the money. I felt Grant was the most exciting chef at the time. For me, this wasn't a lateral move. It was a *leap up*.

"Grant, I'm only making sixteen thousand. How much less are you going to pay me?"

"I'm telling you; you're not going to learn anything here," Grant continued. "You need to go be a chef at your own restaurant."

I persisted, however, and Grant finally broke down.

"I can pay you exactly what you're making now—sixteen thousand a year," he said.

I agreed to the sum, and he hired me as a pastry chef.

ALTHOUGH I KNEW that Charlie Trotter wasn't as possessive as John Souza, he could be a real hothead. Charlie was a man who supposedly throttled beloved chef and reality TV guy Graham Elliot in front of the kitchen staff. My old pal Homaro "Omar" Cantu told me that he was there with Graham when it happened.

Omar and Elliot were joking in the kitchen and Charlie didn't like that, so Charlie walked up to Graham, put his hands around Graham's neck in a mock stranglehold and said, "Don't you know that I will fucking kill you right now?"

Charlie got salty when any of his employees left. His attitude was, "Fuck you. Don't bother putting a notice in. You already decided that you're done, so just cut the shit and go."

Charlie dodged me for a while. It was like he sensed my exit was imminent. I planned to give him four weeks notice. For a cook, two weeks notice was normal. Out of respect, I wanted to give him more time to fill my position. That's always been my M.O.—respect for the chef. Today, I always tell my cooks when they leave, "It doesn't matter if you spend ten years at my company, fifteen years, or four months—the *last two weeks* of your time are what will be remembered. So, kill it. Outwork everybody. Walk out of here with your head high."

I wanted Charlie to know first. I didn't want to tell the *chef de cuisine* because he might tell Charlie and there was no way I wanted that to happen.

Finally, I caught up with Charlie as I swept the hallway between the restaurant and the chef's office. He was running past and I said, "Chef, I need five minutes with you." And any time you tell the chef, "I need five minutes with you," he knows what you're going to say. Of course, I had to say it anyway. "You know, Chef, it's been an incredible experience here, but … I feel that it's time to move on."

"Okay, Duffy. You want to go now? That's fine. Go get changed out of your uniform."

"No. I want to give you plenty of time and notice. A month."

"I don't need that. You're welcome to stay but I don't really need it."

I ended up staying and worked my ass off—my goal was to fucking crush it. I always want people to say, "Man, I wish that guy still worked here."

A few years after I left, in September 2003, Charlie was served with a massive class action lawsuit, which was big news in Chicago and the culinary world. Unfortunately, though I don't remember signing anything to be a part of it, my name was somehow on the plaintiffs' list—which incited Charlie's fury. It inflicted a permanent strain on our relationship.

I know the chef who filed the class action suit. Her name is Beverly Kim. She filed in Cook County Circuit Court and then it moved to federal court a month later. The complaint said back of the house employees were expected to work twelve-to-fourteen-hour shifts, six days a week, without overtime pay. Someone else from the service staff—a.k.a. the front-of-the-house—also filed a class action suit over tip distribution. Two different class action lawsuits hit Trotter like a one-two punch.

To my mind, if you're at the restaurant, you're *there*, period. No matter what. Don't bitch. You know what you're getting into and O.T. is a given. Everybody worked for shift pay back then. You didn't clock in;

you didn't clock out. You showed up, you got paid a certain amount of money—which was sixty dollars a day.

Granted, it should be called *shit pay*, not *shift pay*. But Charlie was upfront about the deal when you started.

If you don't like it, don't fucking work here.

Trotter's was open on random Mondays throughout the year in order to make up for those two-week summer closures. Eventually you'd work ten six-workday weeks and revenue would be back where it would've been if you worked through the summer. Smart.

To staff up those Mondays, Charlie would come around and say, "You want to volunteer your time on Monday? The restaurant's open." Of course, I wasn't going to say "No" to Charlie Trotter. The restaurant's open so I'm going to work. *Everyone* is going to work. Oh, and if you didn't show up, it's a no-brainer that you're going to lose your job. Again, Charlie was straightforward about all this the day he hired you. It wasn't a surprise. There's a pile of sacrifices and challenges you need to commit to if you really have the desire to be a next-level chef in a next-level restaurant.

Charlie Trotter's wasn't some normal nine-to-five workplace, know what I mean?

One day I got this check that was mailed to my house, and when I saw it, I didn't ask any questions: When you're twenty-five years old and making sixteen grand a year and you suddenly get a check in the mail for seventeen thousand, guess what? You're gonna cash that check.

That's what I did.

I used the money to educate myself. I bought books and read. Kim and I traveled to Paris for two weeks and then Spain for two weeks all so I could learn more about—and dine at—legendary restaurants I had only dreamed of experiencing, where my food gods dwelled. I learned so much and I never would've been able to do that without that check.

And Charlie Trotter?

He was understandably pissed and bitter.

In the documentary *For Grace*, there's a tense scene between Charlie Trotter and me at the front door of his restaurant.

Some months after Charlie announced in 2012 that he'd be closing his restaurant after twenty-five years, Michael Muser and I thought we'd go there one last time and bring the camera crew along to capture what we thought would be a special moment. I'd been to Charlie Trotter's many times after I'd left and he'd always welcomed me back—even *after* the 2003 class action lawsuit. Shit, I did events with Alinea—more on this restaurant in a moment—at Charlie Trotter's. Charlie was always cordial. He'd say, "Hey Chef, how are you? Nice to see you."

So, imagine my surprise when Charlie tore into me and refused to allow me inside. The camera crew filmed this along with him cussing me out about joining the class action lawsuit and taking a check for $50,000 dollars.

I *never* received a $50,000 check.

I don't know if it was my camera crew or if he was maybe feeling some kind of extra *fuck-it* amidst his Trotter swan song. Whatever his reason, if Charlie's intention was to wound me, he succeeded …

I was hurt and super-embarrassed.

I wish we could've mended that fence because, as you already know, Charlie was a huge inspiration and so much more to me.

Sadly, it wasn't long after that nasty encounter that Charlie died. He was fifty-four years old.

TWENTY
EDIBLE ETHICS

I fear pinnacles—professional and otherwise.
Why?
Because I know in my heart that satisfaction would be the death of my desire.

I want to stay hungry ... I never want that flame to burn out.

~

SOMETIME IN 2004 while I was at Trio, an issue of *Food & Wine* hit stands ranking me as one of the top ten pastry chefs in North America. Which would've been fine except ... *I never wanted to be a pastry chef!*

Now, I admit, there are worse problems. My fear of being pigeon-holed, however, was very real.

I needn't have worried, really. At Trio, I was at the bottom of the food chain—and I ironically was freed up to create more. And to reach your full creative potential as a chef, you need to be well-rounded.

Eventually, I felt comfortable in my skin *anywhere* in the restaurant. I'd made it a mission to learn and master all aspects of the restaurant team's roles, whether it be dropping silver on a table, removing a glass, pouring wine, or caramelizing. And if later down the line I hired a pastry chef I could do exactly what he or she could—maybe even better. That, to me, was what made a well-rounded chef. I spent time just honing and honing and honing.

While Grant Achatz was at Trio, he gained national renown. The Mobil Travel Guide awarded the restaurant five stars. Grant's big hits were famous—the black truffle explosion, which was ravioli filled with black truffle; caramelized Sri Lankan eggplant; chicharrons con salsa; Moulard duck foie gras with blueberries and cinnamon tapioca; and on and on—all paired with fine wines from Europe. Much like Charlie Trotter's, Trio is also credited for launching the careers of other Chicago culinary superstars: Rick Tramonto, Gale Gand, Shawn McClain, and Dale Levitski.

Grant left at the end of 2004 and Trio's owner Henry Adaniya closed the twelve-year-old restaurant in 2006.

I was still working as the pastry chef at Trio, just shy of my two-year anniversary, when Grant came in with some exciting news. He had met this investor, Nick Kokonas, and they were planning on opening a new restaurant together.

Kokonas was not just a money man, he was also an entrepreneur with a deep understanding of the restaurant industry. The restaurants he co-founded with Grant Achatz also served as development and testing grounds for a revolutionary, proprietary ticketing system he invented called Tock, which helps restaurants determine dynamic pricing, store guest preferences, create memorable events, automate tasks and reminders, and streamline the reservations and takeout processes. It's a system we use today at Ever, and it was successful from the get-go. In 2021, Tock was acquired by SquareSpace for more than $400 million.

Back then, though, we knew him as just the kind of guy who understood an innovative vision for a new restaurant—and had the cash to help bring it to life.

"I want two people to come with me," Grant said.

I was one, a chef named John Peters was the other.

We spent the next two years working mostly out of a Starbucks before we finally got offices and, together, built the restaurant: *Alinea*. Alinea would be a big step toward my later vision: Grace.

I was at Alinea from the ground floor up as the *chef de cuisine*, and I spent the first three years it was open there.

It was cool to see Grant kicking things up with his innovations. His creativity applied not only to dishes, but also to plateware; like arranging oak leaves to dine off of or having guests eat crab out of a glass crab. Alinea was offering ten-to-fourteen and sixteen-to-eighteen-course options. Grant's recipes were astounding; he brought along his black truffle explosion and did up steelhead roe with coconut, curry, and yuzu; razor clam with shiso, soy, and daikon; wooly pig with fennel, orange, and squid; and a 'balloon' made of a green apple taffy and filled with helium, connected to a string made from apple fruit leather.

Un-fucking-real!

Alinea launched in 2005. By October 2006, *Gourmet* magazine named it the best restaurant in America. In 2011, Alinea became a three-Michelin-Star-rated restaurant.

Grant Achatz has said of me:

"He's very disciplined, and that comes off, really. He's fit. He exercises. He lifts weights. He runs. His hair is always clean cut. He's solid. Everything about him gives a persona that he's just meticulous, detail-oriented, ready to go. His reputation is brilliant. I mean, I've eaten his food many, many times, and he's just such a huge force to be reckoned with as far as his talent goes. His food is very thoughtful. It's very thought out. And it's a very credible concentration of flavors, and the look is beautiful. Beautiful, beautiful look."

I have great admiration for Grant, so his amazing and kind words about me as a chef mean so much to me.

People ask if Grant and I are still tight. Yeah, we are. The vibe is *friendly competition.* We're both in Chicago; we're still connected. He's dined at Grace. I've gone back to Alinea as a guest. We're not super tight and hanging out together like the old days, but I love and respect the guy.

Grant also showed up at my restaurant, Ever, in a unique way in the form of a cameo in the TV series, *The Bear.* In Episode 10, characters are hanging at a star-studded dinner to honor the legacy of the fictionalized version of Ever, and the character Luca (played by actor Will Poulter) chats Grant up about his edible helium balloons, lavender pillows, and black truffles explosion—all of which are real-life dishes at Alinea.

Speaking of Grant, I have him on a list of my personal favorite worldwide chefs that I'll share here:

- **Michel Bras, Le Suquet**: A brilliant chef, incredible restaurant, incredible food. He's an innovator. He created an institution. I had the opportunity to go to France and eat at his restaurant years ago. He blew me away.
- **Peter Gilmore, Quay**: I love the cuisine of Peter Gilmore. He's a chef in Sydney, Australia. I love his approach and his style of food. They offer a wonderful vegetarian menu with six- and ten-course options as well as fish and meat options. An original.
- **Charlie Trotter, Charlie Trotter's**: Obviously.
- **Albert Adriá, El Bulli**: I *must* mention Albert. He's an astonishing chef. Albert and his brother, Ferran, used to have a three-Michelin-starred restaurant called El Bulli in Spain. It was one of the best restaurants in the world for many, many years. I was fortunate enough to eat his cuisine and loved it.
- **Thomas Keller, The French Laundry**: He continues to evolve and inspire and has a way with food unlike anyone else.
- **Grant Achatz, Alinea**: Again, obviously.
- **Juan Mari Arzak, Arzak**: Arzak is in San Sebastián, Spain. It was awarded three Michelin stars and it's one of the greatest restaurants in the world. The menu features a "New Basque Cuisine." Chef Juan is unmatched at innovation.
- **Dan Bark, Upstairs at Mikkeller**: I give a shout-out to my buddy, Chef Dan Bark, a Korean-American who was born in Chicago. He was also the first person I hired when I worked at Avenues, the restaurant I helmed at the Peninsula Hotel (which you will hear about soon). After his first week there, I thought to myself, *Why did I hire this kid?* He couldn't do the simple things. But once he got it, he excelled—just crushed it. Dan ended up being one of the best people I've ever hired. He worked at Avenues for three or four years and spent another two working with me at Grace, moving up to a *sous* chef position. While at Avenues, he met his now-wife, who is from Bangkok, and when they relocated there, he opened this super-small place called Upstairs at Mikkeller and it earned a Michelin star. I ate there and it was next-level. Unfortunately,

this impressive restaurant has closed, but I'm so proud of Dan and I can't wait to see what he does next.

TWENTY-ONE
IT'S THE JOURNEY, NOT THE RESERVATION

"I can do better than this."

I had told my wife Kim this as I considered leaving Alinea to try something bigger.

"That's nice."

Kim didn't share my enthusiasm. Truth be told, she hadn't been excited about me or my career for a couple years at this point. I get it. She moved to Chicago and our family took a huge pay cut so I could pursue my dream. And her reward for supporting my success was …being married to a ghost. I was working too much—and I knew it.

And yet …

"Does this mean you've finally 'made it?'" There was an edge to her voice. "You're done trying to be the finest chef in the world?"

I looked at Kim, holding her gaze for a second.

"Fuck, no. Not by a long shot."

WHY CAN'T *I do my own restaurant?*

I got the itch, finally, while at Alinea. It had always seemed to a lot of people—starting with Grant himself, back when I'd applied for that job at Trio—that I really should have my own restaurant. More and more, my colleagues wanted to know *when*, not *if*, I'd do it. But I hadn't felt ready until this point. Now, I was ready to scratch that itch and express my own voice.

I've always been very strategic as to my career path, knowing where I wanted to go. And I knew that by leaving Alinea—which had such a spotlight on it—the question would arise, "What happens to the *chef de cuisine* when he leaves a restaurant of this caliber?" The culinary world wants to know, the media wants to know, and the guests—who mean everything—certainly want to know. They're all going to follow that chef and see what he's going to do next.

All of us would soon have an answer.

THE PEOPLE AT AVENUES, the celebrated restaurant in The Peninsula Chicago hotel helmed by the beloved, four-star chef, Graham Elliot Bowles, contacted me while I was still Alinea's *chef de cuisine*. Bowles was leaving to open a new place under his own name. I went in and cooked for them, and they immediately offered me a job. For the next three years, I was the executive chef at Avenues. For the first time in my career, the entire menu featured my cuisine.

At thirty-two years old, I had become *the* chef. Because of the restaurant's reputation, the culinary world took notice and I was suddenly catapulted into comparisons with legendary Chicago chefs I had worked for and with, including Trotter, Achatz and Bowles, and I was gratified when the critics viewed my work as comprising creative, imaginative, intricate dishes with perfect pairings.

Delicious was a word I aspired to—one that I strove to hear from the guests.

Delicious means that you really enjoy it—that what you're eating hits every note in your mouth.

From sweet to savory to bitter to salty and sour, *delicious* means you want more of it.

Avenues was a completely blank canvas. Upon it I could paint a gustatory portrait for Chicago and the rest of the world of my vision and capabilities. And it was where I first became aware that I could earn recognition for them.

As a young cook, Michelin-starred chefs overseas inspired me. I looked up to these amazing chefs as if they were gods and thought, *Man, I wish someday Michelin would come to the U.S. Why are they only in Europe? We should have this.*

In honor of my old teacher John Saunders, I'll give you a little Michelin history here ...

The Michelin Guide originated in Europe in 1900, created by André and Édouard Michelin—two guys who also changed the world with their tire technology. Relevant to their international travel guide, they first created their small Michelin book as a guide for motorists, giving them helpful info for their trip, including maps, tips on how to change a tire, and the locations of petrol stations, hotels, lodges, and restaurants.

This, of course, was also a savvy way to increase car sales, which would in turn result in the demand for tires.

Twenty years later, the restaurant section had grown in popularity and the Michelin boys decided to round up a group of secret diners—clandestine restaurant inspectors—who'd visit and review restaurants.

A new Michelin Guide was born.

In 1926, the Michelin Guide began awarding stars for fine dining establishments, all in France, originally marking them only with a single star signifying a "fine dining establishment."

Around 1931, a ranking of zero, one, two, and three stars was popularized. Which eventually morphed into the three-star rating guests and chefs know to this day.

Good move. There have been more than thirty million Michelin Guides sold to-date. Today, it rates over thirty thousand establishments around the world—with more and more cities being added all the time.

The United States finally got its first guide in 2005, initially covering approximately 500 restaurants in New York City and surrounding areas. San Francisco, L.A., and Las Vegas followed. Finally, in 2010, Chicago was included.

And in 2010, I earned two Michelin stars at Avenues.

I still marvel at it.

Believe it or not, there are restaurant owners and chefs who didn't want the stars they were awarded. Some have experienced personal strain and depression from the accolades. The pressure of the high expectations from a new clientele after being Michelin-starred are very real: Those stars place you in an elite class with a high-price model that'll fuck you up if you're not prepared to roll with the attention.

Me? I never felt that pressure. I wanted those stars. I had worked my ass off for more than twenty years to be prepare for that. And that wasn't the only accolade my crew and I received. We also won the AAA Five Diamond Award and were recognized with perfect four-star ratings from *Chicago Magazine* and the *Chicago Tribune*.

That same year, for the twentieth anniversary of the James Beard Awards, the foundation reached out to previous winners of the Outstanding Chef Award and asked them to select a chef they mentored who they believed would have a major impact on the culinary world. Grant Achatz at Alinea recommended me, which is how I earned the honor of being named a Legacy Chef.

If ever I had felt I'd arrived, this was the time.

As a Legacy Chef, I was given the opportunity to prepare samplings of one of my menu items for more than a thousand James Beard Awards attendees. So, my team and I served up this mini-rendition of the Alaskan king crab dish that was a guest favorite on my Avenues menu.

Moreover, a nice bonus was some unexpected love I got from a writer for *Food & Wine* magazine that night. Travel Editor Jen Murphy wrote in her blog the next day that, "Of all the food I've eaten in the last 48 hours I can't stop thinking about the insanely brilliant Alaskan king crab dish Curtis Duffy and his talented crew from Avenues in Chicago were serving after last night's awards gala ...lovely chunks of Alaskan king crab were served in a cucumber consommé topped with a delicate three-sugar tuile that was garnished with wild-steelhead roe, kalamansi and lemon balm. The dish was complex, refreshing, artistic and came served in a little plastic cup that conveniently cradled into the top of my wine glass. I was beyond impressed, to the point where I had to have seconds."

She had asked me if making this complex-yet-miniature dish for over a thousand people was perhaps a tad grandiose.

"If I'm going to New York City to cook for the James Beard Awards," I replied, "I'm going to go big."

That's how I roll.

~

It was at Avenues where I also met Michael Muser—a.k.a. the Muze—who, as the wine director for the Peninsula Hotel, headed up that program at Avenues. And he *really* knows wine, and understands how to make both Old World and New World offerings from around the globe approachable and enjoyable for both fellow connoisseurs and those who don't have experience with it.

Our bond began over food and wine then expanded to … well, everything else. His energy is so infectious. This is especially important for me because I'm a complete introvert. I'm the quiet guy while Michael's this huge, outgoing and bubbly personality who can handle the guests with pure confidence.

Whenever we were together, we were tight as hell—yin and yang.

Michael's also an incomparable restaurant manager. At Avenues, the higher-ups didn't let me a hire a front-of-the-house person to lean on to enforce my standards. This was a sore spot for Michael. "Fuck this!" he said. "We have to change things ourselves." He took on that role in addition to his main responsibilities. That initiative made him a superstar in my eyes.

DIY, right?

Although Michael and I took charge of Avenues as best we could, the restaurant's high command remained chaotic and misguided. Even to get the most basic items—say, enough coffee cups or forks and knives—I'd have to fill out a purchase order and then the general manager would have to sign it. The food and beverage guys have to sign it. The executive chef of the hotel has to sign it. The purchasing guy has to sign it.

Truth is, though, you could get an order pushed through this exasperating pipeline, but then it might just get buried under a paper mountain of previous requests.

It wasn't that it was just a nuisance, like, if you're going to be a world-class restaurant, you need to pull triggers right away.

When I was at Charlie Trotter's, I learned to take pride in making every inch of the restaurant as close to flawless as possible. I wield that pride today. It might sound crazy outside the kitchen family, but even seeing a single light bulb burnt out or a scuffed chair or a chipped cup can knock the morale out of my team. It breaks the spell. I always push for and insist on the fine points in any restaurant I command. Guests and employees notice details. I wouldn't tolerate it … but even these simple maintenance requirements were a constant battle to remedy.

That's the problem with hotel restaurants, man. They want the prestige of a two-or-three-Michelin-starred restaurant in their hotel or under the brand, but don't want to invest in what it takes to get it. The restaurant is the first place where the owners and managers would bring VIPs to dinner and blow a fortune, but the next morning they'd bitch about the number of staff on hand.

Pray tell, you want to say, *how the fuck do you think this all gets done?*

～

MUSER and I were at Avenues, talking shit—again. The vibration this time, however, was a little different, a little higher.

"Ever think of *really* doing better, Michael?"

"What? Like buying Avenues and firing the management team?"

I laughed but pressed on. "Muze, I'm talking about making our *own* restaurant. What we're doing here is great—but it's not *great enough*. I want to have the best restaurant in the country, brother, and I think you and I could make that happen. Somehow …"

"Hey, you consistently achieve what you set your mind to," Muser said. Always a believer, that one.

"It's gonna take more than just setting my mind to it." I held my hand up, rubbing my thumb and finger on an invisible wad of money.

"So what?" Muser shrugged. "Let's do this. Figure it out."

Perhaps this would've remained idle talk except that moments later, a big ball of fate and Fuck You money waltzed through the door.

～

"GUY HERE, a customer. He insists on meeting you."

"Okay … can it wait?" I was busy preparing for service. The prep work was just heating up and I was in "the zone."

"Not really," Muze replied. "Just spend a couple minutes, real quick. He's really pushing to see you. The guy seems like a big shot."

I smoothed out my chef's coat and prepared to meet a stranger whose role in my life would later become both a dream come true—and a fucking nightmare of epic proportions.

"I think his name is Dolos," Muser said.

Or that's what Muze *would've* said if "Dolos" was this man's real name. I've changed it here for a couple reasons: one being that the guest who came to me that day fits the definition of Dolos—the Greek spirit who was the personification of trickery, cunning, deception, treachery, and guile, for those who haven't read classical mythology—and the second reason, out of fear that if I actually speak the Devil's true name, he may reappear.

In fact, I can smell the brimstone simply *thinking* about him now.

EVIDENTLY, Dolos had only wanted to go somewhere for a steak and potato that night; he wasn't in the mood for fancy food. But his wife wanted him to broaden his culinary horizons and insisted they eat at Avenues.

A real estate capitalist who lived in a huge mansion in the western suburbs of Chicago, Dolos would come into the city for the weekend with his family and stay at the Peninsula Chicago. He preferred the penthouse suite, which, at the time it was eighty-five hundred a night. His wife and daughters would go off shopping on Michigan Avenue and spend his money all weekend, whatever.

On that particular night, however, I found myself standing in front of Mr. Steak and Potato and he's telling me, "I've never had food like this before, Chef!"

Over the next two months, Dolos became something of a regular. Whenever he came in, I'd change up my dishes, taking advantage of the premium ingredients coming my way just as they were being harvested. One visit, I might offer simple things like salmon and cooked carrot, along with grains, nuts, seeds, and toasted meringue. The next, smoked paprika, medjool dates, parsley roots, black truffles, scallions, braised pistachios, and morel mushrooms.

Around November 2010, Dolos asked me if I'd do a private dinner at his house. My Spidey-senses were tingling.

This could be a wonderful opportunity.

This guy immediately made me think of investor and entrepreneur Nick Kokonas, who had partnered with Chef Grant Achatz to build Alinea—and they had gone on to monumental success.

Anyway, I created an invoice detailing what it would cost for Muser and me to go to his house up in the burbs with my staff and the finest china, and custom-cater this entire dinner for around fifteen guests. He immediately signed it and made a deposit.

After that dinner, Dolos pulled Muser and me aside in his home and said, "I really want to do something special with you guys if you're interested. I'm talking about partnering with you to make a restaurant."

Now, it wasn't as if I hadn't already had wealthy people jaw on about what we could do together in the afterglow of an epic meal. But Dolos was different. Persistent. Determined to present himself to me as a stand-up family man, complete with a wife, three kids, and a dog. A nice guy in a town full of wise guys. I knew he was a successful businessman with the money to do something real and I took him seriously.

Muser and I were invited back up to his house to discuss restaurant ideas. He's talking about conquering the world with us, building off my name and my reputation. Pretty soon we're getting deep into details, discussing a vision for a ten-thousand-square-foot restaurant with a gorgeous, seventy-five seat dining room, a lounge and a state-of-the-art kitchen.

Hey, if we started soon, it'd open by 2012!

We figured he'd write up a proposal for us to review and we'd go from there. But suddenly, from out of nowhere, he whips out these contracts.

"What's this?"

"Oh, you know, it's just an employment agreement. No big deal. Everybody does it."

Unfortunately, Muser and I had drunk so much of the Kool-Aid and were so blinded by the razzle-dazzle bullshit blitz, we signed.

Without hiring lawyers.

We were so fucking stupid.

I remember Muser and I grabbing coffee before we got onto the highway to head home to the city, looking at each other, excited but perplexed.

We asked each other, "What just happened? What did we just sign?"

After I got home, I sat down and read the employment agreement in detail. Red flags *everywhere*. There were issues specific to the actual partnership, salaries and bonuses, profit-sharing, and more. I'm suddenly not okay with this. I sent an email to both Muser and Dolos. "I have concerns."

"Come on back out to the house." Dolos replied. "We'll talk about it."

Once again, Muser and I made the trip to the Dolos estate.

This time, Dolos was no longer the smiling, ass-kissing family man. He was glowering, offended Muser and I would question such a generous contract. He had changed into Mr. Hyde then. Loud. Irate. Threatening, even. Muser and I should've just ripped the deal up and walked out right then. But, no, we just sucked it up and went back home.

Dolos had handed me the proverbial apple. And yes, I took a bite.

PART FIVE

Grace

TWENTY-TWO
WHAT'S IN A NAME?

G*race.*

    A single word encapsulating the code by which I live. It means that I do right in everything for guests and staff with dignity, elegance, refinement, beauty, class, and service.

Grace.

A single word that defines how I conduct myself and what I put into every detail of my cuisine.

Grace.

A single word, the name I gave to my beloved Chicago restaurant. The establishment is a literal dream come true. It's everything I ever envisioned and wanted in my own restaurant.

WHEN WE STARTED the Grace build, I was still working at Avenues. But that wasn't fair to either establishment, so when we got a little deeper into the process, I gave Avenues a three-month notice and hammered out an agreement to take a salary to manage the Grace build-out. Generally, that's what people do—the process of creating a first-class restaurant is, after all, a full-time job long before its doors open. Muser joined Grace's payroll as well.

"Start over from scratch." That's what I told Avenues management when they asked what their next move should be as I made my exit. "Get away from the chef aspect of it. Make this place a concept restaurant—a seafood restaurant, a steakhouse, Italian. Just hire a good chef, not one with a 'name,' so that when they leave, it's not this big ordeal to replace him or her."

By the end of the summer of 2011, I was cooking my final service at Avenues. When I walked, the restaurant closed for good. Ultimately, management decided to turn it into a simple banquet facility.

The Chicago Tribune reported on my plans to create my own West Loop restaurant in 2012. I boasted to the reporter that it would be the best restaurant in the country as dreams of a third Michelin star danced in my head.

Well, be careful what you wish for.

The Canadian writer Lawrence Hill said, *"Sometimes a deal with the Devil is better than no deal at all."*

But I had no idea how rotten our end of the bargain would turn out to be.

TWENTY-THREE
CHICAGO'S OWN

I regard Chicago as the greatest city in the world—and the greatest culinary destination as well. And I don't discriminate: Chinese, Mexican, Italian, Greek, Thai, Indian, pizza, burgers, sushi—each of them appeals to me. And the variety of what's available here keeps me on my toes. It keeps my creative fires burning.

The city really loves and celebrates its incredible food scene. And it has become a must-visit food destination, too, with an eager and ravenous clientele of both residents and tourists that allows you to—indeed, *expects* you to—express yourself and follow the muse. They don't want "safe"—and neither do I.

~

AT THE RESTAURANTS I FREQUENT, I stay under the radar and don't blab about them later, unless someone asks me where I love to go. I just like to enjoy my experience.

But, you know, it's my book, so I'm going to make an exception.

I've been back to my former home Alinea numerous times. I've always enjoyed my experiences there. Is it my favorite dining place? No. That's not a diss because I absolutely love Alinea and my mentor Grant

Achatz's cuisine. It's just that I can't be pinned down to a single *favorite* place in Chicago.

I know there are a million pizza places in Chicago, but I gotta give props to Pequod's.

Then there's a place in the Fulton Market area called Proxi that I'm crazy about. It's a Japanese robatayaki restaurant with a southeast Asian scene. They do some grill, some sushi, some sashimi. It's one of a chain from L.A. with multiple restaurants there. This is their first "concept" restaurant and they're opening a couple more in Chicago.

I love Asian food. It's the best style of food in my opinion. I would say Japan is the leader in Asian cuisine and Thailand is number two. I enjoy Thai food more than Japanese food, but unfortunately, it doesn't have the refinement that Japanese cuisine does—the care and precision and the clean flavors. The Japanese have that nailed. But the flavors you get with Thai cuisine are fucking impeccable.

I'll digress here, but some of the best dishes I've had here are Japanese and some of the most revolting dishes I've sampled are also Japanese. The weirdest thing I've ever had? Black cod sperm—that's one. The first time I experienced that was at Charlie Trotter's. Sounds really appetizing, right? In Japan it's a delicacy and, normally in Japan if you're a guest, you get a larger portion of anything. The second time I had black cod sperm was in Japan. I didn't enjoy it the first time, so to get it in a larger portion the second time? *Fuck my life.* It looks like a brain! And I remember the texture of it … firm on the outside, but when you break it open, gooey and slimy. It's nasty looking and it tastes nasty.

A delicacy, I guess.

I hate stuffed green bell peppers more than anything—thanks to Jan-mom forcing me to eat them during my childhood, the one thing she ever tried to make from scratch—but if I had to choose between green bell peppers or black cod sperm, I'd probably choose the gag-inducing peppers Jan made.

Then there's *natto*, Japanese fermented soybeans. When they start to ferment, they create this slime that's hard to stomach. Natto's super snotty and the more you screw with it, the more it becomes this gooey, boogery stuff with chunky bits in it. But if you can get past the texture, the flavor is really good—like roasted coffee bean almost.

Okay … back to Chicago:

One of my favorite Chicago restaurants is Tiparos, which serves Thai food. I've been going there for about nineteen years and I love their coconut chicken Tom Kha Gai soup—the best I've had in the city. Side note: I love coconut in any form. It not only fills you up, but it also explodes with flavor every time you take a spoonful.

Tiparos is consistently delicious, and their peanut sauce is really good, too.

Once, on an episode of *Parts Unknown*, Anthony Bourdain went to Vietnam, chowed down on pho broth and noodles and then went off about pho being the best noodles in the world. I agree.

On that note, one of my favorite spots in Chicago is this amazing Vietnamese restaurant down in Pilsen called HaiSous. The chef's name is Thai Dang and I have *always* loved his food—many of his dishes stick in my mind for days after I've had them. He cooks from the heart, and you can see and taste it.

Unfortunately, Thai and his wife got really destroyed by their business partner in their last restaurant, Embeya, which, coincidentally, was located a block away from Grace. It was ugly—a story straight out of *American Greed*. You can almost hear Stacy Keach narrating the tale.

If it doesn't sound familiar now, it will soon enough.

TWENTY-FOUR
BABY STEPS IN BIG SHOES

To find Grace's home, Michael Muser and I looked at more than eighty locations around the city. We worked with real estate agents who showed us properties that weren't even on the market yet, and some turnkey restaurants. But I'd always had a vision of my restaurant being in a beautiful, multilevel brownstone with small, intimate rooms.

The way I saw it, this was my shot. I was going to take it my way.

Before long, I realized that I was never going to find the perfect space. It didn't exist. Also, I figured out that if I got the beautiful brownstone I fancied, I'd have to put the kitchen in the basement and I started to realize that didn't make sense.

I had already experienced multi-level dining issues firsthand at Charlie Trotter's—that's kinda where I got the idea, and my dream had first surpassed what I knew wasn't practical. I started thinking of how the the staff, would just be running up and down, up and down, up and down. It's never good when the food travels up from the depths of the kitchen to guests waiting one or two or more floors above. What's that food going to look like when it gets to the top of the steps?

Alinea is set up that multi-level way, but they make it work, and there's probably some kinda Grant Achatz genius as to why it works.

For me? I decided I just couldn't see us doing that at Grace.

Once we decided we'd go one level only, I figured we'd need at least five thousand square feet for Grace. My agent did some searching and told us there were only three spaces available that met our criteria. We looked at them all, but after visiting 652 West Randolph four times it was clear—weirdly— that this was it.

I never envisioned Grace would be a storefront setting in a blocky box of a building with other shit attached.

Yet here we were.

The building offered everything we needed: a big empty space, with five thousand square feet all on one level, and another four thousand feet downstairs. The lease was also very sexy at sixty-five hundred a month— and we didn't have to pay rent for the downstairs space.

Back when we began building, I kept telling everyone that I wanted to be the best restaurant in the world. Then, shortly after we opened, I changed my thinking:

We don't need to be the best restaurant in the world. We first need to be the best restaurant at 652 West Randolph ... the best restaurant within these four walls. Everything else doesn't matter, because if we're the best here, everything else will take care of itself.

With the space acquired and the construction underway, I turned my attention to getting the people I needed—my "get-shit-done" crew.

When you're a chef leaving a restaurant, you consider yourself fortunate if some of the team moves on with you. When Avenues closed, I took nearly everyone with me over to Grace. Nick Romero was my opening *chef de cuisine.* I also had two *sous* chefs and a pastry chef who came from Avenues and stayed at Grace for a couple of years. Any chef would want to be surrounded with this team. They're self-motivated. I never need to tell them to go off and create something. They just *do.*

David Connell became my right-hand guy because he always delivered, no matter how difficult the mission was. He's a *yes* guy; he *never* says *no.* I take him on all my cooking trips around the world. I can drop him off in Hong Kong and say, "All right, I'm cutting you loose on this city to take care of what I need done. I'll see you in a day, David." And off he'll go, finding what's required and exceeding all my expectations. It's awesome. Long before David was in a management position, when he was a cook on everybody else's level, I'd sit in my office at the end of the night and I'd hear him telling people what needed to be done.

"Everyone, let's hustle!" Technically, he shouldn't have been doing that … but nobody complained because he strengthened the team.

Amy Cordell is another vital member of my inner circle—she's still with me to this day. Amy came to us at Avenues—from Charlie Trotter's of all places, where she'd been waiting tables, and she has that extraordinary, unique mentality one acquires from working at Charlie Trotter's. I met her and immediately thought: *She gets it—that pursuit of excellence and service.* At Avenues she worked as a captain, a front waiter.

As time went on, Amy, Muser, and I developed a great, familial relationship. When the time came for Muser and me to leave Avenues and build Grace, Amy said, "I'm coming with you guys! Whatever it takes, whatever you need." We obliged and soon she was managing the dining room, training everybody. She knew the expectation that Muser and I had, which was to constantly refine, refine, refine. She's very personable, too—guests love the hell out of her. She's an incredible person, really, and I'd do anything for her.

Matt Danko was another member of my dream team for Grace. When Nick Romero left, David Connell had begun taking over many of those responsibilities, but I had different, bigger plans for David so Matt became the new *chef de cuisine*. Matt's a talented guy. He's driven. He's smart. People really like him; the cooks like him. He has a *voice*, which is important. There's nothing worse than having someone running your kitchen who doesn't express himself.

On the flip side, I've seen others lapse into complacency, which can come into play with longevity. I certainly don't want to have to be the guy to kick you in your ass to get you out of that comfort zone.

I'll do it, but I don't want to. That's the only downside of long-term relationships. But it's not a big concern with my team.

I do actually love it when my people are invited to go to other restaurants with me for some "guest chef" deal and have to work in a new environment. I love that because they realize how spoiled they are with me. I give them every tool they need to be successful and I take away any excuses to fail. In my kitchen, they only have one way to go: Up to the next level. When they leave with me to do something for other restaurants, I observe them running around different kitchens looking around for a deli container … or a lid that fits properly … or the right-size pot. It's culture shock—and not in a good way.

If you're creating amazing food, you shouldn't have to struggle to do it.

I love taking my new people abroad to work in some lower-than-standard kitchens. Places where they don't even know what a mixing bowl is. Kitchens that don't even have whisks! Yes, places where it's really *that* bad. Kitchens like that really opens the eyes of my crew.

I had my team in some Asian kitchen once, trying to put together noodles and rice and sweet and savory hot chili sauces with candied haws and curry leaves and various other local ingredients and spices, and they couldn't even cut up kimchi or mix up satay because they didn't have the tools. An experience like that makes my team appreciate where they come from all the more.

TWENTY-FIVE
THE FOUR PILLARS

Muser and I sat at a conference table with Dolos in an office in Chicago's West Loop. He was dressed to the nines, his sleek suit bulging, over-strained—as if his tailor screwed up the measurements but still managed to shoehorn his stout body into it. Under the office lights, Dolos's tanned scalp shone and the mammoth ring on his large right hand sparkled as he frowned and swept up a sheaf of papers from the table, setting aside the accounting sheets that enumerated the expenses that Grace had accrued so far as it was still under construction,

"Again, with the fucking menu paper?" Dolos waved a fistful of menu samples and their associated cost estimates, glaring at me as though he wanted to punch me. "Curtis, you keep coming back with this and I keep telling you, 'No.' What gives?"

Up until now, Dolos had given me full control to use my vision and build Grace as I saw fit—and man, I was so grateful to him for that. I had stepped out of my role as an executive chef at Avenues and had become a legit restaurant builder and owner.

But the menu paper, of all things, became a sore spot for Dolos, a real estate investor with zero fucking restaurant experience.

Why?

Dolos didn't raise an eyebrow when I had bought a hundred dining chairs at a thousand dollars a pop. Or used expensive materials for Grace's luxurious restrooms. Or spent a small fortune on the finest dinnerware.

But for some reason, the paper I wanted to use for our guests menus was a huge stone in his luxury dress shoe.

"We've discussed this for the last year, Dolos. We agreed that no expense should be spared in the build, right? All the furniture, the kitchen appliances, the drywall and linen and all the shit in between. Every detail must be the absolute *best*."

"Sure, but this ... this is just stupid." Dolos threw the menu sample and estimates across the table and they drifted toward Muser. Muser arched his eyebrows but said nothing. "Every single sheet you want for the menu costs $1.10 apiece. Correct?"

"That's right."

"And every day, we will have to print your fancy menu on this expensive fucking paper that requires a special printer because it's so high end?"

I shrugged. "Something like that."

"And every night our guests will wanna take these menus home as some"—here, he rolled his eyes—"*souvenir*. I got that right? So they can remember what a great time they had here?"

"Exactly." I had already explained all of this in detail numerous times. "I get it, Dolos; it's a lot of money to spend on menus that guests may take home or may get tossed. But it's like everything else with Grace, it's *quality*. These menus will *feel* amazing to our guests, Dolos. It's called *milk paper*. They'll have an embossed Grace logo, which has ... *weight*. It's art! It means something! It's another small detail that will make the guest experience even more special—which is what Grace is going to be all about!"

The concept didn't seem that outlandish to me: Would Dolos rather sleep on thousand thread count sheets or a scratchy set from a discount outlet? Same idea.

"You lost me at 'milk paper.'" Dolos stood up and waved a dismissive hand at me. "Fine. Go ahead with your fancy printed menu. It's *your* fucking restaurant, after all."

He turned and walked out.

Muser exhaled and smiled. "Talk about not seeing the forest for the trees, huh?"

I laughed but while the pun was clever, the analogy left me feeling uneasy.

~

GRACE WAS BUILT on my four pillars:

Ambience, Service, Cuisine, and the Wine program.

Why do people come?

For the food?

Sure.

Are the other three pillars just a bonus?

No, they're all *equally* important.

If the cuisine outshines the service; it's unbalanced.

If the wine program is stronger than the food program, it's also unbalanced.

In a restaurant, everything must be cohesive. It's like a good menu—a natural progression and flow should take over; you should start to eat dessert without realizing that you're already having dessert. It's the pastry not outshining the savory food and the savory food not outshining the pastries. The marinated duck isn't taking away from the vibe or the bottle of 2009 Villa Calcinaia Chianti Classico on your table. Of course, you might have dishes that you like more than others. That's always going to happen. It's just your preference. But it should still be consistently, stylistically the same.

AMBIENCE. The *ambience* is obviously the setting of the room, the setting of the experience. A restaurant that's very minimal in décor, but warm and welcoming has always been my approach. It's essential to ensure that everything you touch is luxurious—that everything in the restaurant has been designed from a guest's perspective. The chairs are comfortable —you can sit in them for three hours. The table linens are pressed and soft. The china is of the highest quality. Same goes for the stemware. The silverware is balanced and properly weighted—that maybe sounds silly, but it's an uncomfortable moment when you pick up a knife and it's heavier on one end. The carpet in the room is nice. The acoustics in the ceiling have been attended to. The lighting is right. If there's music playing, it's at the right level.

We're not using shit from IKEA; we're using luxury furniture. You know what I mean? It's got to be of the highest quality.

At Grace, we spent so much money on acoustic paneling: All the drywall was double drywall. We paid extra to deaden the sound. We didn't want sound to bounce off so you could hear other people's conversations. It was important to us for guests to feel that their experience at that table was like having their own little restaurant. The background noise? You shouldn't even notice it. That's what I mean by *ambience*.

SERVICE. The best *service* is *unnoticed*. Your water glass is always full, but you never saw the person fill it. To me, great service is anticipating what a guest wants before they even know they want it. Also, just *being there*— delivering and explaining the dishes thoroughly, yes, but also reading the guest. One table might be on a date night while the next is a business dinner. The service team needs to quickly discern that, so everyone has their individual needs met. If you're eating fast, we serve you fast. But if you're eating slowly and taking your time, we're not going to rush you. You're at your own tempo.

CUISINE. *Cuisine* is food of the highest possible quality. It's all about elegance. Moreover, it's about the team and me respecting the ingredients —being ingredient-forward, if you will. Their quality is far more important than the technique. I have a romantic love for food—as does my team. It's what allows us to apply what we know within the cooking world and make it better.

WINE. My food is super-light and herbaceous, so the wine program needs to be just as exciting. It's about finding unique, exciting wines from all over the world that pair with my cuisine. It doesn't stop with the wine itself: The team plays a major role in how it's presented, talked about, and paired with the food—all those moments that get it from the bottle to the glass to the guest. People come into our restaurant hoping not to make decisions. Taking that wine decision off their hands is great for us, but we have to offer them small vintages from around the world that they've never seen or could probably never buy here.

Otherwise?

Again, the spell is broken.

Obviously, there are reasons we pair certain dishes with certain wines —the notes in the wine match those in the dish. When we pick wines, we sit down with multiple bottles and say, "Okay. Let's taste this with the scallop." That said, I've always been an advocate of asking a guest what they like to drink and eat, and *then* pairing. I'm not here to tell you, "Oh, you *must* drink a Pinot Noir with this salmon because only this red wine will go with this salmon." Who's to say someone can't drink a big-ass Bordeaux with a light seafood scallop dish if that's what they want? Enjoy it. Michael Muser might not *recommend* that—but if that's what you knew you wanted, he would be delighted that we could make that happen for you.

As you may have guessed by this point, I'm not one to spare an expense. I certainly aimed high when building Grace.

From a diner's perspective, when you're dropping more than two hundred dollars a plate and you walk out of that experience feeling it wasn't worth it, we lose you as a customer. My goal is to have guests who *always* want to come back, who tell everyone they know about us, who *want* to spend the money every time because they know the way the experience makes them feel is worth it in the end. I've been to many restaurants where I've had a bad experience. I've been given the check and thought, *I can't believe I'm paying this much money for that shit.*

Not on my watch.

In 2022, the culinary horror-comedy movie *The Menu* was released. Directed by Mark Mylod, the movie is an outrageous depiction of the gourmet dining world which takes place in an exclusive restaurant with guests being served a multi-course tasting menu hosted by a psychopathic *chef de cuisine,* played by Ralph Fiennes. I found it wildly entertaining. When the movie came out, *Bon Appétit* magazine interviewed screenwriters Will Tracy and Seth Reiss, who told the magazine that Grace restaurant had "informed the kind of fine dining restaurant they'd set out to both celebrate and sear." Reiss said, "[Grace], to me, was the epitome of fine dining. Everything (was) synchronized. Everything makes perfect sense, top to bottom."

It's amazing, but also gratifying, that people still talk about Grace with such reverence.

For me, when I look back on my years at Grace, there's a lot of emotion to unpack. Muser and I often talk about it. Grace was our baby; it was our hearts. We were two kids building our dream restaurant—and we made it happen. We brought our vision to life in myriad ways. We've since learned a lot more about everything it takes to own a restaurant. We know the building process. We know what to expect from the architects and the design team, and how everything comes together. I was there every day when Grace was being built. I watched *every* fucking screw go in.

Ego aside, this is the truth: We built a masterpiece with Grace.

TWENTY-SIX
SHOOTING STARS

"We're calling with some amazing news," the woman from the Michelin Guide said. It's the fall of 2014. I had her on speaker. Muser and I, and the rest of the staff hung on her every word. "In the new edition, you're being awarded three Michelin Stars for Grace. Congratulations!"

I was over the moon. The press was on site with us, taking photos and videos as the call came in. Muser and I were barely able to contain our joy. The staff cheered and hugged. French Champagne was flowing …

I considered three Michelin stars a huge win, not just for myself and Grace, but also for Chicago. The Second City had now been recognized by Michelin as home to two of the world's best restaurants—Grace and Alinea. Michelin Guide's international director Michael Ellis named Chicago as one of the most dynamic and exciting places to dine.

One thing bothered me amid the celebration. I didn't understand why Dolos hadn't come. Surely, he would want to be seen with Muser and me since we'd just put his restaurant on the map as one of the best restaurants in the world. Right?

Instead, I received a brief call in which he congratulated … himself.

Dolos had never been the nicest guy to deal with and almost everyone on our team felt uncomfortable around him, so him literally phoning it in that day was probably for the better. Hell, he phoned it in quite often, rarely showing his face at the restaurant since we'd opened in 2012. Instead, Dolos would send his bagman down to collect cash, and sometimes Muser would have to chase him down to pay off Grace's past-due invoices. More and more, I started to feel that Grace's owner had zero interest in Grace other than squeezing it for cash.

Even if Dolos didn't appreciate Grace, I took comfort knowing my team and I put genuine love and emotion into all Grace did. I was able to innovate, creating such dishes as strawberry, kaffir, and balm; or the Alaskan king crab, calamansi, cucumber and lemon mint; or the pig tail, endive, cauliflower, oxalis; or the Miyazaki beef. It was me, not Dolos, whom Michael Ellis of the Michelin Guide mentioned in an interview with the *Chicago Tribune*, saying that I created "contemporary seasonal tasting menus that are both intricate and elaborately structured."

Still, I wondered if Dolos's behavior would force me to walk away from Grace one day.

I hated the thought. I feared if I left, Grace would close forever, just as Avenues did. I'd be killing the greatest dream I ever had.

But could I avoid it?

MAYBE PART of the reason Dolos's disinterest bothered me was personal. Sometimes, I'll admit, I feel some kind of imposter syndrome when Curtis Duffy from Johnstown, Ohio makes a successful leap or comeback. He doesn't understand what it is to gain approval from anyone in his family or to be permitted to feel joy—those things are completely alien to him. It's not easy to get out from under the shadow of my youth; to let old ghosts rest.

Deep down, I'm ecstatic. I mean, it was an incredible achievement for me to be considered one of only twelve three-Michelin-starred chefs in the U.S. and one of fewer than a hundred worldwide at that time. That's pretty damn crazy. I wanted it. I worked so hard for it.

But when it happened, I didn't feel worthy. It's an internal struggle with that impostor syndrome.

A tool I've been using to help me through this type of thing is what I call an "accountability board." It's in my bedroom. I have a list of things written on it. At the top is a reminder to make sure that I'm forgiving of the past and accepting that I deserve good things, that I can be present at all times and enjoy and appreciate the wonderful things in my life.

I owe that accountability to my family—my wife, Jen, and our kids.

And I owe it to myself—to the kid who grew up being told by the people who should've been his biggest supporters that he would *never* become anything.

My accountability board changes when I feel something is out of balance. I put my problem on it to see if I can come up with a solution that restores the balance. That way, it's right there in my face, every single day, and not dancing in my head without resolution.

Some of the things on my board are goals, ways to better myself:

"Stop to observe."

"Read more books."

"Laugh and play more."

"Get better at public speaking."

"Enunciate better."

"Eat fewer sweets."

The top of the list, however, is reserved for more foundational exhortations and affirmations:

"Forgiving of the past."

"Deserving."

To be able to forgive the past is to allow myself to enjoy and appreciate things in my present, right? It's hard for me to forget that my father had told me I'm not worthy of anything, but the hurdle I've cleared is knowing that those words are not fact—that I *am* worthy of the success I achieve.

Being awarded three Michelin stars at Grace was something I'll cherish forever. No one can take that pride and joy of having earned them away from me. Michelin *can* take the stars away, though.

Michelin did it to Jiro Ono—the most famous sushi chef on the planet.

Chef Ono began his culinary path by working at a local restaurant at the age of seven. He became a qualified sushi chef in 1951 and in 1965 opened his own restaurant, Sukiyabashi Jiro, in Ginza, Tokyo. It is considered the world's most legendary sushi restaurant. The 2011 documentary, *Jiro Dreams of Sushi*, made him an international celebrity. Jiro's reputation was further enhanced when President Obama dined at his restaurant in 2014 with Japanese Prime Minister Shinzo Abe. Obama was quoted as saying Jiro's sushi was the *best* he'd ever had.

Jiro's a true *shokunin*, man. I embrace and respect that *shokunin* spirit —to be someone who relentlessly pursues perfection in his craft. Jiro would always go the extra mile to create that delicately flavored sushi with those fabled umami flavors. He would massage an octopus for forty minutes to give it a softer texture and a better taste. His rice was legendary; methodically cooked, then fanned to a precise temperature and sherry-vinegared. He pressed the sushi together with a precise tenderness. He sourced his tuna, eel, red sea bream, octopus, and shrimp from the legendary Tsukiji fish market in Tokyo, which had replaced a similar bustling bazaar destroyed in the Great Kantō earthquake in 1923. (It ultimately closed on October 6, 2018.) Jiro always sampled the ingredients that came into his kitchen to ensure that the quality and flavor were up to his expectations.

Sukiyabashi Jiro was the first sushi restaurant in the world to receive three Michelin stars—and one of the hardest places in the world to secure a reservation. Because of that, in November 2019, it was removed from the Michelin Guide—not from any drop in excellence whatsoever, but because they no longer accept reservations from the general public or through hotel concierges: The restaurant seats only ten people at a time, which makes it impossible for the average Joe to eat there.

The Michelin Guide frowns on such exclusivity.

So, yes, the Michelin Guide can certainly take stars away from a restaurant. But they'll never rescind the achievement. At Grace, we had set what we thought was a lofty goal to try to achieve the distinction in five years but we earned those three stars after being open just two years. *Un-fucking-real.*

While I respect the Guide with all my heart, I never understood why its only focus is on the food when it rates a restaurant. I've always felt strongly that everything *inside* the restaurant that makes the food shine is also important.

My food is combined with an accumulation of everything that supports it—my four pillars. If you had my crab dish and it was delivered to you in a nasty-ass dining room that stank like a sewer and had shitty plastic chairs, you might not think my dish was so great because of the environment that came with it. You could lose so much with that bad ambience or a chipped piece of china, or silver that's not polished. If the wine didn't pair well with that crab dish, or the service wasn't great because we were off in that area one night, I guarantee we'd get dinged for a bad review even if the food was amazing.

Grace, like any three-Michelin-starred restaurant, was an *experience*.

I'm happiest at work at about eight o'clock at night.

That's when I'm able to start inviting the guests to come back to the kitchen. I love to see how excited they are to be there and to share their experience with them—which I always hope has been great. It's then that I can see the fruit of our labor.

My other happy kitchen time is being able to create food during the day. I don't like to sit behind a desk or in front of a computer. I've never followed trends in wine or food. I have no interest in yesterday, and I have no predictions for the future of restaurants and dining.

I'm about the *now*.

I like to be in the kitchen, cooking. I like to hear the sounds. I like to be in there, in the trenches—firmly in the present, creating.

If I were an engineer or an architect, I wouldn't get to see those creative results for many years. In my kitchen, I can take delicious ingredients and, in moments, transform them all into something extraordinary that then can make somebody happy.

That's everything to me.

Being a chef is my creative outlet, my way to say something without having to say anything.

Know what I mean?

It's my art.

TWENTY-SEVEN
A RESPONSIBILITY FOR GREATNESS

Two years after I was awarded those three Michelin stars, I was riding high on a nomination for the 2016 James Beard Awards. Most any chef will tell you that a James Beard Award is the Oscar of the culinary world, one of the most prestigious awards a chef can receive. The 2016 James Beard Foundation Restaurant and Chef Awards all went down in a black-tie ceremony at the Civic Opera House in Chicago, with general public tickets at $500 a pop. This marked the second year that the ceremony was held in the Second City after more than twenty years in New York. The show that night was amazing.

It delighted me to see Chicago host the event, and also to see Chicago score big right out of the gate, with Alinea winning for Outstanding Restaurant. Like the class act he is, Alinea's executive chef and owner, Grant Achatz, thanked his team and the city of Chicago when he accepted his award. Grant had previously won three James Beard awards: Rising Star Chef of the Year, Best Chef: Great Lakes, and Outstanding Chef. That night was the first restaurant win for Alinea itself, which impressed me. I knew a restaurant could only be nominated after being open for ten years, but that alone did not make it eligible. You had to flourish for all those years while constantly pioneering new and exciting offerings in the culinary world. Alinea had *all* that. I considered

Grant a culinary genius and was happy for my friend. Grant and Alinea deserved everything they got.

The second win for Chicago went to me. I was awarded Best Chef: Great Lakes. In order to even be nominated, you had to meet these requirements: setting new and consistent standards of excellence in my respective region; working at a dining establishment; and working as a chef for more than five years with the three most recent years spent in the region, which included Illinois, Indiana, Michigan, and Ohio.

I'd been nominated many times before—back at Avenues as well— but this time, I edged out four other chefs to win. I was euphoric. And the icing on the cake was that my daughters—Ava and Eden—joined me at the podium to accept my award. I love them so much and it lifted my heart to see them glow with pride that night.

In my speech, I thanked my business partners and the people I considered the most amazing restaurant staff in the country. "I've been wanting a James Beard Award for a very long time," I said. "You gotta be patient for these things. Finally, it's my year. We have the best team —'cause it really is; it's an entire team that goes beyond what I do every single day and they support me one-hundred percent."

Ava and Eden told a journalist that they knew their dad would win. They also revealed that their dad's French toast and pancakes were their favorite Duffy-made dishes. And why not? Not much makes me happier than simply soaking thick slices of bread in a creamy egg custard, pan-frying them, and seeing my girls smile with delight as they cover the slices in a cascade of maple syrup.

Who the hell doesn't like French toast?

It's a breakfast win for kids and adults alike.

After stepping away from the podium, I told the press the award was, "very personal to me. Before Michelin ever came to the U.S., James Beard was already here, and for a young cook, this award is the pinnacle."

"You put in your work and do what you should be doing and hope-fully it pays off," I told another journalist. "This is something as a young cook that you always aspire to do, to win a James Beard Award. Tonight is that night."

I was riding high in 2016.

∼

AROUND THIS TIME, *For Grace*, the documentary film, had been released. The film only glossed over the surface of my life story—hence me wanting to have author Jeremy Wagner write this memoir for me. What happened in my life before 2016—and everything after—was so much deeper and personal, so much more insane and inspiring, that I feel the film failed to tell my *real* story.

So here we are …

No matter where I went, the kitchen would always remain my refuge, my passion, and my salvation. And to keep it that way, I always want to look back at my roots and continue to work hard, to aspire to greatness.

I don't remember ever learning the *importance* of working hard from my parents, but I believe that my work ethic comes directly from observing their struggle, their desperate need to survive.

I always say to my cooks: "You have a *responsibility* for greatness." That's something that I've always lived by. That responsibility is yours and no one else's and you owe it to yourself. The responsibility could be for anything. You could be great at drawing, music, photography, public speaking. Set the bar high and go for it.

And I always want to keep raising the bar, higher and higher.

TWENTY-EIGHT
FALL FROM GRACE

F*all 2017*
     I'm inside the offices of a Chicago law firm with Michael Muser. We're meeting with our new lawyers for the first time. We've just explained how our efforts to purchase Grace restaurant from the owner, Dolos, have failed. We've disclosed how our working relationship with Dolos has deteriorated abysmally. We're owed salary increases, ownership, and profit-sharing ... and have seen absolutely *nothing* from Dolos.

Now we've secured new counsel in hopes that these fresh lawyers will help broker a deal with Dolos to make good on his promises, to do right by us, to keep us on board, and to keep Grace alive.

Keep Grace alive ... that's all I cared about.

∾

I'LL TELL you where I believe the end of Grace began.

And it kinda began to end as it was just starting ...

Rewind to when Muser and I were deep into building Grace. Dolos shows up one day at the restaurant space that's under construction and he has us sign contracts *again*.

"Oh, I lost the originals and my copies. I just need these for my file."

Dolos comes at us with that line and we simply tell him that we'll make him copies of our original contracts. Well, Dolos throws a hell of a tantrum at that suggestion. Muser was going through a divorce at this time, so with his mind on his marriage ending and all the details in the Grace build, he just cuts the crap and signs the contract, right there … he doesn't want to deal with any extra bullshit.

I do the same and sign. We stop questioning Dolos.

"I'll get copies of this to you guys."

Of course, that never happened. We believe Dolos had changed something in these new papers to benefit himself financially but we have nothing to compare it to.

I sent the original deal to our lawyers. They looked at it and asked, "What did you sign this for?"

Fool me once, shame on you.

Fool me twice, shame on me.

I know, Muser and I look like the two most gullible dudes on the planet, right?

As we were building Grace, Dolos came around again one day and said, "I'll take care of the Grace LLC and roll you guys into it." So, he created and signed the LLC—but he's the sole member and president. Our names are *nowhere* on there. All the while, he was telling me, "You're not just the chef at Grace, okay? Curtis, you're the chef/owner. Make sure everything you use to promote yourself clearly states: CHEF/OWNER, CURTIS DUFFY. Put that in your title, on your business cards, and across all your social media stuff."

Much later, when we'd just begun fighting each other in court, Dolos's lawyer started barking at our lawyers, "You need your client to stop lying to the public. Curtis Duffy's *not* an owner!"

Dolos's lawyer made it clear that Muser was not an owner, either.

Dolos had made sure that Grace was one hundred percent *his* business.

∼

FROM THE FIRST day Grace's construction began to the first dish we served, Dolos couldn't have cared less about the restaurant itself. He was never making an effort to be in the trenches with me and the team.

Once we were in business, months went by without us ever actually seeing or speaking to Dolos. However, there was one area that he *did* speak up about and micromanage—the *financial* side.

Muser and I would put together numbers based on restaurant expenses. We managed the money coming in. For instance, if the restaurant rang up $40,000 on a normal night, we accounted for that. We knew what we spent in food, what money came in at the restaurant that day. We knew how much labor we employed that day and how much it cost. We accounted for every single bill that came through the door. We packaged everything for Dolos—including cash—and, at his request, gave it all to him through some bagman he sent over every Friday.

But there were some areas that remained a mystery.

We weren't too clear as to what Grace was paying in taxes every month.

How much were labor taxes?

We didn't know.

Also, what were the premiums for the insurance Dolos had taken out on the business?

Something about it all smelled worse than week-old hamachi. And those weren't our only financial concerns.

We had made the accounts payable process as easy as possible for Dolos, breaking it down in the most basic layman's terms: Here's every bill that's due seven days from now; here's every bill that's overdue; here's every bill that's fourteen days, twenty-one days, each one based on the vendor's terms.

Maybe a week later, we'd get a packet from Dolos full of checks and invoices to be paid—he'd send the invoices back to us with checks written out for what he *wanted* to pay. I'd say ninety percent of the time they were for incorrect amounts.

It was a real pain in the ass!

If vendors were billing us a thousand bucks, Dolos would refuse to write a thousand-dollar check. The check would be for nine-ninety-eight.

He'd short pay *everything*.

We always had problems with the vendors. It was exasperating. We're in a high-class, fast-paced work environment ... and then suddenly we come to a complete stop because we need produce that isn't there.

That's a terrible feeling.

It was that way *all ... the ... time.*

Every other day, we were trying to find a new produce company or a new beef guy—and we wanted the very best. Burning a bridge with *any* vendor sucks. But when you burn a bridge with a specialized vendor, it *really* sucks.

What Dolos failed to understand was, the restaurant community in Chicago is so small that when you burn one vendor, they're *all* talking about your shitty business practices.

Why is it so hard to pay the bills, you ask?

I wondered the same thing a million times.

Even after all these years—to this very day—I'm still hearing about lawsuits and invoices from people he screwed over, including a produce company still seeking eleven fucking grand.

Though Dolos would bully staff—particularly, my *sous* chef, David Connell, whom he went after behind my back—we thankfully never had an issue with labor pay. It was always the vendors and contractors who suffered, and that was happening from the very beginning of the build.

And there were consequences. Screwing the companies doing the construction in turn fucked *us*, because, when you don't pay them, they don't want to work. Everyone has agreed upon three pay draws: one at the beginning to start work, one in the middle to continue, and one in the end. Say the middle stage is over and the contractors still haven't gotten their second draw. Guess what? They're not coming back to work for free.

Dolos would finally pay the contractors—but only after these long, drawn-out fights. And even when these guys would come back to work after being paid late, they wouldn't work hard for us anymore—they're on constant cigarette or coffee breaks. They no longer have care or urgency for us.

I get it ...

Grace was forced to open six to nine months behind the planned opening date.

I remember how bad things got with one of the contractors. We were maybe about a quarter of the way into construction, meeting with our two architects and some other contractors. The meeting included Muser and me, Dolos, and a man I'll call "Patton," the general contractor for the entire build who oversaw the project on a day-to-day basis. He'd begun construction and hired all the subcontractors—plumbers, electricians, the HVAC guys. They were all on board. Plus, he had a separate tile guy, a lighting guy, a low voltage guy, you name it. There's thirty or more people going to town on building Grace.

Within minutes of us all sitting down, Dolos got into a heated argument with Patton about some agreement that had been broken, a mistake that had been made. Fingers were pointed, screams exchanged across the table. It all got hotter and hotter until Dolos finally exploded and *shoved* Patton as hard as he could.

Now, understand, Dolos is a big, fat guy. Wide and tall, right? He's probably six-feet, two-fifty-plus pounds and he put everything he had into shoving Patton, who lost his balance, almost fell down.

Patton said, "Fuck you, Dolos!" He turned to his guys and roared, "Round up all your shit! We're outta here!'" As his crew gathered their tools and started walking out, Dolos got in Patton's face, spewing a torrent of nasty words as the crew marched out the front door. They packed up all their extension cords, drills, saws, everything, and *walked*.

Muser and I just looked at each other like, *Well, there goes our restaurant.*

Dolos chased Patton down the street. They stood at the end of the block for a good hour or so talking, gesturing and pointing, and then, somehow, some way, Dolos convinced Patton to come back to work!

And guess what?

Patton and his crew got fucked in the end.

But they were hardly alone.

The electrician, for example: All the beautiful lights he installed for the restaurant, all those miles of excellent wiring, it's all done. Now he's ready to collect his final check and Dolos cuts him short.

Then there's the wood master—I'll call him "Woodchip." A supremely dedicated and talented artisan, he crafted every single piece that made up the walls and all the handrails. Such *beautiful* stuff. The day after the build was finished, Woodchip and his business partner came in for his final payout—around $70,000.

Everybody was happy because Grace looked amazing.

Well, almost everybody.

Dolos grabbed Muser and me. "I want you guys to see this," he said, excited to show off god-knew-what. A few minutes later, he was waving a blank check at Woodchip and launching into a tirade about higher-than-expected material costs and missed deadlines.

"I'll give you ten thousand firm," Dolos said at last, folding his arms and staring down at Woodchip, "and you can suck on that."

"Fuck, no," Woodchip replied. "You're going to pay us the full seventy grand right now."

"*No.*" Dolos shook his head. Then he grinned. "How 'bout you shit in one hand and wish in the other? I'm not paying seventy-k. In fact, now I'm pissed off. I'm not paying you at all. How's that?" He then waved the check in the air and says, "Tell you what, I'll give you guys one last chance. You guys go off, talk amongst yourselves, figure out a number you'd be happy with. We'll see if we can agree on it."

Woodchip and his partner looked at Dolos in disbelief, as did Muser and I. But they came back five minutes later with a number. Dolos of course didn't agree to their new number, so they went lower. Dolos *still* wouldn't agree. Finally, Dolos wrote out the check and forced it into Woodchip's hand. "That's it. Come after me for the rest of your money if you want. Go ahead, I'll see you in court. It'll be my pleasure. Trust me, I have more fucking money than *you*."

Fuck You money—the true last refuge of the scoundrel.

From what I understand, Woodchip closed shop right after that and they are no longer in business. For fucks sake, $70,000 is a lot of money to float and lose. It probably cost them even more than that, I'm sure. The whole thing nauseates me.

Growing up, I'd dealt with the *crème de la crème* of bullies.

Dolos could teach all of them a thing or two.

And his vile behavior didn't stop there.

On his infrequent visits to Grace, he crossed other lines. Amy Cordell and the wonderful woman who ran our offices complained to us multiple times about how he would make crass comments to them and other women about their appearances, place an unwanted hand on them, and say inappropriate things to them about how big his dick was and how lucky his wife was to be blessed with it.

"You're disgusting," Amy finally snapped at him. "Stop touching me. Stop making offensive comments. Stop being so rude and nasty. Don't *ever* do that shit again."

Another Dolos habit got under everyone's skin—his tendency to brag about his wealth. This one time, he was bitching about how one of his luxury houses was being ravaged by a hurricane, loudly airing it out to everyone as if he wanted sympathy. Now, all my cooks were making a minimum wage and never got raises. Why? Because Dolos refused to pay them anything more, even though they were working eighty hours a week. So, when you get a bull-in-a-china-shop guy coming in and complaining about his fourth mansion in the Keys sustaining damage from a hurricane, guess what? Nobody gives a fuck!

"Good thing you're lucky enough to have three other houses for back-up," one of my guys finally told him. "I'm struggling to make next month's rent."

It got to the point that if Dolos called the restaurant to say he was coming down, the entire staff would scramble. Amy would go hide in the wine cellar and do her work down there. She knew Dolos had a bad knee and would never walk his stiff, hefty, apathetic ass downstairs to find anybody.

Eventually, I had to step in and insist that Dolos have no further contact with anyone on my team other than Muser or me. As expected, it further strained our already rocky relationship.

Over and over again, Muser and I asked one another, "How could we have partnered with such an asshole? How did this guy prove to be such an infernal chameleon?"

AND THEN SUDDENLY, the energy surrounding Grace began to feel more serene and *normal* …

Dolos was paying bills on time. He stopped asking us to change the companies we sourced from. He stopped haggling over prices with every vendor every week. He blessedly stopped coming in to Grace. He stopped calling and interfering—doing the shitty things we'd come to expect as routine.

Dolos was MIA—and it felt fucking *great* … at first.

And then my Spidey-senses—sharpened at an early age in those other toxic environments—began to tingle.

Why isn't *Dolos concerned about labor anymore?*

Why isn't he worried about how much I'm spending on food anymore?

Muser and I started crunching the numbers and realized that this fucker's been *paid!* He's been made whole. He'd gotten his three-million-dollar investment back in two-and-a-half years, which was great because we'd forecasted for a five-year return.

So why wasn't Dolos crowing to everyone about not being in the red any longer?

A little history: The original agreement we'd made in his house was that he'd get a *seven-percent return* on investment.

Then it was *eleven percent*.

Then, in the last conversation we had, it was a *fifteen-percent return*.

Now, any investor deserves to make their initial outlay back with a profit. That's how ROI's works and we were grateful for Dolos's investment.

The manner of the taking wasn't making sense, however: For years he'd pocket *all* the profits to reach that fifteen percent—just taking *everything*, every day. He'd say in July, "Oh, the fifteen percent isn't paid back yet, but I predict it's will be in November." Well, when November came and went, Dolos would claim he still wasn't paid: "No, fellas, by my calculation there's about a hundred thousand left owed to me." He'd throw that out there, but never share exactly how he'd made these calculations.

Muser and I started working this out, doing the math with our accountant. We brought the numbers to Dolos and told him we were sure he'd gotten paid off two months ago. He just fought it, said we're wrong.

The *CPA* is wrong?

There was always an excuse.

We were *never* going to reach it—just a golden carrot dangling in front of our noses while Dolos constantly took whatever he felt he was owed.

But now that Dolos had made his money back, he was no longer nitpicking every expense. He stopped sending his bagman over to collect those big packets of papers and cash every week—the cash was now being deposited by us into the company bank, but we were still sending him checks. It wasn't perfect; no money was going into capital reserves to cover unforeseen expenses, for example. But he was actually getting the invoices paid on time.

It seemed he—and all of us—were sitting really nice. But Dolos wasn't done.

As Dolos recouped his investment and was collecting towards his fifteen percent return, wintertime 2016 rolled around. Now, the last three months of the year are the busiest time for any restaurant. That's when businesses start renting the restaurant out in its entirety for days at a time. And that's a forty-or-fifty-thousand-dollar check per night. Whether it's ten people or sixty, the price is the same because on a Saturday night, that's what the restaurant would have generated anyway. So, you get paid that and maybe a little more to do a customized menu or add other special touches.

A company called Salesforce rented Grace restaurant out every year. Now, Salesforce knows how to throw a party—they once hired Metallica —with a million-dollar guarantee to play a private, corporate event in San Francisco, just for their employees. This particular year, 2016, they did two buyouts with Grace—$45,000 apiece, back-to-back—$90,000 total. The invoices go in an envelope; the envelope goes out on Friday— nothing any different than what we normally do.

Then, in April of the following year, we got a phone call from Sales-force. "Hey, we're trying to close our books. Is Mr. Dolos going to cash that last check we wrote him?"

We connect Salesforce to Dolos. "What last check?" he asks.

The company tells him he cashed the check for the November second dinner, but not November third.

Dolos had lost the $45,000 check and didn't even know it! That's a brand-new sports car—or half of my salary!

It's almost comical until you ask yourself, *What else is he mishandling?*

Muser and I had had enough of Dolos's misappropriation of funds, his general carelessness, and his neglect. Grace was a restaurant of uncommon excellence, reputation, and class. But Dolos didn't realize what he had. He didn't put any sweat equity into it; he'd never worked a day on it. He had nothing emotionally invested in it. To him it was just an ATM. He took what he could and stepped on everyone there while he looted the place. And on top of all that, none of us were being fairly compensated.

We scheduled a sit-down to discuss these concerns. Dolos was flippant about his handling of the check—and indifferent when it came to making good on what we were owed.

Muser exploded.

"Your disregard for us and for Grace isn't working for us anymore," he said. "There are so many things wrong here. You're paid off, Dolos, and now you're taking more than the agreed ROI. You're taking tons of cash that appears to be unreported. And Curtis and I and our staff need to be paid what we're owed, and what we're worth."

In typical fashion, Dolos went nuts over everything so we'd back down. He roared at me about what an ungrateful prick I was, expecting me to give in—as Muser and I usually did so that we could escape him retaliating in some way that harmed the restaurant or our ability to do our work. So, I got up, fists clenched, ready to lay his ass out right there. Just as I got in his face, he put his hands up. His tone shifted and he began to backpedal, trying to make everything he'd done sound harmless.

"Okay, okay," he purred. "You're right. Look, I'll make good on everything. I'll give each of you guys a hundred-and-sixteen grand a year now, okay? From now on, boys, everything's gonna be on the up-and-up. Hey … we're *family*, right?"

He prattled on, pitching us all kinds of bullshit that didn't make sense or hold water—and then he split so fast that he left smoking tire marks.

Muser and I were still seething. We now knew this was all just another song and dance—with nothing locked in legally.

Well, we didn't drink the Kool-Aid this time.

When we began the restaurant, Dolos wouldn't let us run any of the buyouts—and we're talking at least $250,000 worth—through the POS system. Imagine where that money went. I would love for someone to go back and audit Dolos and Grace to see what's really up.

All that cash I watched Dolos's bagman take … Muser and I were like those men in the counting room in the Scorsese movie *Casino*, preparing all the millions skimmed off the casino's profits for the Chicago Outfit, doing as we were instructed while Dolos took every liquid penny home

—and I'm talking about anywhere from fifteen-to-twenty grand in cash a *day*!

Eventually, Muser and I came at Dolos with an offer to buy Grace from him.

"Okay, let's talk about it," Dolos said.

We all met at our lawyer's office. It was Muser and me, our lawyer, and Dolos, who showed up alone. No lawyer.

The hubris, man.

"All right," he said. "What's the number?"

"It's realistic. We'd like to know your number first."

"Ten million."

I almost blurted out, "Are you high?"

We kept talking. He finally got down to a price of three-and-a-quarter million, the number Muser and I and our lawyers thought was fair. We verbally agreed and began searching for investors. Our lawyer stepped up, supposedly knowing somebody with money who might be interested, but the terms were too crazy. Another guy was introduced and we got really close to making a deal with him. Unfortunately, he wanted a huge percentage of the restaurant for life. We didn't want to go there because it would be just like dealing with Dolos.

Constant dead ends, in other words.

So, Muser and I reached out to Dolos personally and asked him to meet us *mano a mano*.

Dolos agreed.

We met with Dolos again at some point around November 2017 to discuss buying Grace under different terms. The three of us met at a local Chicago dive—no lawyers, no handlers, just face-to-face with me hoping a personal sit-down would make a difference.

Muser and I pitched Dolos with the friendliest vibe we could.

"All we want to do is separate, Dolos," Muser said. "That's it. We are so very grateful that you made Grace happen. But now we gotta go our way, you go yours. We all want to be happy with this endgame … Duffy and me have great things planned and we'd appreciate it if you'd help us through this process."

"Go your own way?" Dolos said. It was clear from his tone he'd once again chosen to take kindness for weakness. "Uh-uh. I'm going to get a percentage on *all* the future stuff you guys *ever* do." Dolos drilled his eyes into us. "I made all this happen. You wanna go off and do all these great things? Well … what do I get? I don't wanna just sell Grace to you. I want a *piece*."

And Dolos wasn't just talking about getting a piece of the restaurant. He wanted a piece of anything Muser and I did for perpetuity.

The devil wants all souls for eternity, I thought.

I didn't bother to comment aloud. Muser did the talking and kept his temper in check.

"Dolos, we're talking about purchasing Grace from you with no catch, no tricks," he said. "There's no way that you're owning us. You're not Vito Corleone."

"Fuck you guys." Dolos said his voice rising. "I ain't done with you two assholes by a long shot!"

Muser's expression changed. He shook his head and glared at Dolos. "You're the Devil, man!" he said, reading my mind. "I mean, you really *are* the fuckin' Devil. You're totally clawing your way into things that just have *nothing* to do with you beyond Grace. We have families we're trying to provide for here. We don't need you. We just want you to go away."

Our personable olive branch had instantly turned into a dead limb.

Dolos stood up and slammed his fists on the table. "Let's go, Muser! Let's fucking go to the parking lot right-fucking-now so I can kick your fucking ass!"

"Dude, are you okay?" Muser replied. "Sincerely. Are you actually feeling okay? Are you on drugs? You on medication or something else right now? I ask because you're not acting sane in the slightest."

The question triggered an even larger meltdown. Dolos's eyes bulged. He shook with rage. "You better fucking believe it! I *am* the Devil!" he shouted. "And Satan fucks my wife and I bathe in babies' blood, motherfucker!"

You can't make this shit up.

To this day, Muser and I remember Dolos's unhinged outburst, going Defcon 1 and name-dropping Satan and turning our well-intended business conversation into some vulgar display of machismo.

Muser and I got up and left.

We were still employees of Grace.

After that demented confrontation, I just wanted to throw myself into my work. I wanted peace; wanted Dolos to calm down. But there was now a thick and constant unease in the air. Dolos had once again cast a very dark cloud over 652 West Randolph Street. Muser and I worried he would pull some unscrupulous shit—a fear that continued to increase as two weeks passed without hearing a damn thing from him.

On the 1st of December, 2017, Dolos resurfaced.

Muser and I had just retained new counsel. We were, in fact, set to meet with the new lawyers for the first time on the very day Dolos made contact—he phoned Muser directly out of the blue, but Muser wouldn't answer.

"I want you at the restaurant at one o'clock today," Dolos told Muser via voicemail. "You need to be there to meet me. *No exceptions.*"

Muser was rattled. Understandably so after that Satanic sit-down weeks before and by the dread-laden tone in the voicemail Dolos left on Muser's voicemail.

Despite leaving a clear voice-message, Dolos persistently called Muser over and over.

"Dude ..." Muser said when he finally answered. "I got your message. I know you want me to meet you at the restaurant, but it's always a hostile environment when we meet and I don't feel comfortable being around you by myself—especially since the last time we met. I'm going to bring Curtis and our lawyers."

"Fine," Dolos said. "Bring whoever you want. I don't give a fuck. Go ahead, bring your pal and your fucking lawyers."

At one o'clock in the afternoon, Muser and I—along with our new legal team—walked over to Grace.

We took our lawyers into the Private Dining Room, where there was a big table in place for large dinner parties.

Our two lawyers sat down. Muser went over to the corner. I was standing in the doorway chatting with all of them when I heard Dolos coming through the kitchen, talking to the staff in an extra-loud voice, trying to be all friendly and jolly with them. Let's not forget, my staff absolutely hated this guy. They wouldn't even say hello to him as he slapped them on the back, saying, "Attaboy! Good job, guys! You all are doing amazing!"

Fake as they come.

Anyway, Dolos barreled into the PDR—and everything after that happened in minutes. Dolos ordered me to exit the room, saying that he'd summoned Muser *only*. For some reason he allowed our lawyers to stay and they asked Dolos if he was comfortable talking without his own counsel present.

"I don't need a fucking lawyer. You guys fucking represent Muser, huh?"

"We actually represent both Michael and Curtis now."

"Good luck with that." Dolos turned to Muser and threw a packet full of paperwork at his face. "Here you go."

Muser grabbed the packet as it hit him. "What's this?"

"You're terminated, asshole." Dolos pointed a fat finger at Muser. "You're *fired*, get it? Now get the fuck outta *my* restaurant!"

Muser was dumbfounded. "Why am I being fired?"

Muser never got an answer. Dolos simply stood up, ordered everyone in the PDR to leave Grace immediately—and told them all to never come back.

It all happened *that fast*.

Oh, and that packet Dolos threw in Muser's face? It was full of a bunch of Dolos bullshit: justification for termination, threats, false accusations and so on.

When I was ordered out of the PDR before the meeting started, I'd made my way into the service bar. Not even a minute later, my phone started ringing. It was Muser. My first thought was that he was secretly calling me on the down-low with his phone under the table so I could hear the Dolos conversation as it's going down. So, I picked up and didn't say anything.

"Duffy!" Muser shouted. "You there?"

"Yeah, I'm here. Where are you, brother?"

"Dude, I'm out back in the alley behind the restaurant. I just got fired."

"What the fuck?!"

"I'm walking home right now. I'm out and the lawyers just left. Come over to my house later."

Dolos had left quickly, too—a human tornado who came in, destroyed shit, then was gone in a flash—leaving me to pick up the pieces.

If the atmosphere had been tense beforehand, I knew it was going to get even worse … the kitchen was gonna feel more uncomfortable now that Muser was fired. At this point, it was just Amy Cordell and I left working at Grace from the original "Fab Three" trio who had first united to run this restaurant of our dreams.

I immediately pulled Amy aside and told her what happened.

"Keep quiet about this," I said. "No one here needs to know what happened to Muser today. You and I know for now and that's it. I don't wanna ruin the confidence of the team. This is probably a temporary thing, anyway."

I had hoped that it was temporary. Always wishful thinking …

Days went by. At first, the rest of the Grace staff suspected nothing. Muser had often been doing a lot of work on offsite events, so he was always in and out of the restaurant. For him to not be part of dinner service every night was kind of normal.

By the second week, however, the questions started …

What's up?

Where's Muser?

What's going on?

I reconvened the lawyers.

"All right, Curtis," one said to me. "Here's a list of the things that you insist Dolos needs to change. Your priority is that Muser has to be brought back. If Dolos isn't willing to budge at all, what's your move?"

"Then I'll have to leave Grace. I can't stay there and work with Dolos by myself. If there's no Muser in the mix, then there's not gonna be Curtis working at Grace."

Dolos had soon begun talking about hiring a new manager to replace Muser. The idea was predictably DOA for me.

First of all, I figured that Dolos would almost certainly poison my good name with the new manager, making a working relationship nearly impossible. But even if Dolos sang my praises to the new guy, my team would give no quarter to Muser's replacement. It was more than just the "Fab Three" here. My entire team was family to us. It could get ugly. Dolos was already leaning even more heavily into the power trips and ultimatums.

"Just shut up and cook," Dolos said to me one day when I mentioned he'd have a mutiny on his hands soon. I was so goddamned furious when he spoke to me like that … I wanted to get medieval on his ass and walk off into the sunset.

We gave Dolos the opportunity to come to the table one last time to mend this fucked up situation. Muser and I—through our lawyers—requested that Dolos really rethink things ... we wanted Muser back, we wanted acknowledgment that Grace wasn't tangible without Muser—and especially without me. I wanted my rightful salary and my promised share of Grace—along with an accounting of Dolos's intentions for Grace's future if I were to stay. We also asked if Dolos would reconsider an offer to buy the restaurant from him if we had a new investor.

It was another olive branch extended, one I hoped would salvage everything we'd built and accomplished so that we could continue to create more synergies and opportunities.

"FUCK YOU."

That was Dolos's reply to our demands.

After that, Dolos flat-out stopped talking to me or my lawyers. He didn't respond to emails. He didn't do anything. Just radio silence from his end, period.

I had to walk away.

Muser got fired on December 1, 2017. I stayed on and steered the ship for a couple weeks longer before I officially quit on December 18. As I planned my official exit, my lawyers and PR team drafted a statement for *The New York Times* and planned to publish it the day I quit.

With the heat turned up high and the end in sight, I wanted so badly to address my staff and tell them what was going down, but I wasn't allowed to say anything to my team per instructions from my lawyers. Just before my exit, and before the press release dropped, we had our annual Grace Christmas party with all the staff. Dolos announced the holiday gathering would be at a bowling alley and it was the first time he ever got personally involved with a company Christmas party. He'd *never* gone to any of our Grace get-togethers before, never mind ever making an effort to plan one. He'd never cared before. *Never.* But for the first time ever, he actually showed up, acting like big man on campus; bragging about everything, trying to be cool, making sure everyone knew that it was *his* party. He was handing out Jäger bomb shots all around, slapping everyone on the back, saying he loved everyone, just crop-dusting all of his fake bullshit on everyone as always.

At one moment that night, I was bowling with my daughters and I felt Dolos' eyes burning a hole in my back. My Spidey-senses, right? I turned around and sure enough, there Dolos was, staring right at me.

The stare-down alone told me everything was over. It was an unsettling end to a sordid, ugly, and unfortunate drama. And what makes it even more sad is that I loved Grace with every fiber of my being. I loved my team. I loved *our restaurant* ... what we did there, it was so very special. People came in from all over the country and from overseas. Some of our guests dined in our restaurant more than *thirty times*. That sounds outrageous, but they did it because they loved the experience, and to us, our guests also felt like family.

At Grace, I had fully achieved my own identity as a chef, and my work had been appropriately recognized. That James Beard Award hangs on my door. Grace also won one for Best Restaurant Design—but the architectural design team deserves that one.

Rahm Emanuel, then the mayor of Chicago, said Grace and our team made the city proud. The international press celebrated our cuisine and achievements. Four stars from the *Chicago Tribune* was amazing, right? But to earn three Michelin stars four years in a row was something else. We did that from 2014 to 2018.

Johnstown boy done good? I'd say so.

I thought of how far I'd come ... I thought of my beloved parents, Ruth Snider, Kathy Zay, Regan Koivisto, John Saunders, John Souza, Charlie Trotter, Matthias Merges, Omar Cantu, Grant Achatz, and everyone else who played a role in getting me here.

And now, to end like this? Was I done for?

Fuck no.

No matter what happened, the death of Grace wouldn't be the end of me. None of the betrayal and drama recounted above was going to change my path and my drive at all—it's the crumbs left behind after the meal, not the meal itself.

It was a weekend in December 2017. Christmas was around the corner. I was with my then-girlfriend—now wife—Jennifer in our room at a hotel in downtown Chicago, which was hosting an event for the Boys and Girls Club of Chicago that was set to begin within the hour.

Earlier that day, I had finalized a statement that would officially announce my departure from Grace. My publicists were going to release it to the *Chicago Tribune* and *The New York Times* the following week.

But as we finished getting ready for the evening, I suddenly had second thoughts. As I sat on the bed, I looked over at Jennifer, my trusted confidant. "Jen, I'm going to call Dolos one last time," I said. "Try to talk some sense with him. You know, before I officially release anything."

Jen was doing her makeup at a vanity and stopped to look back at me in the mirror. "Do it." She shrugged and pressed her lips together. "Just call him. Maybe you guys can work it out. I mean, Grace is your baby. You *are* Grace. That guy's a businessman, right? He'd be stupid to blow it with you, *cariño*. If you can't buy the place, maybe stay on if he does right by you and your demands from here on out—like you wanted."

How much do I love this woman? Jen's my rock. How'd I get so lucky? I'm so grateful I have her—especially so on this poignant night.

Jen got up and stood next to me, giving me silent encouragement as I pulled up Dolos's number on my phone and called him.

"Yeah?"

"Dolos … it's Curtis. Got a minute?"

I remember there was a pause on his end that felt like eternity. How many times had I done this same act of reaching out with an olive branch to save things and put things right? I hate confrontation. I hate bad blood. This call was making me anxious as hell.

Finally, Dolos spoke. "Yeah. What?"

"You know … things have collapsed between us and we need to work out a fair deal for us to buy Grace before they deteriorate further. I'm uncomfortable because you fired Muser on the very day he was to get his profit-sharing. You've begun alienating me and the strain is felt throughout the kitchen …"

Dolos didn't offer a response beyond a heavy sigh.

"I *don't* want to leave, Dolos, but I'm going to if things don't change. And if I do that, it's not going to be good for you."

"Is that a fact?" Dolos suddenly piped up. "Don't you fucking tell me what's good for me or not."

Always the tough guy.

"Dolos, I didn't call to get into a fight with you. I'm trying to come at you with logic. Look, I know you have nobody on your side who's given you any educational advice in terms of understanding how a restaurant with Grace's prestige is built and the consequences that come with it if your chef leaves. Basically, if your chef leaves, the restaurant will close. No one else is telling you this."

"What? You think you're Grace? *I'm* Grace. You're just a face with a spatula and an ego."

I tried to remind him that *he* had wanted to open the restaurant with *me* for a reason. I reminded him of this epic thing we made. I tried to warn him of the stakes—that the restaurant would likely close forever if I was gone. I tried to be as vulnerable as possible and to tell him just how much I did *not* want any of this bad shit to happen.

"You think you're so damn special," Dolos said after a long pause. "You're not. Go ahead and leave. I don't need you ... don't want you. I've already got a lotta chefs in line to take your place. So, fuck you, and fuck Grace. Let it fucking burn."

Dolos hung up on me.

"It's all over," I told Jen. "It's all really gone ..."

I dropped my phone and began to weep. Jen sat down and held me.

I was a blubbering mess. But I had to get my shit together because Jen and I had to attend the Boys and Girls Club of Chicago event going on downstairs. I was going there to represent the restaurant, to be the face of Grace—and Jennifer was there representing the company she worked for.

It was an incredibly rough evening, attending this event and hearing people praise me and Grace. Many of the people who approached me with praise had been guests at Grace dozens of times. I nodded and smiled and shook their hands. "Thank you so much. We're so grateful to have wonderful guests like you in our restaurant. Your support means everything to me, thank you."

This charade really sucked. I couldn't wait to get back upstairs because I felt I was lying to everyone and I hated every minute of it.

After that weekend, I gave Dolos my official notice—which he accepted immediately. I never went back. The *New York Times* dropped my press release on Wednesday, December 20.

I had officially made my exit, and as it turned out, I wasn't alone.

Forty members of the Grace staff walked out after hearing the news.

Dolos's gamble to bring in new management and a new chef had failed. No one he tried to bring in could acclimatize to one square inch of the place quickly—or understand how to use that kitchen.

He maintained his bravado to the bitterest of ends.

Dolos had told me, "Let it fucking burn," and that wasn't just talk, it was a cruel way of forcing my hand—because it was ME who had to burn it all down.

∼

IN THE OFFICIAL statement that Michael Muser and I gave to *The New York Times*, we said:

"It became evident that our evolving goals and aspirations were no longer aligned with the restaurant and its future, making this change necessary. As this chapter ends, another begins. We plan to spend quality time with our families as we develop our next project."

∼

IN THE OFFICIAL statement that Dolos gave to *The New York Times*, he said:

"Grace had an incredible run and everyone who had a role in it, from the front of the house and kitchen staff to Curtis and myself, should hold their heads up high, but that run has come to an end. This space will live to see another day with yet another great restaurant headed by a new team that will make Chicago and the restaurant community proud."

∼

GRACE IS *the beauty of form, under the influence of freedom.*

That famous quote from German philosopher Friedrich Schiller—which I have tattooed on my forearm in script—was my inspiration for the restaurant's name. For me, Grace was my freedom to express everything I want to express in a kitchen.

Imagine a painter in a studio that's full of every possible color he could ever dream of to use for everything he ever wanted to paint.

Unfortunately, the restaurant died, but Grace's *spirit* remains and I carry that with me along with that spirit of freedom on which it was created.

To me, the word *Grace* also meant *refinement*. It's about taking a dish and working carefully to enhance it. Grace was never a "spontaneous restaurant." Spontaneity doesn't bode well for refinement. The Japanese, whom I admire greatly, will take a dish that's a hundred-and-fifty years old and still try to make it better every single day. And that's my philosophy within my own food world—taking our dishes and making them better every single day. Constantly tweaking them to a place where we're happy with them.

That's *refinement*—in food *and* in life … and I *never* stop refining my own life, no matter the odds.

PART SIX

Far Beyond Driven

TWENTY-NINE
THE PHOENIX IN LOVE

Over my quarter century-plus as a chef, I've learned that this career involves a lot of sacrifice—but the definition of "sacrifice" is open to interpretation.

I remember a passage in *Kitchen Confidential* where Anthony Bourdain rattles off a list of questions for wannabe chefs, including if they are prepared to give up every relationship they have with family and significant others. Are they willing to work eighteen hours a day and night? I know the weight of those questions, understanding how deep inside you need to look before making a commitment to the kitchen—all the while making less than you would in any other business.

Quite honestly, I'd love for people to stop talking about it—even though I realize I'm doing that right now. I *chose* to do this and knew what it required. But it's true in any profession. You want to be a great musician? You're going to play your guitar, the drums, whatever instrument it is, until your fingers bleed from those strings or your lips bleed from blowing that horn so much. If you want to be great at *anything*, you're going to do *whatever* it takes. You're not going to stop.

It's all about mindset: There are humble beginnings for most of us because we must work just to survive. Then, at some point, you're getting better at what you're doing and then suddenly, you find yourself doing what you love. I have never thought of the work I've done as a job.

I was lucky enough to get paid—albeit sometimes minimally—to do what I loved.

I can see where the culinary world can be hard for young people. If you're a cook in your teens or twenties, you're not going to the clubs with your friends. You're missing concerts, weddings, birthday parties, family dinners; you can't even go to the movies on a date. You work on Christmas Day because the restaurants are open then. You must work when everybody else gets to play. And it's human to not want to miss out on the fun.

When you're a chef, your playtime is everybody else's sleepy time, right? This is when the vices can creep in. As a chef, you spend all this time and energy taking care of other people day and night, because that's what we do in our industry. We're hospitality—so we're hospitable. We're always nurturing other people. So, it can breed that sense of entitlement, where you say, *Well, when's someone gonna take care of me? Now it's my turn. I'm going out and you bet your ass I'm gonna feel good.*

That's fine, but you're seeking this entitlement at … *two o'clock in the morning.*

If you're meeting your friends out at the bar, you're playing catch-up. You're downing shots, guzzling cocktails, pounding beers because the bar closes soon and your buddies are already in the bag. You're just trying to feel what everybody else is feeling: drunk and happy—which leads to bad decisions.

I certainly partied as a younger cook. Fortunately, I got it out of my system very early. Being surrounded by my older and more mature friends and mentors who weren't going out and getting fucked up helped to steer me straight.

I've read studies showing that individuals in the food service industry have the highest rate of illicit drug use and one of the highest rates of heavy alcohol consumption among all major occupations. And while I've avoided that trap, my love life and family life have certainly taken a beating. There are hours, days, moments, and years I can never get back.

~

I BRING ALL this up as a preamble to say I never thought I'd have another meaningful relationship—much less a marriage—given my dedication to my work and the damage it had wrought.

Growing up in Johnstown and St. Louisville, Ohio, I did attempt to juggle cooking with romance. I had a few girlfriends when I was a teenager. I went through the rite of passage of trying to find something to mask love bites ... rifling through Jan's stuff in the bathroom, searching for my mom's foundation, whatever, in order to cover the hickeys on my neck.

I never took any girls home to my place—for many reasons. I would arrange to meet girlfriends at the local skating rink on a Friday night or hang out at parks or go over to their houses or anywhere else—as long as we never met up at *my* home.

I was terrified to expose any girlfriend to my parents. That was both weird and disappointing for me.

Besides, as you may recall, there was zero privacy at the Duffy's!

In junior high, I dated a girl for a few months, and I thought that was long term! Then, in high school, I started seeing an older girl. I was fifteen and she was eighteen. I wasn't able to drive yet but she was a senior and she drove us around. I lost my virginity to her.

Another girl I dated for a short period of time was from one of the wealthiest families in central Ohio—while I was as dirt poor as you can get. I always thought how crazy it was that my parent's apartment felt like it was the size of a Smart car and my girlfriend's was the size of the Taj Mahal. We'd go to her house and never cross paths with her parents anywhere ... we'd never even hear them because the place was so huge. Then I'd go back home to sleep in a fucking closet while she had a bedroom where her walk-in closet was twice the size of my parents entire apartment!

Later I had a relationship with a girl for four years—my first serious relationship—and that was Nikki. I'll never forget how she and her parents were so very supportive of and helpful to me when my parents died.

As I grew older, cooking became more important than girls—and that food obsession and the time it required didn't benefit my love life. And my hours in the kitchen made it difficult to meet anyone.

Also, most girls I met didn't think much of dating someone who worked in a kitchen. In the early nineties, Food TV wasn't as big as it is now, so girls didn't think my being a chef was a "cool" thing—unlike in today's culture where the perception is that it's glamorous and amazing.

But, hey, I knew what I was getting into, so I couldn't blame anybody but myself. I dove into this profession with the knowledge that I was going to put this career before *anything* … and I was fine with that.

Which brings me to my first wife, Kim.

You already know how that story began.

Here's how it ended.

After we settled in Chicago, our family started to grow. We had two daughters as I was making my way up Chicago's culinary ladder—Ava was born while I was at Alinea and then Eden came along while I was at Avenues.

It was at this time, going into our tenth year in Chicago, that our marriage began to crumble.

By 2010, I was engrossed in my work and striving to become a well-known chef, both in Chicago and out in the larger world. At Alinea we were working six days a week for ninety-five-plus hours, keeping that ship moving forward, and, to be honest, it's all I wanted to do.

Once I broke through with my own voice and left Alinea for Avenues, the microscope was focused on me and I suddenly had a lot to prove. I put in over a hundred hours of work per week just to develop the style of food that I wanted—and to establish a reputation.

You just don't leave a restaurant of Alinea's caliber without people watching you, wondering, *What's this guy going to do?*

As time went on, I was increasingly absent from my home physically —a ghost, basically living in the Avenues kitchen—but also emotionally, fixated on professional challenges and opportunities.

Kim, meanwhile, was working a normal nine to five, so she'd be asleep when I rolled in from work. And not long after I'd finally get home and in bed, Kim's alarm would go off and she would get up and get our daughters ready for nursery school and grade school. I got up with her because that was the only time during the Monday to Friday work week that I'd be able to spend some brief quality time with the girls. Unfortunately, my relationship with my wife took a backseat.

We had already been struggling for a while—when Eden came along, Kim and I hoped that another child could maybe save our marriage. I've learned that many married couples in trouble think that, and it isn't a solution. I mean, it does provide distraction for a while, of course, because you're incredibly excited about the new baby. But at the end of the day, you still have to deal with the issues in front of you.

Kim and I did try marriage counseling, but the cracks in the foundation had already become too wide to patch.

~

I GOT off work one night, arrived at my front door, checked the time on my phone. It was three in the morning—the usual time. I entered my home and Kim was sitting at our kitchen table, waiting for me.

"What are you doing up?" I asked as I set a gym bag full of my dirty workout clothes on the floor. "You still have a few hours before your alarm goes off."

Kim looked unhappy. "I'm tired of this, Curt. The girls and I don't see you but for a moment each day."

"I'm building our future, Kim, and my hours are nothing new. You know it comes with the territory."

"Yeah, that 'comes with the territory' excuse again." Kim rubbed her temples. "I left Ohio for you, supported your dream, but there's no reciprocity for the 'you-and-me.' I've been the backdrop to your career for long enough. I'm done.'"

"Don't say that." I felt a stab in my heart. But my next thought was that Kim and I had been in a bad place before. Maybe I could fix it. "Let's go back to counseling."

"No, Curt. We've been there, done that. It didn't work. We were good for a short time after Eden was born, but it's slowly gone back to the same shit. Things went downhill when you took over Avenues, and it's gotten even worse since you got involved in building Grace."

"But I'm doing it all for you and the girls."

"That doesn't change the fact that you're a part-time father and completely absent as a husband." She sniffled, and I could tell she was trying not to cry. "You're more of a roommate here than anything else."

I couldn't argue with that. I remember wishing that I could just have it all—the girls and my career, all of it together, happily.

"What do you want?"

"I want a divorce, Curt. It's long overdue."

That day, I slept on the couch. Before long, I moved into a friend's place for a while to try to get my shit together. A year later, our divorce was finalized and I doubled down on my commitment to focus on my kids. The little time I was now going to have with them was more precious than ever.

I had a friend who had a condo in the city but didn't live there. She kindly invited me to stay there until I found an apartment. I moved in and stayed there for about five months. I made sure that I saw my daughters every morning. I hated not waking up to them in our house, not being able to see them and hear their sweet voices as they rose in the morning. But I took them to school and prioritized seeing them on Sundays when I wasn't working.

With the divorce behind me, I began dating. My dates were nothing serious—and I made sure that I never dated anyone in the food scene!

Hell, no.

Kim and I agreed that our daughters were our number one priority, so we squashed our resentments and remained civil for our daughters' sakes. The attitude was to move forward and show our kids that we're friendly and on good terms. I wanted Kim and me to have a healthy relationship with each other and be the best for our girls.

We've certainly done right by them in that way.

I MET Jennifer Perez through her job. Jen's the Global Director of "The World." The World is the largest privately owned residential yacht on earth. It's 644 feet long and has a hundred-and-sixty-five luxury residences on board. People from about nineteen countries circumnavigate the globe while staying in residences that they own, exploring amazing destinations every few years via an epic itinerary that they choose.

I first saw Jennifer in early 2015 while I was working an event down in Naples, Florida, for the Winter Wine Festival, which is the highest-grossing charity wine auction in North America. The WWF auctions everything from bottles of wine to Rolls Royces and McLaren sports cars, along with many more luxury items. One of the auction items that year was a two-week voyage on The World. And that's why Jennifer was there—to represent her company and to see many of her clients who were there, too.

This festival is full of incredibly affluent people, the upper echelon of wealth in Naples. They hire chefs to come and cook exclusive dinners at their houses the week of the event. To that end, I was asked to come down and cook for Bob and Joan Clifford. Bob Clifford is a well-known attorney in Chicago; he and Joan would come to Avenues and Grace often, and I had done this for them before, when I was still at Avenues.

Now this gig didn't pay me—the chef—any fee. My expenses were covered, but I was donating all my time and I was fine with that. It was just a great opportunity to spend the weekend in Florida weather, be around the auction—pretty damn amazing in and of itself—and it was also a great way to network and promote Grace and the Grace *brand*. I didn't actually *meet* Jen there, but we locked eyes as she was sitting outside at one of the tables, talking with a client. I had come in from the outside patio in jeans and a T-shirt—she thought I was a busboy or "the help," as she likes to joke.

Fast forward a few months and Jen's in Chicago for business. She sees a photo of me in a pamphlet from the Chicago Lyric Opera—with which I was affiliated because that is where the James Beard Awards hosts its black-tie galas—and thinks that I look oddly familiar.

Maybe she should get this much-heralded chef onto The World to cook for her residents?

Jen called Grace and got on the phone with Michael Muser. It was a Sunday— a day we're closed and it's a miracle anyone was at the restaurant to answer the phone. She wanted to meet that day.

"I'm busy, Muze," I protested. "I don't wanna meet this lady now. I don't have time. Please, just go meet her yourself and see what this is all about."

Muser met her for a bite to eat, heard her out. The next day Jen came by the restaurant and walked into the kitchen.

"Holy shit!" she exclaimed. "You! You're the busboy! The busboy from Naples."

We hadn't even talked in Naples. We had only made eye contact, but it was enough for her—and me—to simultaneously remember. She asked me for a dinner recommendation—Grace was closed on Mondays—so I set her up at another restaurant and we exchanged numbers. We kept in touch, talking on the phone, texting ... and it all started picking up speed as we became interested in each other on a personal level.

And then Jennifer invited me to cook for guests on The World.

The World travels the globe 365 days a year. The schedule is made out two years in advance so everybody who owns a residence on the ship knows where it's going to be. As an owner, you can decide where you want to get on and off at international ports. You stay on there as long as you want. It's your house. If you own one of these, you can live on this thing year-round and keep waking up in your own home in another country. I've never seen anything like it.

"Pick any spot you want to jump aboard, wherever you want it to be on the planet," Jennifer said. "We'll make sure to get you on the ship at that point."

The deal was, I'd be on board, along with Muser and hand-picked cooks during the yacht's voyage from Porto, Portugal to Bilbao, Spain from July 19—24, 2015.

Owners of condos on The World will sometimes donate their residences for a week or two when they're not on the ship, so my cooks and I got to stay in one of those. Also, much like at the Winter Wine Festival, The World paid for all the travel and food expenses for me and my team while I donated my time and skills and cuisine. And again, as with the festival, it was a phenomenal opportunity to promote Grace and our brand.

By this point, Jen and I had already developed a solid connection and I couldn't get her out of my head. We'd had chemistry right off the bat—she's a drop-dead gorgeous woman. We got together romantically around the time we were floating away on The World, but because this ship is her job, everything had to be super discreet. We had to remain publicly professional despite being completely crazy for each other. But it was more than just physical attraction and steamy intimacy, it was all about her beautiful, warm heart and mind ... she's such an incredible, positive, and good person. Plus, she's talented, driven, and so very smart. She's everything I want to be surrounded with.

Unfortunately, logistics was going to be a hurdle. Jen lived in Miami while I was firmly rooted in Chicago. But as our relationship became serious, we weren't about to let any obstacles get in the way. It's only a two-hour flight from Chicago to Miami, so, to this day, we regularly travel between Chicago and Miami and spend time with all our kids. Jennifer has a boy, Van, and a girl, Jolie, and while this arrangement may not be traditional, it all works wonderfully well for us.

As Jennifer and I fell deeper in love, all of our kids grew close as well. Before long, I decided to propose marriage and give matrimony another try. I bought a ring and then held on to it for some time, waiting for the right moment.

When I think about my first marriage, I'm sure I was subconsciously drawn toward the idea of it because I'd been stripped of my family. And my buddy, Regan Korovisto, who's ten years older than I am, kept telling me when I was back in Ohio, "It's time for a family of your own. Nothing's more important than that. You need to start that life." I was just finishing college then and even though I was still so young, it all sounded great; a way to try to fill the void left by what I'd lost.

This time, with Jen, my approach to marriage would be different. Jen and Grace both dominated my heart … and everything worked together beautifully. I didn't tell anybody that I was going to propose—not even Muser—because I wanted to be one-hundred percent sure that this was what I wanted in my own heart.

In 2018, Jen and I went to Greece and Italy together, along with a couple of my cooks—David and Matt. One morning in Venice, after breakfast, I said, "Hey, Jen. Let's go hit the city early and walk around."

Around noon we stopped to share a bottle of Champagne out on the patio at some little restaurant we'd found. I'll never forget that day, not only for the significance this date had with regard to my proposal, but also, because this was when the news of Anthony Bourdain's death broke. Jen had been on her phone, sipping bubbly, and she showed the news to me.

Holy shit! Bourdain killed himself? He hanged himself in a hotel room? No … no way!

I really loved Bourdain for so many reasons and it hit me hard. The details of his suicide triggered dark thoughts and memories of other chefs' suicides and, of course, my parents deaths. The afternoon grew dark for me as I sat there, taking it all in.

Jen and I talked for a while about life as we finished the bottle of Champagne. Before we knew it, the day was over. At night, Venice becomes romantic and quiet. We began walking and stopped at a bridge to take in the view. There are more than four hundred bridges linking Venice's canals and streets and squares, but the one we were on—made of stone and wrought iron, and arcing over this serene canal—hit me as the magic spot. Jen and I had plans to meet two of my cooks later, so time was of the essence if I was going to propose privately. I reached into my pocket and discreetly slipped the ring on my pinky finger—the only finger on which it fit because it was so damn small. As we were talking, I quietly held it out and presented it to Jen.

"What's that?" Jen's face froze in mid-gesture for a sec, her eyes wide. "Curtis? What's happening here? Is this for real?"

"Absolutely. I want you to be my wife. I love who you are. I love your children. You make me so happy. Let's do this together." I felt tears sting my eyes. "Will you marry me?'

For what felt like an eternity, Jen didn't say anything. I was unsure what she was thinking, but I could see she was stunned—I hoped, in a good way.

"Jen, there's only two answers to this question. It's either yes or no."

"Oh my God, yes, of course! Yes, yes, YES!"

We stood on that bridge by ourselves for another thirty minutes, just laughing and talking, hugging, kissing—and also crying and excited and so happy. Then we went on to meet up with the guys from the restaurant, David and Matt, as planned. We told them about our engagement and from there, we all celebrated.

Our wedding took place in 2019. It was small because we'd both been married before and we wanted to keep it intimate, with close friends and family in Miami only. We honeymooned in the Maldives.

Jen and I have become The Brady Bunch with our kids. They're all excited to be brother and sisters and they get on so well. There's lots of love between them all. My girls love Jen and I love her kids. They're all "our" kids and we're one big, happy family.

For now, we're going to continue alternating between Chicago and Miami. Jen's whole family is down in Miami and Van and Jolie are well-acclimated in school there, so I make time to travel to Miami for a weekend whenever I can. Because of Ever, though, I have to be based in Chicago. However, because Jen works remotely, and her family gives us a tremendous amount of support and help with the children, she can often fly up to Chicago for a week at a time. The kids come with her, too, whenever possible. The situation isn't conventional but it has always worked for us.

The longtime food critic for the *Chicago Tribune*, the great Phil Vettel, often traveled back and forth from Chicago to San Francisco, where his wife worked a great deal. The flight to San Francisco is a hell of a lot longer than the flight to Miami. You're adding two more hours each way. I figure if it worked for Phil Vettel and his wife, it'll work for Jennifer and me.

We always look at it as when we're away from each other, we're hustling, we're working our asses off. And when we're together, we're still working our asses off but we're enjoying each other's company in person, too. We look at these moments as quality over quantity. For us, it's about making sure that the time we spend together is exactly what we want it to be.

THIRTY
SHARKS ON THE MENU

Despite my newfound happiness with Jen at this time, in 2019, I was still embroiled in legal and financial trouble.

Grace was done. I couldn't collect unemployment because I had quit and I wasn't allowed to work because of a non-compete agreement with Dolos. Yet I needed—and wanted—to pay child support every month. But my savings were dwindling and my attempts to talk with Kim about restructuring my payments until I could get back on my feet had failed, even though I had always paid on time and been generous. It got so tight at one point, when Kim asked me to pick up the cost for our daughter's dance class (in addition to my legal obligations), I didn't know what I was going to do because I was basically flat broke.

The dejection and stress of being unable to collaborate with Kim to properly provide for my children sent me into a downward spiral, but just as it began to approach a breaking point, Jen stepped up and offered to pay for my daughter's dance classes—and then did so. Of course, I paid Jen back later, but at the time, I was floored, but also so grateful. When it mattered most, Jen lifted me … had my back.

My angel.

∼

ONE OF THE reasons I was so strapped for money was because of that non-compete clause I'd mentioned, which prevented me from working in any Chicago-area restaurants for eighteen months. In the aftermath of Grace's demise, a slew of legal actions went down between Dolos and Muser and me. We filed for the non-compete clause to be dissolved because at this point, with Grace closed, there was nothing to compete against.

In response, Dolos sued us for half a million dollars, alleging a hundred different misdeeds in hopes that something would stick: accusations of stolen Wagyu beef and truffles, misappropriated ingredients, and other wild claims, including unexcused absences and the assertion that Muser and I had hatched a scheme to solicit Grace's employees to walk out and mutiny against him.

And I had warned Dolos of an imminent mutiny ... not one that I concocted or incited. No, that staff walk out was going all natural as my team could think for themselves, and between their love for Muser and me and their hatred for Dolos, it was predictable they'd follow me out the door.

Our lawyers fought back with invoices from the restaurant and from the food purveyors—the truffle company, the beef company, all our suppliers for Grace. Dolos claimed I was stealing all kinds of stuff on specific dates—which were contradicted by evidence in court proving that I wasn't even working at the restaurant on the dates he referred to. Over and over, Muser and I had to pay our lawyers to prove in court that Dolos's claims were lies.

Dolos also accused Muser of stealing wine for his personal use. Michael wasn't even drinking at that point—he'd stopped shortly after Grace opened (and, as a result, had lost eighty pounds and gotten quite thin). As a sommelier, he continued to taste wine, of course—it was an important part of his job—but the process is to taste the wine and then spit it out. The idea of him stealing wine for personal use was ludicrous, but Dolos didn't care enough about either of us to be aware of this.

Let the petty lawsuits flow!

Dolos then filed a complaint about me doing events outside of Grace with restaurant products. I'll tell you right now that *yes*, I did that—that's how you promote globally when you're representing a three-Michelin-starred restaurant. And, *of course,* Dolos *knew* about these events; he gave me his blessing to do them.

Because some of Dolos's accusations were for actual crimes, our lawyers suggested we counter-sue for defamation of character. But we didn't have the money for it, and to be honest, we really just wanted to settle our affairs with him, cut the ties and move on with our lives. But Dolos is a blowhard. He was huffing and puffing and pushing his chest out and throwing money into legal fees just to ruin Muser and me any way he could.

Thankfully, the judge—who knew that our contract was with Grace and that Grace was no longer open—wasn't having any of Dolos's bullshit. The judge hit his gavel and declared, "Your business, Mr. Dolos, is closed. Mr. Curtis Duffy is free to work *anywhere* in Chicago."

You know, my story is akin to other bad business experiences chefs have had to suffer. I wasn't the only Chicago restaurateur who went through hell at the hands of an unscrupulous "partner."

I frown when I think about how my friend, Thai Dang, along with his older brother, Kenny, partnered with a flashy Hungarian businessman, Attila Gyulai, to open the revolutionary and acclaimed Asian restaurant, Embeya, only to have Gyulai and his wife, Komal Patel, steal more than $1.5 million from Thai, Kenny and the restaurant, and disappear.

There are things in Thai Dang's backstory that hit home for me. His journey is similar to mine, one that I can relate to, a story that shocks me and yet also makes me smile. Thai came from a rough background in Vietnam. I came from a rough background in Ohio. Thai's life was like mine growing up—extremely hard. His mom and dad were farmers and traders who fled Vietnam with their six children and landed in a Philippine refugee camp. From what I know, his time there sounded brutal. Then, miraculously—in part because Vietnam had been a French protectorate and was primarily a Catholic country—the family was given an opportunity to come to the States through a Catholic non-profit organization that set them up here.

In the States, Thai went to school, graduated, and got a scholarship for the L'Academie de Cuisine, in Maryland. He learned French technique, learned to speak French, worked in French restaurants, and then he went off and toured Spain and France. All of this inspired him to go to work for Michelin-starred restaurants and finally open his own place in Chicago, which was Embeya.

But success to some is blood in the water to others. Thai became concerned because he and the Embeya shareholders were seeing none of the profits from the restaurant's success, while Gyulai and his wife were taking lavish personal vacations and flaunting expensive clothing and jewelry. The minute Thai and his wife, Danielle—who was the restaurant's beverage director—confronted Gyulai about this, he fired them. Thai then sued for $90,000 in unpaid wages, which was when his lawyers discovered that Gyulai had been stealing money.

Gyulai was indicted for fraud and Cook County court documents detail how Gyulai and Patel had also created a mountain of personal and business debts to merchants, banks, vendors, landlords, personal attorneys, and credit card companies—while also defrauding former colleagues, friends, family members, and neighbors. The Dangs were awarded more than $1.4 million.

At that point, the Feds took notice, and Gyulai, who'd been charged with fraud but released on bond despite being deemed a flight risk, fled the country with Patel, prompting his appearance on FBI Most Wanted posters in government buildings across the country.

The Feds discovered Gyulai had also misappropriated more than $300,000 in illegal transactions and paid $140,000 to himself and Patel as part of a disbursement to shareholders—a disbursement they weren't qualified to receive. That same year, Gyulai allegedly transferred $65,000 from Embeya's accounts into his own. Cash ping-ponged between Gyulai's U.S. account and another in Hungary, before he withdrew $15,000 in cash and put $55,000 into an E-Trade account. Just days before Embeya shuttered forever, Gyulai put another $103,750 into his personal account and wired most of it to Canada and Budapest.

Gyulai and Patel were eventually spotted in Canada, Mexico, and Ecuador—and by February 2020, the law had caught up with them. Gyulai, who spent some months in a Spanish jail and then some more under house arrest in Chicago, pled guilty to wire fraud and was sentenced to three years of probation and ordered to pay $125,000 in restitution.

In my opinion, Attila Gyulani got off way too fucking easy. But I believe in karma. It's a *thing* ... it gets them all in the end.

I can do nothing but admire Thai Dang. His dream was destroyed by a criminal business partner who stole everything, a guy who'd fuck you over for a dollar. How do you deal with bullshit like that?

Thai took it on the chin and he kept on keeping on.

Thai and Danielle didn't let the shit storm from Embeya's fallout define them. They were resilient, they rose above it and they're thriving with their new restaurant, HaiSous, in Pilsen. It's recognized as one of the best Vietnamese restaurants in the city. And as if that wasn't enough, they've also opened a café next to HaiSous called Cà Phê Đá. It's inspiring and it lifts my spirits to witness their success.

In America—in life—*anything* is possible. I believe that with all my heart. It's especially true for those who come to Chicago with ambition, determination, and a very thick skin.

THIRTY-ONE
LONELY AT THE TOP

I n the summer of 2019, I was hustling, getting ready to rock the city with my new restaurant, Ever.

I would usually meet with Michael Muser every morning. The design for Ever restaurant was finished, new investors had come through to make it a reality, and the build had begun. I was married to the love of my life—Mrs. Jennifer Duffy. My two daughters were staying at my apartment on the city's North Side every weekend. The girls were excited to have a new stepmom and new siblings—and, also, their summer break had just started.

I couldn't believe how fast time had flown over those last twelve months and I was extremely grateful for everything.

I regard my trials and victories from 2018 to 2019 with mixed feelings. There's a lot of love in what I've been through, and also a lot of difficulty. Despite all I'd lost and endured throughout the Grace saga, I'd stayed the course and seen it through. I like to think that I've always been strong. I've *had* to be strong since I was a kid.

But there have been others who, for whatever reasons, checked out early. Suicide among chefs is rising, and no matter who takes their life, inevitably, it always hits close to home for me. Off the top of my head, so many who died by suicide come to mind, like Bernard Loiseau, François Vatel, Anthony Bourdain, and Homaro Cantu.

Homaro Cantu.

Omar.

That one hurts me most of all.

I first met Chef Homaro Cantu in the early 2000s at Charlie Trotter's, where we cooked together for three years. I had connected with Omar right away. He'd been a problem child who'd ended up homeless for a while in grade school and had used that shitty upbringing as inspiration to make cooking his life and become an entrepreneur. He lived down the street from me and I'd go over to his house to hang out and party. His turbulent childhood experiences were so similar to my own and we had a lot in common as young chefs hoping to make it in Chicago. And Omar certainly made it.

Omar was a real innovator, a genius mad scientist. Someone had dubbed him the "Edison of the Edible," which was an extremely accurate nickname. We were working together around the time that Elon Musk founded SpaceX and I kept thinking then about how Omar would've loved to make interplanetary snacks for that program. He always came into the kitchen with these crazy ideas. And of course, because Charlie Trotter's name was on the door, a lot of that creative shit didn't fly. So, Omar, who was wicked smart and had the confidence to cut an original path, eventually went on to do his own thing.

Around 2004, he opened his own place, and it was the *first* restaurant to go into the Fulton Market district in Chicago's West Loop. It's now hopping with 200 restaurants, but back then, no one opened a restaurant in that area—there was nothing else over there—and Omar was the first one to go in. It was a really big deal. For him to launch an avant-garde restaurant over there was ballsy. He was always ahead of us all.

It was a place where he could unleash his ideas and realize his potential and, ultimately, blow up the dining scene. Grant Achatz referred to Omar as "an ambassador of creative food." His restaurant, Moto, kicked ass, and they were awarded a Michelin star in 2012.

He was a pioneer in the areas of meatless burgers and zero food-mile gastronomy, where he envisioned everyone creating every component of their meals in-house. From synthetic meat and vegan eggs to aeroponic farming and cooking with laser beams to using ion-particle guns to levitate food, his work exemplified the very definition of molecular gastronomy.

Even now I can recall how Omar would make menus on large tortilla chips with his dishes printed on them in comestible ink. He created edible Polaroids, which were maki roll photographs made of rice paper and laminated in a nori seaweed and soy sauce; they tasted like crab, avocado, and cucumber. He had a dish of butter-poached lobster tail with crème fraîche, trout roe, and carbonated grapes that would evoke the fizz of a soda, and another of confit duck on a plate of juniper berry sauce that had been made to look like a horror movie.

Omar didn't operate with rules. He wanted to shake up the human relationship with food by revolutionizing and transforming food and the way diners experienced it. He famously said that he wanted to make food *float*, disappear, and reappear.

We're talking magic here.

Omar wanted to make edible utensils, plates, and furniture. He wanted to elevate haute cuisine to a level that verged on science fiction. More than that, Omar dreamed of stamping out disease and hunger to save Mother Earth. An obsessive inventor, he had four concept patents to his credit and many more in the pipeline when he died.

He was only thirty-eight years old when he was found hanging in a building on Chicago's Northwest Side. Omar didn't leave a suicide note; nothing to explain why he wanted to die.

I still can't get my head around it. I want to know why someone who fought so hard to achieve his dreams—like I did—would kill himself. Omar had successful businesses, he was getting lots of love and attention, and he was excited about many new projects he was developing, but one day he just snapped.

Why?

Was it because of the pressures of the food world? I don't know if he had any substance abuse issues or if he was trying to cope with stress or depression. I never knew him to do anything bad.

I think Omar's suicide had perhaps been provoked by the burden of overextending himself. I do remember him having some problems with the many balls he had in the air.

Moto was a Michelin-starred restaurant, and there's high-expectations that come with that honor; plus, I'd heard later that it had been mired in financial disputes. He'd opened a second restaurant, named iNG, and it had closed the year before. He also had a cookbook in the works, and a coffee shop/café, and he was doing things with some "miracle berry" deal as well. On top of all that, Omar had piled on a brewery, which was about to open up. He had a development lab in the works, too, but the funding had fallen through.

Omar was also behind The Trotter Project, a non-profit built on Chef Trotter's philosophical legacy—which I adopted, too, and still practice after all these years. The philosophy promotes the mindset that one can reach and maximize excellence by providing stellar service to others, mentoring people, and inspiring and encouraging them to pursue their dreams. So ... here's Omar pushing that and doing all these other great things in Chicago. He was rising up fast, a shining star with twenty irons in the fire.

My feeling is that Omar probably had too much on his plate ... and it overwhelmed him.

And, of course, his suicide brings back memories of my parents murder-suicide and I know the answers aren't always there. The human mind is a very fragile thing.

The other sad thing is, Omar was married, with two daughters the same age as my two girls, which adds another level of grief to his death that pains me beyond words. As a parent and as the child of someone who died by suicide, I feel for them ... it's devastating. At Omar's funeral, I saw his daughters crying hysterically. It was heartbreaking. I mean, it really shook me to my core. How this going to affect the rest of their lives? I hope they learn to understand it and to forgive—it takes strength to do so when you're on the living end of that situation. I hope his girls find that strength the way I did.

No matter how bad things get, no matter how strained and burdened I may feel in my role as a chef or business owner, I hold on tightly to all that is *good* in my life. I wish Homaro Cantu had held on. I wish that everyone who's thinking of suicide will find the strength to hold on. I know that's not so easy to do, to summon that strength. I recognize how hard that can be for so many.

Chef suicides have been going on for hundreds of years, all the way back to François Vatel. Vatel was this dude who served as Louis XIV's superintendent in France and was in charge of this wild, magnificent banquet for some two thousand guests at the Château de Chantilly in April 1671. He became so distressed and frazzled over numerous fiascos affecting his banquet preparations that he killed himself with his sword. He just ran into it on purpose.

Another French chef, Bernard Daniel Jacques Loiseau, worked a full day in his kitchen on February 24, 2003, and then shot himself, apparently because of whisperings in the press that his restaurant might lose its three-Michelin-starred status. After the suicide, fellow three-star French chef Jacques Lameloise revealed that Loiseau once told him he'd kill himself if he lost a star.

What the fuck, right?

But Loiseau, who was only fifty-two at the time of his death, was buried in debt, losing customers, and suffering ever-increasing spells of clinical depression. So, of course there was more to the story—although Michelin status may have been the catalyst, it wouldn't have been the cause.

Suicide is an extreme response to extreme situations. Mental illness is a proven factor, of course—and there's a real problem with psychological illness in the restaurant industry—but I believe the stress of a high-pressure job can also grind anyone down until you snap. This is about so much more than one celebrity chef killing himself. There's a legit crisis here. Our work is high-pressure; it's mentally and physically demanding. I've seen my share of meltdowns in the kitchen, for sure.

It's a cliché to say that suicide is selfish. It's also an insensitive judgment, in my opinion. That said, when I was younger, I also used to feel that way, because if you kill yourself and leave all these people behind—children, friends, family, coworkers—they are suddenly forced to deal with the pain and suffering of losing you, while, in their eyes, you're now free.

Why'd you do this to me?

I felt that way with my father's suicide. I was really angry and hurt and confused and I didn't get it. But I now understand and I wholeheartedly sympathize with that situation.

Success brings constant pressure to deliver in huge ways. And it's lonely at the top, right? Because when you're at that peak, you're surrounded by people who want to bring you down, people who envy you and try to get what you have. You're constantly questioning the motives of the people around you. Are they around you for the right reasons? *Do they think I'm a rock star and want to use me?* Mike Tyson once said he was always surrounded by people who wanted to be in his circle only because he was rich and famous. They didn't want to be genuine friends. They didn't want to get to know him. They only wanted to take advantage. And if you're well-known, that perpetual state of mistrust and questioning compounds the mountain of pressure you're experiencing with your celebrity status.

Success doesn't make loneliness go away and some believe that Anthony Bourdain was lonely in some way. Perhaps even Bernard Loiseau was in his time. I try to picture what my friend Homaro Cantu was going through, how he felt inside.

Depression and stress are no joke, believe me. For me, martial arts help; that's my main outlet and release. Being able to kick and punch a heavy bag every day gets out whatever stress and pain I'm going through. I know Anthony Bourdain was also into martial arts, Brazilian jiu-jitsu, but maybe that wasn't enough for him to discharge enough negative energy to clear his mind.

In his younger years, Bourdain said he'd used recreational drugs—cocaine, heroin, mushrooms, weed, LSD—and was high all the time … until it became a problem. Somehow, he worked through all of that. But I've seen too many chefs hit that shit spiral and lose their jobs because they've lost their grip, melted down, gone over the edge. And it's true—the world of food service gives itself over to a lot of loners and nonconformists, many of whom aren't the most emotionally stable.

Every industry probably draws its own handful of eccentrics, but nothing like this culinary one. In the words of Bourdain himself, "In America, the professional kitchen is the last refuge of the misfit." He was so right.

So … here's to my fellow misfits—please, always remember you're not alone—and to Omar and to Anthony and everyone else we've lost: Our world was and still is a better place for having had you in it.

PART SEVEN

Origin of the Sculleries

THIRTY-TWO
CONSUME AND CONNECT

I sometimes go down to Ohio and stand at a stainless-steel table in a kitchen at The Culinary Vegetable Institute—which is an educational arm of The Chef's Garden farm, my longtime source for produce. In front of me will be a small group of young chefs and others interested in educating themselves on the origins of food—and I oblige.

Here's the crib sheet: I tell them it comes down to quality, fresh ingredients. If you use average ingredients, you're gonna make average dishes. Just a little bit of effort in what you buy for your recipes makes all the difference. Respect for the ingredient is everything.

I can take a simple carrot and make a dozen different things from it that'll blow your mind—one way would be to roast it and mix it with whipped mascarpone and Iranian pistachio for my menu.

But knowledge about ingredients is not as common as you might expect.

At The Chef's Garden, for example, I'll ask my class where they're from and they'll usually answer Cleveland, Columbus, Detroit, or another large city. Then I ask how many of them always believed that their vegetables simply came in a bag at the grocery store and didn't have a backstory—and almost everyone raises their hand.

That's okay. I'm more than happy to give them a crash course in Flavor 101.

Man, do I love to talk about *flavor*.

Flavor is paramount. It means everything. The character of whatever you're experiencing on your tongue and palate is going to open doors in your mind. It goes beyond that aesthetic taste. It becomes cerebral and triggers a lot of things—emotions, memories. Think about the part in the animated film *Ratatouille*, when food critic Anton Ego eats a special dish of ratatouille. It reminds him of his mother's cooking, and a flood of memories takes him back to his childhood.

So, when you experience those moments yourself, the trigger is *flavor*.

One thing that I believe makes my cuisine so good is that I use minimal fat so that the flavor profile is accentuated rather than disguised. The moment you start adding fat to anything, you influence flavor perception—and I don't want to take away from the natural tastes of my ingredients. Cooking, with butter and cream? I don't really go there. If I do, it's very minimal. In old-school French cuisine, with every sauce that was made, at the end they would put a ton of cream or butter into it. All that fat deadens your palate and makes it heavy. People *do* want fatty richness, because it's satisfying, but you can add rich unctuousness to a dish without adding fat.

But it comes back to using the right ingredients.

I respect the ingredients and use as much of each as I can for a particular dish.

Take broccoli.

What do you do with broccoli when you buy it from the grocery store? Most people cut the florets off and throw the stem away. Well, to me, that's wasteful. That stem is edible! Even if it's not in the primary dish, let's use it creatively. Shred it and make it coleslaw for tomorrow's staff meal, you know what I mean? Same with fennel, which has, like, a dozen different pieces, so let's find a use for all of them and celebrate what makes it unique and different on the plate.

Cuisine has a personality and it's that personality that I want to get to know as I'm eating and cooking.

I've always relied on the Chef's Garden for my produce. It's an incredible farm. I've been buying from them since '92 and the main guy there, Lee Jones, is a dear friend. I've always had a great relationship with them and when I moved from Ohio to Chicago, I continued to buy from them. I've even had them ship same day/overnight to Hong Kong from Ohio just to use their product. That sounds extreme, but I've always wanted the best produce available, wherever I am in the world.

Years ago, the Chef's Garden created the Culinary Vegetable Institute, a facility with a kitchen where they could educate people about ingredients. In addition to the kitchen classroom, it's basically a mini-hotel with rooms downstairs where you can stay over and sleep, and a chef's suite upstairs with a bedroom, hot tub, and TV, as well as a library.

The idea was to bring chefs here to experiment, to learn and grow—or just disappear for a few days among like-minded food lovers.

I've been bringing my team down there since my Alinea days. It's educational *and* inspiring for everyone. Much like some of the class I mentioned earlier, a number of young people on some of my kitchen teams didn't even know where the food comes from. They'd say, "Wow. That's how a carrot grows? In dirt? Holy shit. I had no idea!"

I'm not joking.

People don't know how potatoes grow. They can't make a connection to where a certain food comes from, but that connection is very important to understand. And for me, each time I've gone back to the basics, I've learned something new.

I met Alice Waters while working at French Laundry during a summer when I was on sabbatical from Charlie Trotter's for two weeks. While there, I ate at her restaurant, Chez Panisse. She wasn't the chef; although she's the owner, she's always had an executive chef in the kitchen.

Alice's food is about as pure in its simplicity as you could possibly cook. You'll get two or three ingredients to a dish and that's it. Think more is better? There can be fifteen, twenty, thirty elements on a dish. But as you get older and wiser as a chef, you may find that you slowly take things away that aren't necessary and you strive to make the dishes more simple. Alice has always cooked that way and her restaurant represents that. I remember my dessert at Chez Panisse was a perfectly ripe peach. That was it. It wasn't cut. It was a peach set onto a plate and it was perfect in every way. A simple, individual fruit. Ripe, in season. Exactly what you want a peach to be.

Alice elevates farmers from anonymity, giving them a face. She has a connection with seventy-five people she sources from. Some of them only provide one thing. One might provide strawberries or tomatoes, and the other seventy-four are where she goes for other components. It's *always* about the ingredients—the best quality, at the height of their season. It's a philosophy I share.

At the same time, it's important for the farmers to understand where their food ends up. Some of our farmers offer only a few items and it's crucial for us to get those exclusive products—the very best they have to offer.

To bring it back to our orange friends, if you're buying carrots from grocery stores, you don't get the history. You don't know anything about them. Whereas if you buy from a small farmer, those carrots represent who the farmers are. And the history of your produce matters. You're not going to make that carrot any better by cooking it and using fancy techniques on it. An old carrot that's been sitting around for two weeks in somebody's warehouse is not the same as a carrot that was pulled from the dirt on a farm yesterday.

Produce represents the supplier. If one of my chefs brings me vegetables that are dark on the edges and picked wrong and of an incorrect size, that's a representation of who the suppliers are. The supplier is telling me that he thinks it's okay to give me a shitty product. I set high standards and I expect my cooks to exceed them. So, when I'm handed a piece of basil that's black, that supplier and its goods don't belong in my kitchen.

Again, it all goes back to your relationship with the farmers. This mindset is straight out Alice Waters' brilliant, avant-garde "farm-to-table" movement. If you have a good relationship directly with a phenomenal farmer, they're not going to send you a substandard product.

Some chefs personally taste test fresh vegetables, fruits, anything and everything coming through the door. I don't always have time to do that, but I'll have one of my team taste it if I can't. When farmers bring in new produce that's coming fresh into season—varieties that maybe we haven't seen in a few years—they're super-excited about it.

"Chef, you've got to taste this—it's amazing! I just picked it this morning! We're only going to have these for another six weeks ..."

Then I taste it and decide whether we can use it.

Does it fit?

Does it make sense with what we're doing at this time?

You can taste-test a vegetable and learn about the region where it's grown. Is it wild or fresh? A wild product is in an environment that's not controlled, which gives it a hell of a lot more flavor than something that's grown in a greenhouse. When, for example, someone says, "Hey, chef. We have something from the valley, mountain, foothills," my interest is definitely piqued.

The chef-farmer relationship isn't a one-way street, either. Farmers are smart and savvy, but they aren't chefs. They need our wisdom and experience to help them broaden their product lines. If you get a chef in there who says he could do something with a farmer's new product, other chefs may follow that lead and start ordering it. If fifteen chefs pass on a product, the farmers won't push it. They'll abandon that idea. They'll produce the food the chefs want, whatever the use may be. They know how to market their produce so that great chefs will use everything they can grow.

Along those lines, I think it's important for chefs to mentor young people who might become future chefs, to teach them the importance of buying from small farms—and not necessarily from only one farm, either—as well as the importance of sourcing consciously so they can help farmers strive for better products.

And I personally love the idea of "edible schoolyards"—the term and idea founded by the great Alice Waters—where students raise fruits and vegetables and, as I mentioned before, learn that such bounties don't originate in a plastic bag.

I now have four kids who've been in school. Cafeteria food is still mostly shit. But, you know, there are schools out there trying to provide healthy food. When you have a certain budget to work with, it's hard. That's why people with lower incomes eat a lot of fast food—you can get an entire meal with a tremendous amount of calories for less than five bucks. But if you go to the grocery store and try to feed yourself a nutritious meal that includes vegetables, grains, protein, fruits, and maybe some dairy with five bucks, it's almost impossible. Unfortunately, schools often can't make it happen, either; they're grappling with that cost dilemma.

I get it. And to be honest, the last thing I want to do is cook at home. I laugh when I say that, but it's true. I don't have a choice because I need to feed my kids and I try and make them the best meals I can, but they challenge me. They're at an age—especially my oldest daughter—where they don't eat just anything.

Do my kids know the caliber of the level at which I can cook?

Yes.

Do they care?

What do *you* think?

Once Ava hit her teens, she wouldn't eat anything but basic stuff—grilled cheese, chicken fingers from a bag, pizza, and fucking peanut butter and jelly sandwiches. And it would drive me crazy. I would look at her and be like, "You're fourteen years old and you wonder why you're so goddamn tired all the time? It's because you're eating nothing that offers real energy." Ava also never ate French fries, didn't like ketchup. What kid doesn't like French fries and ketchup? Every kid eats that shit—not that she needed it. I just spent a lot of time wishing she'd eat better.

The irony here is, I was the exact same way about food when I was that age. My childhood meals weren't great moments for me. First off, going out to dinner didn't exist in my family. My family *never* did that. They couldn't afford to do it even if they wanted to. My mom, Jan, was "cooking" when she could—and by "cooking" I mean that she was feeding us TV dinners. We also ate a lot of frozen pot pies. Who the hell wants to eat a packaged frozen meal that comes from an assembly line, portioned for an individual, with some type of processed meat for the main course, tasteless vegetables, potatoes, and a nasty dessert?

As an educated adult, I've learned a lot about food, and can't believe I had to eat that garbage as a kid. TV dinners suck, and it comes down to how they're made. During the freezing process, the taste of the food degrades, so the meals are processed with tons of extra salt and fat to compensate for the lack of taste. Moreover, they need to be stabilized for long periods of time, so companies use partially hydrogenated vegetable oils in things like the desserts to give them longevity. Partially hydrogenated vegetable oils are super high in trans-fats, which are proven to negatively affect cardiovascular health. The dinners were never nutritious, and they also contained preservatives like butylated hydroxytoluene to make them last if they were stuck in freezers for a long time.

And I think that's why I became so stubborn when it came to eating as a kid because I didn't enjoy the food my mom gave me. I didn't like the taste of it at all. I'd go hours and hours without eating a bite. My parents would say, "Look, you little fucker, you're going to sit there 'til you eat it all or you're going to go to bed hungry." I'd sit and sit and sit. I'd actually fall asleep in my chair at the table sometimes. And God forbid if I laid my head down on the table or put my elbows on the table, for that matter. My parents made a big deal about table manners, which was just absurd because they didn't really give a fuck about decorum or etiquette. They laid out rules that would be broken, and that would give them an excuse to inflict pain. Like, if I put my elbows on the table, without any warning, Bear or Jan would jab a fork as hard as they could into my elbow! They'd embed the prongs deep until they *hit bone.*

I went to bed hurting and hungry all the time.

When I was growing up, I was pretty skinny. My dad called me, "Bones." Obviously, my emaciated body was the result of not eating a lot. But by the time I was fourteen, I started to eat more of what was given to me—and eating more as a teen working in a restaurant.

I just didn't enjoy my mom's food ... and I really hate saying that. I *wish* I had fond memories of delicious homemade meals or favorite dishes from my mom that I could be proud of and miss. But I don't.

I never consumed a lot of dairy. I do like cheese, but I'm not going out of my way to eat it. I like cereal every once in a while. My stepdaughter, Jolie, eats Cocoa Krispies, which I'm a sucker for, but I don't really like milk in my cereal. I'll use nondairy milk, which is great—almond or cashew milk. But it's got to be the type of almond milk that doesn't have all the additives and shit.

When you consume nonfat dairy, look at the ingredients as compared to something that's not nonfat. In some cases, there can be more ingredients than in regular milk to balance the taste. When that happens, it's actually worse for you than regular dairy.

PEOPLE TODAY HAVE MORE access to ingredients that only high-end chefs used to be able to find. For instance, there's the buddha's hand, a citrus fruit from Asia. They appeared on my radar for the first time twenty plus years ago and there was no way you would've seen them in a grocery store then. I mean, it was a big stretch even for a chef to get them. Now you can easily buy them in Chicago at Mariano's or any other grocery chain. It's awesome.

Back in the day, sourcing items used to be a different ball game. Any time you got something new in your restaurant it was a huge deal. For instance, finger limes. We were buying them frozen from Australia when I was at Trio in 2003 and we thought that was extremely special. You would *never* have seen fresh ones anywhere in the U.S. Now you can buy them—and pretty much any other food items you desire—online, and that blows my mind.

I mentioned the importance of cooks connecting to farmers and the food they produce, but it's also important to connect the eater to the ingredients in a dish. Create a dish that people can relate to: consume and connect. When people have no idea what they're eating, they can't connect with it. You lose people when they lose interest in the food. I always try to create a dish that has something creative and different about it while retaining some familiarity for the guest who's eating it. If it's roasted beets, most people know that flavor profile. If you give them a dish with beets in it, the dish needs to taste of beets. You can't be so off the wall with your culinary creativity that the eater can't connect with it.

For me, it's about taking recipe ideas and then using my imagination to figure out what to do differently to create something that's not typical —while avoiding being lumped into the molecular gastronomy move-ment. That movement is great, but it's not how I cook my food.

Take my popular crab dish, for instance; we use only a few ingredi-ents and they're very familiar to people. It starts with cucumber and crab, which is a classic pairing. But then we add an acidic element with calamansi, which is a kind of citrus from the Philippines, and maybe calamansi is something that people don't know. That's one way I can introduce an interesting twist, using calamansi in place of something simpler, like a lemon.

Further into the same dish, we're going to use sugar in a new way: a sugar tuile. And we want to probe the whole chemistry side of it. *How do we make this sugar tuile sit on top of the dish while withstanding humidity and moisture, so it doesn't melt right away?* We don't want it to become tacky and sticky and hard to work with. So, we research sugars and how each one is affected by moisture and humidity.

Then we create a recipe for that application—and no joke, it can take months to figure out how much of each sugar to include. That sugar tuile has three different types of sugar in it, okay? And one of them is used in confectioneries, specifically to keep humidity out. But we can't use just that one sugar because it doesn't allow the correct *texture* once it's in the state where we need it to be. So, we add other sugars to soften it. We're basically playing with food all day to figure those moments out—and once it's documented and we're happy with the result, that's when it becomes a recipe.

Throughout this process, I'm playing the role of a lab technician. I measure out my sugars to arrive at the perfect concoction. With those three different sugars, maybe it's 100 grams of isomalt, 100 grams of glucose, and fifteen grams of granulated sugar—but when we make it, it's not the way we want it to be. So, then we go back and look at it again. What next? Let's try a different measurement of each of those sugars and bump the granulated sugar either up or down and see how it reacts. And that becomes a starting point, until we adjust it to the stage where we're happy with it.

I'll tell you this: with all the dishes I create in my kitchen, two ingredients that are probably always going to be on my menu when they're in season are coconut and fennel. They always win ... those flavors are just out of this world.

I'm cuckoo for coconuts. Coconut is the ultimate luxury food.

The different stages of coconut growth are each so amazing and delicious. And at every stage, all the flesh on the inside is edible. It fascinates me. I love raw coconut. I love coconut water. I love young coconut, old coconut, mature coconut.

In Hawaii, they feed babies young coconut flesh because it's pudding-like. It's rich and fatty and creamy—and it lends itself to so many different things; sweet and savory and everything in between. For me, it's fatty luxury that brings a dish to the ultimate level of decadence.

When something's very fatty, it usually absorbs a lot of flavor—but coconut also masks a lot of flavor, which is a crazy thing. It takes on flavor very easily and it goes well with things. As I said, I'm not a dairy guy, so I replace that with coconut and it becomes a little bit healthier ... but you still get the same texture and feel in your mouth as if you were adding heavy cream.

And it's also vegetarian and vegan-friendly.

THIRTY-THREE
DUCK, DUCK, DINNER

lthough my cuisine relies heavily on vegetables, the vegetarian and vegan lifestyles are not for me.

I tried the vegetarian path for a while and it was really hard, man. I gained more weight going vegetarian than eating a normal diet with meat and I didn't feel good at all.

I do, however, respect the ethical choice of not eating meat because of modern agribusiness, which pollutes our environment and drinking water, ruins rural areas and landscapes, and abuses and traumatizes the animals that are raised and butchered. When corporations dominate our food supply, that's dangerous.

When I approach an animal for use, I first make sure it comes from a humane and ethical source. I use that animal like any other ingredient—in numerous ways. As a chef running a restaurant, I have an obligation to be sustainable. I'm not buying things that are going extinct. There are certain seasons when fishing companies won't harvest specific fish to let those fish spawn and reproduce, for example. You have to be conscious of that.

Sustainability is vital, maybe more than anything. If we like a certain type of fish for the menu but it's barely available because that species has plummeting numbers, we're not going to buy it. That's about making good choices as a chef.

I don't like foie gras. I won't put it on the menu because ducks and geese are inhumanely treated. I had no problems with foie gras when I was a younger chef, but as I got older, the taste made me want to throw up. Plus, knowing the source sickens me and makes me uneasy. I'm not going to serve it because of what I know of that industry. I won't prepare that anywhere.

I know there are some companies who treat the ducks and geese they harvest in a respectful manner—not like the barbaric ways of the past. But I have terrible pictures in my brain of ducks and geese brutally being force-fed grains through a tube inserted down the esophagus—which ultimately caused their livers to balloon to obscene size—all while being held captive in dark rooms. I'm not on board for that. That's not the way farmers do it anymore, thanks to public outrage and animal-rights activists who helped to abolish those inhumane practices from most of the U.S.-based companies. Back in 2012, I remember then-California governor Arnold Schwarzenegger signing a bill outlawing the production and sale of foie gras. And once upon a time, there was a foie gras ban in Chicago but it was repealed after about two years.

And a year before that, Charlie Trotter landed at the center of a heated foie gras issue when he announced to the *Chicago Tribune* that he'd stopped serving it at his restaurant. He had visited a few farms and it kind of fucked his head up. Charlie then took jabs at Chef Rick Tramonto for serving foie gras. Then he jabbed at the American foie gras farmers who disagreed with his harsh descriptions, as they swore that their ducks never suffered cruel treatment.

Those accusations came back to bite Trotter on the ass.

Just weeks after he'd criticized Tramonto and foie gras farmers, Charlie found himself in the hot seat as two guest chefs he'd hosted at his restaurant served foie gras! While this was presumably done without Charlie's knowledge, he still found himself attacked by everyone: *The New York Times*, *The New York Post*, and even Anthony Bourdain, who had always held Charlie in high regard despite his dark temperament and lack of humor.

There are many folks in the restaurant industry who are adamant that conditions are far worse at mass-produced poultry and pig factory farms, and that many chefs who refuse to allow foie gras on their menus are still comfortable using the breasts, legs, and all other edible parts of the duck.

It's a challenge for all chefs to explore—what we determine to be our values and obligations for the food we serve and how we make choices to support that.

In the end, Charlie removed foie gras from his menu forever. He said that decision wouldn't make a chef less of a chef. I get that ... I don't serve it either, and, after all, the culinary world doesn't revolve around it!

THIRTY-FOUR
THE OBSESSED

D o I have an obsession with food?

Yes.

I'm obsessed in a way where I think about food all the time, *creatively*.

I look at different things and wonder, *If that were a piece of food, what would I do with it?* I recently saw a video of a guy screwing around with colored sidewalk chalk. He tied a bunch of colors together and then rubbed the bundle against a traditional kitchen strainer, producing a rainbow of chalk powder. It inspired me! I figured I could take a piece of meringue, scrape it against a strainer, get meringue powder, and do four different flavors and four different colors and achieve exactly what the chalk guy did.

Now I have a new idea to run with, taking that moment of inspiration and creating a dish around it.

There are several different types of meringue. Meringue is basically a technique, taking egg whites and whipping them in a KitchenAid, and mixing sugar in to stabilize them, and sometimes a little bit of lemon. That becomes a *medium*. I like to call it a medium because at that point it's limitless as to whatever flavor you want to put in it. If you want to take smoked paprika and put it in the meringue, you have a smoked paprika meringue.

Let's say you take a big batch of meringue and split it up into five bowls. You have the same meringue, but into each one you put a different spice. Maybe one is coriander, the next is star anise, the next one is black cardamom, the next is cumin, and the last is fennel seed. Now you have all these flavors of meringue. Then you put them in the dehydrator to dry them out. So now you have a crispy meringue that almost resembles that chalk. Then you're scraping it into the kitchen strainer. You could change the color of each one.

When you're open to thinking outside the box, every day brings a million inspirations.

My menus are ever-changing, and I draw inspiration from places unrelated to cuisine, perhaps a video or artwork or music; anywhere, really. Inspiration and creativity are free to embrace when you accept the elements of what surrounds you. Right now, I'm peering up at the light fixture in my dining room at home, which looks like a Gothic mace. There are chains with spikes on the end and a big ball in the middle. And now I'm imagining doing a dish in that shape! It's natural for me to see things this way and you can, too. You simply need to be open with your mind and willing to be aware of your surroundings and accept any ideas that come to you.

When I'm not in the restaurant, I'm not usually searching for recipes; it's more about allowing myself to be open that way. I encourage adults to have a child's imagination. When we do that, it opens us up to amazing things.

As for the creative process that goes into developing my recipes, I'll share that here. It's not just about me writing down two or three ideas, it's taking those two or three ideas and trying to explore them. I'll sometimes get into relating the ingredient combination to something I've done in the past and then twisting it. I'm trying to get the idea to move from paper to what I'll create with my hands.

Take a flavor profile of, say, white chocolate and caviar. If I just write that down, it might be enough for me to look back and go, "Oh, yeah, I know exactly what that was." But I want to connect where my head was at when I wrote it down and why. Whether I ate something that tasted like those two ingredients, or it was an idea that just came to me, I want to explore it more deeply.

Maybe I had something that was crispy and tasted like white chocolate and thought, *Damn, what if I can have this with caviar? I love the texture of both.* That will all make more sense to me than just writing down "chocolate and caviar."

As creative and inspired as I might get, I don't go too far or get crazy-adventurous. I've always walked that fine line, not pushing it. I've mentioned before that what makes my cuisine stand out is the fact that it's *relatable*. I don't think I'd go as far as, say, what Grant Achatz had done at Alinea, where they offer an edible balloon made from green apple taffy and filled with helium. Maybe that's because I was told as a kid to never stick a balloon in my mouth because I'd choke on it! Funny as it sounds, I'm serious. For me, a balloon doesn't relate to food, but someone brilliant like Grant Achatz made it work.

I sometimes have a mental picture of what a new dish might look like, aesthetically, on a plate. Now and again, I'll sketch a small picture of how I'm envisioning it—though the end result could be totally different from that sketch or what was in my head. It could end up on a plate when it was originally supposed to be in a small glass, or vice versa. Maybe it ends up in a bowl because I've decided, as I was messing with ingredients, that I wanted to turn part of the fennel into a broth and now we're pouring a broth tableside. It all takes shape quickly once we get into the kitchen and start translating what's in my head and my notes into actual dishes.

I'll collaborate in the kitchen, but most of the ideas that make it to my menus are mine. I always want to make sure that what I'm offering is done in my voice, the right voice. Toward the end of a dish's creation, I'll maybe collaborate with a couple of my chefs. It's good to have others on hand, because obviously one chef can't think of everything. When you have six people in the room, you get six different ideas. That's fucking great.

At Alinea, Grant and I and a few others would sit together at the end of the night or once or twice a week, and we'd have a specific topic to talk about. Everybody would throw out ideas and it was up to Grant to take some of those ideas and incorporate them.

The collaborative ideas that stuck became a small part of a full dish, a way to better it. It could be a roasted chestnut dish, for example. If we wanted to put chestnuts on the menu, we'd start talking about other elements we could add to them. What flavors go with chestnuts? I'd say,

"Madeira is great with chestnuts," or, "Cabbage is great with chestnuts," or, "Lemon verbena is amazing with chestnuts." Then maybe Grant would be like, "All right, let's make that chestnut dish," and we'd start adding these other elements. But the *final dish* was *all* Achatz.

Follow?

The final dish is always seen as the main, executive chef's creation, even if other chefs—or the whole kitchen—might've contributed to the making of it.

THIRTY-FIVE
REALITY BITES

ichael Muser has tried getting me to participate in reality
TV shows. Even though it's not my bag, I get it—the expo-
sure from these shows is huge. Millions of viewers will see
you and your name will be known in every house. I won't lie—I do think
about what that might do for my brand.

Then again, I didn't come this far just to come this far—know what I
mean?

I don't like the idea of having to duel other chefs to prove who's the
best.

I'm not into celebrity chefs and I don't care for rock-star-wannabe
chefs. A chef should be behind the scenes, creating, working on his craft,
giving diners his or her best cuisine and service. I'd like to show that side
of my craft to viewers, to give them something compelling and educational. But when I've tuned in to many of these chef-based shows, I often
see some loudmouth screaming at the staff, swearing at everyone just to
grind them down. It's pure drama and they're using their platform not to
promote great cooking, but to showcase their name as a star. Totally arrogant shit, man.

Celebrity chefs didn't really even exist when I began my career. Yes,
you had Julia Child and Jacques Pepin and *Yan Can Cook* and *The
Galloping Gourmet*. They were the Big Four and they were doing real

work. They have sometimes been credited with being the first TV celebrity chefs. Then as time went on, in the late eighties and early nineties, the Food Network started to climb in the TV ratings. The focus was shifting to showcase the actual restaurant chef in a professional kitchen as opposed to home cooks teaching you how to make a meal at home. It started to expose the globe to what we do. Back then I thought the Food Network might have something there, a good platform that would educate people.

Now, if you turn on the TV, you'd think every chef out there has his or her own show. The list of ranking celebrity chefs is endless. But the celebrity thing fuels unrealistic expectations. Let me tell you, this industry will eat you alive if you're not in it for the right reasons. If you're going into it just because you think cooking is going to put you on TV, you're in for a surprise—like the nineteen-hour workdays you've got to put in.

I will say, however, that this type of programming has given a greater visibility to the culinary world and its chefs. I do understand that TV has done a lot for the food world; I'm not going to take that away from it. I've seen over the years that diners have become more educated and seem to have a better overall awareness of food. That makes our job more challenging because people are always questioning our products. "Where are you buying your ingredients from?" "Is it sustainable?" I love that, those are great questions about things we should all be aware of anyway.

If any cooking show on TV has appeal for me, it's one that gives me something both I and others can *use*. I love *tasteful* cooking shows. Alton Brown used to do a show for the Food Network, for example. I thought it was whimsical, but more important, it was informative. I respected him because he taught the science side of it and gave the answers as to why things were happening. And I have to say that Rachael Ray deserves some credit: She admits she isn't a certified chef and has often pointed out that she never had any formal culinary training—but she delivers a fun show and promotes good eating. Rick Bayless does a wonderful job. He does a very *educational* show, teaching you about the cuisine or the culture of Mexican food. I love that.

That said, I understand why Muser kept pushing me to participate in a TV show. He was particularly partial to *Iron Chef America*, which is based on the Japanese TV series of the same name. Every week, exceptional chefs from around the world enter a kitchen to battle the great Iron Chefs of America—chefs such as Michael Symon, Geoffrey Zakarian, Bobby Flay, Marc Forgione, Mario Batali, Jose Garces Masaharu, Morimoto, and Cat Cora. Alton Brown does the commentary.

The first time I finally agreed to do *Iron Chef*, they gave me the ingredients of some undetermined recipe that was chosen that day. Then after about a week of going through all the details of what was expected of me and the way I'd have to use ingredients that I didn't choose myself, I decided to not do it. It wasn't for me. My view then was that it didn't resemble what we professional chefs really do every day. To go on that show, throw some shit together very quickly, and try to beat the clock and then beat the other chefs? I get the whole entertainment element, but I take my work and my passion very seriously … and I swore that I'd never appear on a show like that.

Sorry, Muze! I just couldn't do it.

That world just isn't for me.

Or at least it wasn't …

But then, in 2020, I actually *did* appear on Netflix's *Iron Chef: Quest for an Iron Legend*. I admit, despite my reluctance and despite having cancelled years ago, my team and I had an incredible time participating. And I was honored to go up against Dominique Crenn, who is the best of the best.

I was also on *Top Chef* once, but never as a cooking contestant. I was one of the final judges for the last season of 2017 and you barely saw me.

Those experiences helped me loosen up and look at Food Network-style shows in a different way. I stick by my guns about my disappointment with reality TV, networks just dishing out content that doesn't spotlight the craft of world-class chefs in a meaningful way. That said, I thought if I was ever asked to be on *Iron Chef* again, then I'd do it—for fun!

I think of Shep Gordon, whom chef Emeril Lagasse credits as being the guy who created celebrity chefs. In 1972, he set up Alive Culinary Resources, which was the very first talent agency to represent chefs. His roster of clients has included Charlie Trotter, Emeril Lagasse, Lydia Shire, Nobu Matsuhisa, Peter Merriman, Piero Selvaggio, Roy Yamaguchi, Sam Choy, and Wolfgang Puck, among others.

Shep's awesome. He's elevated chefs to a whole new level of visibility and respect. We went from "the help" to distinguished artists and fame followed. But all that respect and recognition isn't earned if you don't put in the work and have an actual passion for cooking. It's not earned if you don't possess any kitchen skills.

When someone walks through the door wanting to work for me, I tell them to break down a chicken and bake me a meringue pie. A lack of skills isn't a deal-breaker for me, but I do want to see if they have some proficiency in the kitchen, an understanding of the fundamentals.

This ain't a TV show.

They might butcher the hell out of a chicken, but do they at least understand the pieces involved and the bone structure? You've got to start in a certain way to begin breaking down a chicken. I had a newbie once tell me, "Well, I just thought chicken came in pieces already."

I'll break down a chicken for you right now.

I get a whole chicken.

I rinse it.

I dry it.

I set up my cutting board. Make sure it's all nice and clean.

I start with the two wing tips.

I take them off. Then I split the skin, push the skin in away from the leg so when you cut through the skin, most of it stays on the breast. The more skin on the breast, the better protection it's going to have.

We all know that the more the muscle was worked, the more flavorful it is—and the longer it takes to cook. This is why the leg and thigh are a bit more forgiving and you can cut some of the skin away. There's always excess on the legs anyway. I'll split the thigh from the drumstick and then take the thigh and push it out of its socket on both sides. That's when you hear that *pop*. That'll allow you to lay the legs flat on the table, which gives the chicken better stability for cutting the breast. Then you flip it around and take the breast off with the keel bone—that's the bone in the middle of the chest plate. And once the breasts are off, you've got, one, two, three, four pieces.

Then I break down the wings. Some people will leave them whole and count it as one. You get the two breasts, the two wings, there's four pieces. I'll finish by cutting the thigh away from the body, separate those two, there's two more pieces. Now you technically have eight. If you want to go deeper, you take off the two wing tips—nine, ten. And then I go for a part known as the *oyster*. If you flip the chicken over, you've got the backbone. And where the legs or the thighs meet the torso, there's a little knuckle of meat called an "oyster." The oysters are the best pieces on the chicken. These nuggets sit underneath, beside the thigh bone, where that joint hits, but they're tucked in, so a lot of people don't cut them off because they don't even know they're there. You can find them, though, especially on a whole roasted bird. They're amazing.

I'LL NEVER FORGET this one guy who came in to apply as a cook during my Avenues days.

I said to him, "Cook me something. Whatever you want to cook. You've got two hours. Make me something."

Right away I could see that this guy was getting flustered and nervous as he went off to the kitchen. Now, I honestly couldn't give a shit if the guy had made me a peanut butter and jelly sandwich, roasted meat, whole cauliflower pizza, sushi, whatever. I didn't care what he did so long as he *did* something. I had already told one of my chefs to give him whatever he wanted or needed. I just wanted to see where he was at with his knowledge and skills.

Well, this guy came out of the kitchen after a bit and he just freaked. I was told by the team later that he'd gone to every one of my chefs for help, running around that kitchen for about an hour, hyperventilating and losing his shit. He finally came up to me as I was sitting in the dining room working on menu stuff. He was crying—hard.

"I … I … I'm sorry, Chef. I have to leave. I'm not going to embarrass myself anymore. I can't do it … I can't cook for you."

I looked up at him and spoke gently. "Sit down, brother. Relax. *Breathe.* Let me explain something to you: You're going to go through these types of challenges through your entire career. You're always going to want to work at other places, and a lot of chefs are going to want to see where your skillset is. That's all I'm doing with you here today. I don't want anything fancy from you, okay? I'm not expecting you to create some magical meal that's going to blow me away. I just want to see what you're going to give me; where you are with your experience and know-how."

"I can't do it."

And that was it. He got up and left Avenues and never tried to come back. I follow this guy via social media to this day and he's doing other things but he's not working in a kitchen at all. I'll never forget him.

THIRTY-SIX
PAINKILLER—ACCENTUATE THE POSITIVE

J ean Banchet owned and operated Le Francais, which was an amazing French restaurant in Chicagoland. Truth be told, there'd probably be no Charlie Trotter in Chicago if Banchet hadn't paved the way.

Le Francais was recognized as the best restaurant in the U.S. for years. Banchet is regarded as Chicago's first celebrity chef, and, yes, I know I just wrote about how much I hate the term "celebrity chef." Maybe the joke's on me because I was given the Jean Banchet Celebrity Chef of the Year award in 2010. But seriously, if anyone deserved that moniker as a compliment—and the induction into the Chicago Chefs Hall of Fame—Banchet did.

So anyway, the Banchet Awards were created in his name maybe twenty years ago to recognize culinary excellence in Chicago. One hundred percent of the money raised at the ceremony goes to this worthy cause. I came onto the board years ago and slowly got Michael Muser involved and then Muser just ran with it. He's the director of it now, which is great. It's near and dear to our hearts.

We both believe that if you have the means to give back, you should do it. I might not have the financial means, but there are times I can contribute through my food. My team and I support many causes and charities—over the years we've helped Meals on Wheels, Share Our

Strength, PAWS Foundation, the Boys and Girls Club, and others. For these events, we donate our time, and the restaurant absorbs the cost of the events; we work charitable expenses into our budget at the beginning of each year. You can only do two or three events a year before you start losing your ass, but trust me, you get asked to do them every day of the week.

Despite this, sometimes we find ourselves dealing with these arrogant assholes who treat my team and me like shit. They show up at the event with no respect for us or the cause. It's all about getting a little social status for themselves and some content for their Instagram page—or at least that's how it feels. Of course, I'm bitching about a select few. But, although a few bad apples won't ruin the whole barrel, they can really turn my mood rotten.

To be one-hundred percent real, generosity can take its toll in myriad ways. Hospitality is a game of give and give and give and very little—if any—*take*. Still, I personally walk away from such events happy that, despite whatever some assholes might've done to rain on my goodwill, I gave my heart and soul for a good cause, to help make the world a better place. And I believe the key to self-preservation is to nurture and care for yourself as you nurture and care for others.

It's easy to look at the negative because it's usually right in front of you, sometimes in the form of a wealthy asshole dissing you. I try to step back and look at my attitude.

How do I cope and move forward? What are the lessons learned here? How do I not let this happen again? How can I be better at managing negativity, taking it for what it is, and turning it around?

I work at it when it happens ... recognizing what might make me angry and then concentrating on defusing it. It's an important exercise because blowing up on some asshole won't turn the situation around. There's some guy who's in your face, telling you that your food and your efforts are shit ... but if you end up bashing his head into a banquet table, that isn't going to help anything—even if it might feel great in the moment.

Everybody has their dark thoughts. I've had the *"me against this shitty world"* moments. It sucked when Grace closed and I wasn't creating and I wasn't drawing an income. I got really down. But I finally had to set aside the self-pity and ask myself, *Why are these hardships happening and what am I going to do to come out of these woes stronger and better?* I didn't have the answers, but it helped me to turn myself around because I knew those dark days out of my kitchen wouldn't go on forever.

When my parents died in the way they did, it made me think hard about how I would navigate my own life. I definitely didn't want to go down the path that my father went down—or his father before him. I was lucky enough to recognize that I had already discovered my passion, and I made choices to actively pursue continued growth in that field, which led me to the satisfying life I have now.

Those moments when you go through a horrible time but then figure out a way to stand up and dust yourself off, they're going to help shape who you are and begin to choose what's next for your life. You *do* have control of your destiny. It's what you do with yourself—and how many times you're willing to pick yourself back up—that determines where you'll go and how you'll get there.

I'm not going to say my life is all roses, but I do think everything happens for a reason. I'm not a religious guy, but I believe there's something greater out there. I'm not saying it's God or some other spiritual figure; I have yet to figure out what that is.

At the end of the day, I honestly don't believe that no good deed goes unpunished. I might say that sometimes, but despite the occasional assholes, *doing good* still feels *really fucking great* to me. It makes me happy. I'm telling you this from my heart.

THIRTY-SEVEN
THE RED BADGE OF INSPIRATION

No one ever gave me anything. I was raised as a bear cub—*Bear's cub*, right? Survival of the fittest and fending for yourself was just how we grew up in the Duffy house. It was all about holding on to what you could as tightly as possible.

What's mine is mine and if anyone thinks about taking my shit, they can do so from my cold, dead fucking hands!

The echo of Bear's bravado bounces off my memory.

I'm nothing like that.

My white chef's uniform hangs inside a clear dry-cleaning bag in my new restaurant office at Ever. I have black uniforms, too. My last uniform had the name Grace on it, this new one is emblazoned with the logo for Ever, the greatest thing to happen to me *again* ...

As I stare at my uniform, I ask myself all kinds of questions.

What will I do differently from my parents?

What will I do differently at my new restaurant?

Well, lots of things. But I sure as hell will *NOT* change my mission.

As always, I'm taking each step steadily to get further in my career and make myself the greatest chef I can be. But there's more to me than that. I became a chef because I was passionate about cooking. Looking into my heart, I also find a deep-seated purpose to nurture and inspire others.

Nurturing is what our industry is all about, and I want to help people share the deep respect that I have for our work. I want to keep that spirit alive. When I see people clowning about, making fun of cooking, or not taking it seriously, I'm affected by that. For me, *nurturing* is not only about giving people amazing cuisine and lifting their spirits through food, but also about mentoring the younger cooks who are enthusiastic about it, so that they can grow and carry on with the tradition of professionalism behind what we do.

Something I've begun to notice over the last ten to fifteen years that really bothers me is when these young cooks don't wear chef jackets anymore. They come in to work outfitted in shitty, shabby pants with holes in them and silly T-shirts that smell because they've worn them for the last three days. They're sporting headbands. These are full-on chefs in restaurants of every degree and they're not taking it seriously; they don't care about appearances.

I know, I sound like an old "get off my lawn!" guy, but hear me out.

I always tell young cooks that your job attire should be no different than that of a businessman or a lawyer or someone who works in a bank. You put on a suit, a tie, nice pants, polished shoes, and go to work. In my restaurant, whether you're in the front of house or in the kitchen, you're wearing clean and sharp attire. I know when I put on a suit, I have greater confidence, period. I take that same philosophy to the kitchen staff and have them put on a nice, pressed white chef's uniform, starched shirt, pressed pants, polished shoes, and a clean, spotless apron. Even in the middle of service, that apron's got to be clean. It'll give you that proud feeling. It doesn't make you a better cook, but that attention to detail identifies you as a professional with high standards and positions you a step up.

I always try to instill respect for the white uniform in my team—that the way you dress and look is the way you will be perceived. It also influences the way that you will cook. If you're sloppy and your shit's everywhere and you have a dirty apron and towel, what does that say about you and your food?

As an executive chef, I aim to use experience and action to create inspiration in everyone who works for me, and to lead by example. I read a lot of people who inspire me, who have guided me through my career.

Zig Ziglar's *See You at the Top* is one of my favorite books; I used to listen to his audio tapes all the time. It's about momentum. You're not going to wake up and have every day be the greatest or best day, one where you're going to achieve great things, but it's the journey to get to where you need to go. It's the little steps. You've got to set your goals high to get there.

As you know, I also love *The Fountainhead* by Ayn Rand.

Then there's *Living With a SEAL: 31 Days Training with the Toughest Man on the Planet*, written by entrepreneur Jesse Itzler, a very wealthy guy who lives in New York. His wife, Sara Blakely, is also super successful—a billionaire, in fact; she's the founder of Spanx. In the book, Itzler invites a Navy SEAL into his house to kick his ass into shape, train him, and push his limits.

The SEAL is a guy named David Goggins. Goggins loves to run. He's a big-time U.S. ultra-marathon runner and distance cyclist … he's also a triathlete, bestselling author, and does motivational speaking and more. On top of all that, he served in Afghanistan and Iraq.

In Itzler's book, Goggins wakes Itzler up at four in the morning for a fifteen-mile run, and then at night, another fifteen-mile run. And he's doing pushups and sit ups and all this shit the whole time he's running through Central Park in New York, even when it's snowing and raining and three degrees.

Goggins holds the record for the most pull-ups in an hour, something like three thousand pull-ups in twelve hours. He exercised when he had two broken feet. He's absolutely inspirational. And the thing is, he inspires others—in this case, Jesse Itzler—to try to become the best they can be, too.

Do I inspire my people? I hope so. I believe that if I do, it's mostly because I'm right in there with them, working, doing the same things they are. I'm not going to ask anyone to do something that I wouldn't do. I'd pick up that piece of paper on the floor if I saw it and I might do it faster than you would because that's my thought process. Go ahead— beat me to it. It's a mental game—and it keeps our kitchen clean!

I want to make sure that when someone on my team leaves my restaurant, they represent who I was and what I gave them. They're taking my name and my values with them down the road. And I hope that I've instilled in them some great qualities that they can pass on to other chefs, bringing them into a place where they're nurturing others as well.

PART EIGHT
Into Everlasting Fire

THIRTY-EIGHT
AFTER...WORD

T he Chef Curtis Duffy Plans His Next Chicago Restaurant
By *The New York Times*
By Amelia Nierenberg
June 24, 2019

CHICAGO, Illinois. The end of Grace, a sleek, modern Chicago restaurant with three Michelin stars and a reputation as one of the nation's best, was quick and messy: The chef, Curtis Duffy, and the general manager, Michael Muser, abruptly stopped working there in December 2017 after a dispute with their business partner. Two days later, Grace unceremoniously closed its doors.

The aftermath, though, has been more deliberative. As Mr. Duffy and Mr. Muser sparred with their former partner in several legal disputes and waited for their noncompete agreements to expire, they planned their next restaurant. It would have the best china, they said, the best furniture ever. They'd use ingredients that were fresher, more seasonal than they ever had before. They'd make a meal more elaborate than anyone had ever seen.

Ever: That word just kept coming up. So, they decided that would be the name.

"It's this little word, this little four-letter thing that we pack into the most epic experiences of our lives," Mr. Muser said in a phone interview.

"This experience, that we're going to put in front of everybody, this is our Ever."

Ever, scheduled to open next spring, will be in Fulton Market, a former meatpacking district that now houses culinary and cultural attractions. The restaurant, in a 6,000-square-foot ground-floor space, is being designed by Lawton Stanley Architects, the firm that also designed and built Grace. Ever will seat about seventy-five people in the main space, with a private dining room for another twelve.

The $300 to $500 tasting menus of twelve to fifteen dishes are similar in cost and structure to Grace's. One menu will focus on seafood and grains, and the other more on vegetables. As at Grace, the food will not center on any one cuisine.

Mr. Duffy, 43, is already known for best-evers. He grew up in central Ohio and came up through some of Chicago's premier restaurants. After working at Charlie Trotter's, he moved to Alinea, the only Chicago restaurant that currently has three Michelin stars.

Mr. Duffy and Mr. Muser won two stars at their first joint venture, Avenues, in 2011. At Grace, food was arranged into edible sculptures on elaborate plates. The cuisine was experimental: The team tried repeatedly to fill a bubble, a dome-like hood made of citrus stock, white wine and several rare fruits, with flavored smoke, but stopped after the bubbles kept popping on their way to the table.

"A lot of it has to do with walking that fine line with giving the guests something that's familiar to them but also taking that familiar away from them," Mr. Duffy said. "They have to be able to connect with it. Otherwise, you lose them."

Since leaving Grace, Mr. Duffy and Mr. Muser have been embroiled in a squall of legal disputes. They have dropped a claim against their former partner, [Dolos], a Chicago real estate broker who invested more than $2.5 million in Grace, over a noncompete clause in their contracts. Another case, currently in appeal, concerns Mr. Muser's unemployment benefits.

Mr. Dolos also says that Mr. Duffy and Mr. Muser had unexplained absences and that expensive ingredients went missing. According to court documents, a lawsuit making those claims was filed with the Circuit Court of Cook County in August 2018. But a manager of the court's Law Division said last week that the suit had been removed from the electronic docket system at the request of the law firm representing Mr. Dolos. Sean O'Callaghan, Mr. Muser and Mr. Duffy's lawyer, said neither he nor his clients had been served with the lawsuit.

Mr. Dolos's lawyer, Victor Pioli, said he did not request the suit be removed. "As far as we're concerned, it's active. We intend to pursue it," he said.

In a phone interview, Mr. Dolos said he wished "Mike and Curtis good luck on all their future endeavors. Chicago is one of the food capitals in the country, and, in my opinion, Grace was the best restaurant in Chicago."

Like Grace, Ever is meant to be an expensive, expansive experience that starts as soon as guests walk through the door.

From a foyer (which Mr. Muser, 45, described as "a decompression chamber") guests will proceed down a hallway so narrow that it almost demands they walk single-file. At the host area, little snacks will be mounted on a wall, ready to be plucked by diners waiting to be seated. Small, citrus-flavored clouds made from cotton candy and dried yuzu rind will hang from the ceiling for diners to reach up and taste.

In the main room, Mr. Duffy and Mr. Muser plan to install acoustic paneling on the ceiling to reduce noise from other tables.

Cooking has always offered Mr. Duffy solace, an escape from a difficult childhood. When he was young, his father fatally shot his mother, and then himself.

"The kitchen has always been my home," he said in a phone interview. "Since my parents had passed away, it became even more of a home to me."

Leaving Grace was also difficult. "We put everything into that restaurant and it's hard to let it go. But it was the right thing. It was the right choice."

He still has the word Grace tattooed on his arm. Sometimes, he said, people ask if he intends to cover it with a new tattoo.

"I'm telling my life story, and I just closed the chapter for Grace," he said. "Is it bitter? Maybe. Parts of it. Is it happy? Absolutely. Now we're writing the next chapter of the story."

THIRTY-NINE
THE RETURN OF THE ZING

I t's October, four months after the story on my planned return was published in *The New York Times*.

Our publicist had reached out to the *Times* and the *Chicago Tribune* to announce Ever. Both agreed to run the story but asked where we were with the lawsuit.

"What lawsuit?" Muser said. "There isn't a lawsuit."

It turned out that Dolos had filed one and sent it to a reporter at the *Chicago Sun Times*—and then sent his lawyer down to the court and had it withdrawn after the article was written.

Our publicist had to explain to *The New York Times* and the *Chicago Tribune* that the story the *Chicago Sun Times* had run—which was also picked up by another dozen or so other publications, all declaring Muser and I were getting sued—was completely wrong. She had to persuade the *Chicago Sun Times* that the entire story was a Dolos fabrication.

We moved on from the false press reports and focused on getting Ever ready to open.

To those who haven't dined at Ever yet, come out to my new restaurant because I'm *back* and doing something special and unique.

What's in a name?

The name *Ever* was bounced around for a while. It started with me saying "evergreen." And then we decided to explore, well, what does it mean if we take the green off? Because evergreen means "forever." It's an ongoing thing; it's a continuation of something.

On a deeper level, what does "ever" mean to me?

Well, think of the context, think how many times you say "ever" in your life. "That was the best concert I've *ever* been to," or, "That's the goddamn best guitarist I've *ever* heard play," and a beloved classic, "That's the best meal I've *ever* had."

You hear these things throughout your life, and experiences are, in fact, everlasting.

"Ever" is the pinnacle of an experience.

Ever.

That's been our spirit and approach to our mission—and that's how the name came about. We explored it, it stuck, and it made sense.

BUILDING world-class restaurants a couple times in row has been a hell of an experience.

All the work involved in building from scratch still blows my mind. Once you begin, things pick up pace. Then, once you've decided on a general contractor, you hit gridlock while their subcontractors take second and third looks at all the systems. None of those tradesmen are going to do that until they really think they're getting the job.

We don't want to mess around with them. So, Muser and I had to ask that GC to sign off on a number with his subcontractors' hard numbers included, same as last time. The build on Ever was set at $2.2 million. That's just *outside* the kitchen—and the GC doesn't want to agree to it unless he knows it's feasible that that number can be hit. And when you're held to a number, you start reconsidering things: Do we really need that sink? Can we go back to the kitchen and maybe pull something out of there and throw it at the dining room?

Soon we're at the point where we're burning the clock. One day we're on the phone with an induction oven company and we get twelve thousand dollars' worth of them for *free*. That's one day, one phone call. It took us an hour-and-a-half or two. A $12,000 reduction in the kitchen price, that's a total win! We can keep doing that, but those calls, those people, those companies, they take forever to get through. You're burning the clock the entire time. And you don't know, until you've invested the time, which efforts will yield that kind of success.

We finally worked the numbers down and pushed the "Go" button on the kitchen equipment, so we weren't dealing with that anymore. On to the next thing. The GC has been given money to start. All the subs went into motion. The plumber's working. The HVAC guy is working.

HVAC, by the way, is the bitch. It sucks spending money on heating and air because the units cost so much. But no one sees them! It's not something that touches the guest, it doesn't make the food any better, but it's got to be perfect. Just the air conditioning for this thing is *four hundred thousand dollars*.

It's been such a wild ride since we began the first outing. Muser and I were just two kids working at the Peninsula way back when, with no experience in business or building—we were still so green, right?

Boy, have we learned a lot over these last several years.

The learning curve has been intense. We went through the entire progression with Grace—designing, building, opening, succeeding, closing. We've gone through the same process again with Ever and putting together our group—and that's taught us a lot, for sure.

I'm telling you, there's been nothing, *nothing* like Ever restaurant, with this style or construction. Our original renderings were so exciting because they showed the promise of a unique restaurant build, and we've made those renderings a reality. We have wood milling pieces that make their way through the dining room and they're fifteen-and-a-half feet tall. They're beautiful, crazy beautiful, man! The ceiling is made of felt acoustic paneling. It's the sexiest thing. It's like your walking into a set of Beats by Dre headphones!

Those white countertops at Grace? Elegant, sleek, gorgeous. But I wanted Ever to have blood-red countertops. Why? Because it's my kitchen and I have an edgy new vision. That said, the blood-red countertops didn't happen. I decided to go back to white. Sometimes practicality must surpass fantasy.

I'm in love with the Maestro stove that Bonnet custom-made for me in France. It's a combination of high quality, modern technology and power, and it's tailored for superior cooking. Aesthetically, this oven is a work of art. From the stainless-steel chassis to the titanium top and the chrome accents and enameled front panels, it looks like a beautiful beast made for a heavy-metal-themed kitchen. And it's the *first* matte-black stove in the United States.

My kitchen, just like the dining room, needs that focus on art.

That's where I'm coming from: My kitchen, my attitude—it's all different from anything I've done before. We're here to make a statement again, and we have the utmost confidence that our team and the guests will help us do it.

∾

MUSER and I talked endlessly about our vision for Ever.

What was going to be different about it?

How were we changing things?

It's not Grace, so what am I going to create that goes above and beyond that? I keep throwing it back at Michael. Grace is just a name, and the furniture and stemware and everything else inside that square box on Randolph Street were Grace.

But the food had *soul*. That food had heart.

I'm remembering it all: Sicilian olives with black truffle puree; my poached Tasmanian trout with Ossetra caviar; or grilled hiramasa; or the pig tail braised with red endive, pickled cauliflower and red wine sauce. It all came alive because of the energy and the dedication I put into it.

Put me anywhere in the world, it's still going to be Curtis Duffy food. Because I cook for me, to please myself. And I'll aim to please our guests with my food as always.

That's it.

Ever has my heart inside it.

FORTY
SOME KIND OF MONSTER

W hen Ever was opening, I had dish ideas bouncing around in my head, but I didn't care to dwell on them. I wanted them to happen naturally. It's the same way jazz musicians interpret their music. Miles Davis never played "My Funny Valentine" the same way twice. He improvised.

I have the same approach in my kitchen.

We're constantly documenting recipes, but I don't sit there every day agonizing over a formula. I only write down recipes when I'm actually making the food. Now an *idea* is a different story. I can jot down an idea in my phone and keep it for a later time. As I've said, I could write down a couple of words, like, *coconut and salmon roe*, and when I go back and see that, I might say, "I don't know what that means." Then I'll revisit it and go, "Oh, shit. I remember that." And then I take it, but maybe now I twist it. That same idea starts to really take on something I didn't expect.

Cuisine changes. We need to have incredible creativity that's edgy, but it still needs it to be refined.

At the same time, we need that to provide the comfort that people always expected from Grace.

Overseeing the restaurant is always my number one priority, but when I'm in the kitchen, my job is to create new dishes. We have to think ahead, right? Once we're into a Spring menu, we have to be working on the Summer menu. In the summer, we need to be working on the Fall and Winter menus. When an ingredient goes out of season, we can address the changes we need to make. And so on. My job is to constantly put new things on the menu; to be ahead of the curve.

How is my food going to be different?

Why does it have to be different?

I love the way I cook and I've come to realize I shouldn't force myself to drastically change just because I'm now in a different box. My food evolves, but you know it's mine—not just by taste but also by aesthetics. If you put ten different photographs of food down on the table, you'll be able to tell which ones are my food. That's what I love about what I do. It's "personality cuisine." If you put a hundred photographs of other chefs' food on the table, I'd be able to tell you: "That's Thomas Keller, that's Charlie Trotter, that's Daniel Boulud, that's Michel Bras food." That's because they cook in their style. We all have a "voice" and a "personality" with our cuisine.

When people ask me what I call my cuisine, I always say, *"thoughtful-progressive."* Our PR team wanted to change that description, and I'm willing to hear someone else's take on how my cuisine should be labeled, but until we have another description that makes sense to me, I'm staying with "thoughtful-progressive."

Well, what the hell does that mean?

Thoughtful means that we're not spontaneous. It's about putting thought and effort and research and time into each dish. We're not the restaurant that goes, "Oh, we've got scallops coming through the back door today, along with carrots. Here's a new dish. Boom!" In that instance, there's no time to hone that dish to where it could be. So that's where the thoughtful part comes into it.

Progressive means we're taking our ingredients and applying new techniques that are available in a way that's exciting from a diner's perspective, but always with respect.

As we were developing Ever, I decided that with my new menu, I don't want to repeat items or be known for one particular dish. I know that my Alaskan king crab dish is beloved by many of my former guests from Grace, but I'm not sure I'll bring it back. If you pinned me down and said, "Curtis you have to have a signature dish," then yeah, I guess that crab dish would be it. However, as I keep saying, I want to be the guy who's thought of as always moving forward, not reliant on the last dish I created. But it's hard because everybody loves that dish—it's a knockout!

Thomas Keller is known for creating a handful of beloved dishes, too: his cone-shaped tuiles topped with crème fraîche and fresh salmon; or his slow-cooked filet of wild Scottish sea trout with red-wine-braised cabbage and *consommé aux choux rouge;* or his basic bread and butter that marries bitter cocoa-laminated brioche and Diane St. Clair's Animal Farm butter. He's very well known for his oysters and pearls, milk and donuts, and his Salmon Cornet. He's been serving them for twenty-some years and they will blow your mind … it's no wonder people want to experience them again and again.

Me? I don't want to be that guy. But there are expectations.

When you go to a restaurant like the French Laundry, the expectation is that you're going to get those dishes because Keller's known for them. So that's a question for me. Are they expecting to get my crab dish at Ever? I wasn't even planning on putting it on the menu. Then again, it's my food. I was the guy who created it at Avenues and then at Grace, so it's still my food. It comes full circle in my life … now we'll see what happens with it.

We have to keep pushing forward and making the cuisine interesting. I do think we'll stick with the Flora and the Fauna themes that we had at Grace for our Ever menus. I don't know if we'll give it the same name, but there's not a lot of restaurants where you can go and have a straight vegetarian meal. A lot of people love that option. I can see why. There's a hell of a lot more you can do with vegetables than with a piece of beef.

Ever's menu stays seasonal. At Grace, we did the same thing. So, in the springtime, you're reaching for spring vegetables—that's easy—but what do you think of on the meat and seafood side? I think of lighter birds, like quail and guinea fowl. Also, rabbit. Or veal, spring lamb, suckling pigs. We start thinking of the seafood as well; what's available to us in those months. But how do you categorize protein seasonally? What does Fall look like in terms of meat? Those are things we have to think about.

Everything starts with the ingredient.

It's conceptualized on paper first. We say, "All right. We want to showcase fennel on the vegetable menu. What are three supporting elements that go with it?" Last year we served it with oranges, olives, and crème fraîche. This year we want to change that up. I might add scallops—which would flip it to the Fauna menu. Staying on the Flora menu, add three elements that would go with fennel, say, tangerine, black olives, mint.

Then we look at those three elements and we start plugging away.

What shape do those elements take?

Is the citrus in its raw form, just segments?

Or do we freeze it in liquid nitrogen to become these little cells?

Do we turn that into a meringue, a savory meringue?

That's where we go with it.

Then … what does the fennel look like? Is it roasted? Raw? Turned into a mousse?

Those are the types of questions that you ask yourself.

And once you're happy with the answers, you start experimenting with it in the kitchen.

I can say that ninety-nine percent of the time it doesn't turn out the way it's conceptualized on paper, because the real truth is that when it's in your hands, you start messing with it. Ideas come into play.

Textures pop up.

I can do this instead of that, I thought about this but maybe I'll do this. It's the interchangeability of it all.

That's how you eventually get to a menu like this one from Grace:

FLORA

MILK: Blood orange, black olive, citrus herbs

WATERMELON RADISH: Green strawberry, ginger, fennel

ENGLISH PEA: Rhubarb, burrata, apple mint

COCONUT: Kumquat, carrot, hoja santa

MOREL: Ramp, potato, chive

DESSERT

Chocolate or Vanilla Ice Cream

Banana—Blueberry, cashew, Thai basil

Passion fruit—Pineapple, lemongrass, coriander blooms

FAUNA

TROUT: Ossetra caviar, lychee, chive

MIYAZAKI BEEF: Romaine, peanut, Vietnamese herbs

DESSERT

Chocolate or Vanilla Ice Cream
Strawberry—Chartreuse, kaffir, balm
Chocolate—Coconut, finger lime, basil

AT NIGHT, when guests are in the restaurant, my first priority is to ensure everything is operating smoothly, from the front of the house to the back, from the dishwasher to the host or hostess.

That responsibility actually falls squarely on the shoulders of my right hand guy / FOH and the general manager—but I'm still in the mix, making sure all is good everywhere. We work together to ensure that the guests are leaving happy.

I love to be in the trenches, as they say. I dig in and talk to the chefs and meet guests. I taste food. I adjust and taste, taste, taste, it all, making sure it's right. And if I'm absent for some reason, my *chef de cuisine*, the guy I've put in charge, is doing exactly what I do to ensure the whole night rocks.

Even when I am there, he is wandering and tasting things and adjusting things, too. We're all over that kitchen.

The whole idea behind wandering, tasting, and adjusting is to ensure the quality of our ingredients and dishes, but it's also all about the *umami*.

Throughout the process, I'm making sure dishes are achieving the correct flavor balance. I will identify the most dominant flavor, and if it's heavy, I will balance it out with other flavors. No matter what the recipe and techniques are, we must be ready to adjust primary tastes in our dishes. Of course, taste preferences differ with diners, but I do my part to ensure that the dish they experience is wonderful and the components have been properly adjusted.

I've always had this philosophy that if I won't taste something or eat it myself, I'm not going to serve it. For instance, I'll never serve shrimp in my restaurant because I'm allergic to it and I'm not going to serve something when I can't ensure it's to the level where I feel it should be.

There are other items that I don't enjoy cooking with or eating. I like uni when somebody offers it to me at a restaurant, but I'm not going to go out and order it unless I'm really in the mood to eat it. So very rarely will you see it at my restaurant.

271

Of course, you'll *never* see a green bell pepper on my freaking menu, that I can promise you! Sorry, Jan!

~

LET'S talk about multi courses.

At Ever, a two-and-a-half-hour experience is about the threshold we want. Anything beyond that, we start to lose you. Ideally, it would be anywhere from eight to fifteen courses, depending on the size. You could have a bunch of small, one-bite courses and if you were to put everything —all those dishes—onto the scale it wouldn't seem like a lot. But suddenly everything together weighs two pounds. Two pounds of food is a lot of food to consume—even if you don't include the wine, water, and coffee or drink at the end of the night.

Say there's sixteen courses. There's sixteen ounces in a pound. A single ounce of food isn't a lot. You know how big an ounce is—two tablespoons. So that's like two bites. If you have sixteen of those, that's a pound of food. Now double that. Two pounds of food, that's a lot. When someone orders an eight-ounce filet mignon or a sixteen-ounce T-bone steak, you're already a half-pound or one pound of food in—and that's just the steak by itself without the sides. Now, traditionally, in a tasting menu, we would cut that down into a one-or-two-ounce portion.

The number one complaint at a tasting-menu restaurant is the guests going away hungry. It's a fine balance. We need to ensure guest expectations are met by providing enough courses and food. We don't want anyone walking away saying that nightmare of a cliche, "I gotta hit a McDonald's on the way home."

At Grace, no guests left the restaurant hungry—and they'll never go away hungry at Ever. For the money guests pay for the experience, we would absolutely fail if they felt otherwise.

On the other side of the ledger, as a chef, you want to present as many modest courses as possible—two to three bites and then you're done. Because when a guest is finished you want her or him to say, "That was amazing. I want to come back for that dish again!"

We all know when we eat something delicious that the first bite tastes great, the second bite's great, the third bite is okay, and the fourth and fifth bites … well, you're starting to get over it. They say the more you have of something, the less you want it.

I make sure that my guests are stimulated but also satisfied. Again, those courses are only one of my four pillars. The beverage team needs to be there and blow you away with the wine pairings. The service team needs to blow you away with smooth and efficient care. And the aesthetics of the restaurant will immerse you in a comforting vibe. Guests have to be wowed the moment they walk in our door—and I guarantee they will.

Back to the subject of wine, it's all about making sure that if a dish or an element in a dish changes we have the correct wine ready. The scallop dish has grapefruit on it, so we find a beautiful Riesling that has grapefruit notes. Then we take the grapefruit off the dish and now we're serving, I don't know, blood orange instead. It's important that both the wine and service teams know that because then we can go, "Okay. Let's relook at some of the wines we have and see if something else goes with it."

It's easy to change the profile of the food, but you can't change the profile of the wine. Sometimes people will order two bottles of wine *they* want. In that case, we have to change our approach a little bit and cook to that bottle.

FOR THE RECORD, I don't drink alcohol anymore at this point in my life, but I have always appreciated the experience of drinking wine.

If I was sitting down at dinner, I'd enjoy the wine pairings or a wine tasting, or just choosing something for the table. I like lighter red wines. For me, heavier, full-bodied Cabernets and Bordeaux were always too much, too hard to drink. It would feel like I was chewing on the wine instead of sipping it. I prefer the fruit-forward Syrahs and Merlots, and the Pinot Noirs have always been a favorite.

Those seem to be my go-tos. You know, just in case you were curious.

EVER IS LOCATED at 1340 West Fulton Street in Chicago, in the corner of the first floor. It has taller ceilings than Grace did, maximizing the space. My kitchen is a gorgeous triumph of functionality and sexiness. Even the guest restrooms are works of art—one of them is inspired by Yves Saint Laurent with black walls and thin, blue-lit lines crisscrossing the darkness. Another restroom is dubbed "Raw," with a giant boulder in a corner and a sink crudely chiseled out from it. The bathrooms all play the audiobook version of Matthew McConaughey's autobiography, *Greenlights*, read by the actor and on a continuous loop. Muser had suggested it because, at the time we opened, the city was feeling dark, sad, and broken, with riots and post-COVID-19 blues, and we needed to show we hadn't lost our sense of humor—to keep the guests laughing, to send them back to their tables with a smile.

We went for that modern approach. We made it to be warm and welcoming. We used a lot of raw material, but we're trying to have that juxtaposition of something that's raw but also elegant and refined. Having those two elements meet in the middle, so to speak. But the color tone is also muted enough where it's not overkill, so guests can stay focused on the food and wine—the reason they're joining us.

There's more excitement going on *above* the restaurant, too. We have a garden on the roof, along with beehives and composting areas. Many chefs dream of having a beautiful garden they can pull ingredients from to integrate into their food. The closer we can get to the earth, the better we are as chefs, because it strengthens our connection to the origins of our ingredients.

So, Ever has an open-air herb garden up there to foster that relationship: When you know exactly where the ingredients come from, you respect them. And it teaches the younger cooks that we're not just opening packages to get our ingredients. We know how they're grown.

How wonderful would it be as an intern to spend four months in my restaurant? During your first month, you're not even cooking. You're maintaining the garden and learning about growing, watering, clipping herbs, and more. Again, I can't stress enough how important that is.

Along those lines, the majority of our herbs—upwards of ninety-nine percent—still come from the Chef's Garden in Ohio. They rock! If we want a hundred dime-sized nasturtium leaves, then we'll get a hundred dime-sized nasturtium leaves, every single time.

Chef's Garden has taken up the idea of growing products for the chef customized to their desired sizes and particular uses. It comes with a premium cost, but I'll always use them. At least during the summer months, when we grow our own herbs on the rooftop, we can minimize some of the expense.

We entertain guests up on that roof—it's not just for VIPs because every guest is special to us. We'll have tours and opportunities to have some Champagne or after-dinner drinks. Eventually, I'd love to put a table in the middle of the garden and give people a dining experience up there with the view, because another plus of our roof area is the most beautiful view of Chicago you could ask for. It's an amazing north-to-south panorama of the city, facing east. We look out at the skyline and see where our roots are set. That's cool. As we approached the opening date of Ever, we had constant staff training—training, training, training, training! We brought in our staff for test runs, with friends and family as guests, before we opened to the public. We practiced over and over again on everything: host and hostess responsibilities, greeting, reservations, waiting lists, telephone procedures, personal appearance and dress codes, stemware, china, linen, guest service, service standards, diplomacy and tact, credit cards, checks, cash, bidding farewell, eating, drinking, alcohol awareness, menu knowledge, culture, in-house behavior, opening duties, running duties, closing duties.

You get the idea.

Ever restaurant is like running a state-of-the art luxury yacht—all hands on deck, performing at their very best to keep the ship from sinking.

Traditionally, most restaurants will do one, maybe two services for friends and family.

Beyond that, when you open the doors to paying customers, you need to be ready—they're paying a premium and they deserve excellence.

Also, you think food critics will give you months to get everything just right?

Think again.

Not these days: On the opening night of Grace, we had a guest from *Chicago* magazine show up. It went well but it exemplifies why we had *three* nights of friends and family service at Ever before we opened to the public.

Practice really does make perfect.

Having my own kitchen again and reuniting with the old crew was such a big deal. I had missed it all so much.

"We're putting the band back together," I said with a nod to *The Blues Brothers* in there when I was building Ever …

It feels like destiny fulfilled.

FORTY-ONE
FOR. EVER.

O n June 11, 2020 the *Chicago Tribune* announced Ever would open to the public on July 28.

Online reservations went live at 7:00 a.m.

By 9:00 a.m., every table for two had been booked through September. And every other table on weekends was booked through October.

And the reservations kept coming.

The place turned out amazing, surpassing my expectations. That said, we were all wearing masks because COVID-19 was still a major concern. The first U.S. case had only been identified six months earlier. But we kept our heads down and moved ahead.

The dining room at Ever seats seventy-five people. The Private Dining Room accommodates twelve guests. The table in the PDR arrived in three pieces and weighs over one ton. Lawton Stanley Architects designed this place for us—the same architectural team that designed Grace. It's incredible. So many curves. Every inch is elegance. The final product turned out even better than our aspirational computer-designed renderings.

Ever is friendly, warm, and inviting. It's modern.

The ceilings are so tall!

We made the decisions on all the Ever designs, picked out the furniture and appliances, chose the color and décor … everything down to that menu paper. The walls are works of art unto themselves, designed and created by wall-maker Vladimir Kharitonsky.

Michael Muser first headed the wine program at Ever with a couple of in-house sommeliers. The wine program has since grown and is bigger and better than anything we'd done before. We have a room for red wine only, and a state-of-the-art cooler for white wine and fine French Champagnes.

The pairings are out of this world.

As for the menu, we began with an eight-to-ten-course tasting menu that offers dishes in both Flora and Fauna. Vegetables and meat. Seafood. It's always going to be brand-new, but with my same progressive approach.

～

I RECALL a rock star once saying something along the lines of, "You've gotta go away for a while so people will miss you."

That's how it was with Ever.

When we came back, it was on! A flood of reservations, guests, and, most importantly, *love*.

Ever was a wonderful mountain to scale, bigger than anything I'd done before. And I had to work harder than I *ever* did because, as I said, I knew I was extremely fortunate to have this second opportunity.

I partnered with a great production company—Aphotic Media—and with the amazing director, Frankie Nasso—and my co-writer, Jeremy Wagner here—we made a new in-depth documentary and captured the complete building and design of Ever, alongside deep insights into my personal life that match this memoir, and we titled it *Ever After*. I believe we pulled it all off in an interesting, cinematic way.

A newer, *better* film update felt necessary to cover my culinary and life experiences in a more profound and meaningful way—exactly like this memoir. The first documentary ever made about me and Grace restaurant wasn't a great experience for me, to be honest. Muser and I signed off on a film made off of our backs with no financial benefit. Sounds like repeating joke in my Grace-era life. When the film was released, I didn't even get a free DVD! Yeah … I had to buy my own movie even though the director promised me one.

I also had no editorial control and felt used once more.

This is where I cue The Who: *"Won't Get Fooled Again!"*

I'M SOMETIMES ASKED what I might've done if I had taken a different path in life: What if I had never discovered or enjoyed Home Ec class or gotten that first restaurant job? What else would I have done to escape my life in Johnstown? What other dreams did I have?

Honestly, I'd love to have been a rock star. But who wouldn't? The idea of being on the stage and touching so many people with music is amazing.

Aside from that, I'd do professional motocross in a second. I love being on bikes, period—and that all goes back to my dad.

Bear was the baddest and truest biker I've ever known. The biker blood flowed through his veins. He was a One Percenter to the end. I lived my early life among bikers and that gave me that bug, to be on a roaring motorcycle in the wind—on the road or off-road.

I could do that all day.

FORTY-TWO
FUTURE SHOCK

I want to be the guy who is predictably unpredictable—the one everyone counts on to do everything differently.

I don't need to be the most creative guy in the world, I need to be only creative for *me*. I want to keep myself stimulated, to keep my intellect moving and happy.

Ever is the ultimate intellectual outlet for me. I always said that I just needed two restaurants: One to feed my intellect and one to put money in my pocket for my children's future.

Now, my goals with this life are bigger. We've begun to expand and I'm envisioning even more possibilities for the future.

Our mothership is Ever, which I've always said had to be in Chicago. Chicago's such a great city because the clientele supports what the chef is doing. And when you get that support, you get amazing results. You win. A chief inspector from the Michelin Guide recently said there's an energy and creativity that's very particular to Chicago. I've always thought that.

At some point I want to focus on my next goal, to create a solid restaurant group where I continue to surround ourselves with great people and build a culture that people won't want to leave. Everybody who's loyal to us should share in our success, too, and we'll want them to have a piece of it.

If you're a chef who has proven yourself, and you say to me, "Chef, I want to open a seafood-focused restaurant where I can cook and learn and grow in a new environment," then, if we have the means, absolutely! Let's see if we can build a seafood restaurant together. Let's give you some ownership and keep you invested.

If that person just walks away and goes somewhere else, we fail. But if we can lift that person up and give him or her a restaurant with ownership and a stake in the game, but still under our big umbrella? Everybody wins. The chef wins; it's his or her restaurant. The company wins because it's profiting from the restaurant. That's how I see us growing.

Mentoring others is at the center of all this. You see something in someone, it's a natural thing to take them under your wing. And in my experience, it's so very easy to encourage people.

I also want to publish cookbooks and perhaps write an educational book and a philosophy book on cuisine and the mindset of how to do something in the restaurant to the best of your ability.

And I would love to do a completely new, non-traditional TV cooking show that incorporates a little bit of both home cooking and restaurant cooking. No "celebrity chef" hype. I'm talking about something *meaningful*, with a format that might include integrating another type of art so that it's not just cooking—so that we could add another level of connection. Maybe it's an artist series where we're designing a menu around visual art, or we're creating food around music. From week to week, maybe we'd have different musicians, from jazz to heavy metal to classical—how does the audience react to that and the food?

Wouldn't that be intriguing?

～

AT THIS POINT, nothing is more important to me than doing right by my family. I feel so lucky and grateful. My wife Jennifer has given me so much. "Amazing" doesn't even come close to describing what she's done for my life. I have two wonderful step-kids and my daughters. I want the best for all of them, to give them the opportunities I didn't have and help structure their minds so that they can discover something they're going to be great at to pursue—something they'll enjoy for the rest of their lives. I can't accomplish that sitting on the couch flipping through

YouTube. And so, I try to provide for them the best I can and then lead by example.

I'm very proud of the father that I am, but I also am keenly aware that I'm not around a lot. It's not an easy balance to strike. You are often forced to choose between steering your kitchen and seeing your family.

Can I live with those choices?

For now.

Maybe I won't be able to later.

There might be a time when I look back and go, "I should've been there more for my family," and rearrange how I work—but not any time soon.

You do have to get up and grind every day to take care of your family responsibilities. But I love what I do and never think of it as a sacrifice. Though there's time I'll never get back, I wouldn't trade my trajectory.

The dynamic with my first two daughters has changed now that Ever is up and running. After Grace, while I wasn't working, I had a lot of flexibility about when I was able to hang with my daughters. But with Ever open, I'm back to seeing them a lot when I'm off on Sunday and Monday.

With Ava in college now, that dynamic is shifting once again.

I hope as my girls are becoming adults, they'll understand that everything that I do as a chef is for them.

When I'm asked if I'd encourage any of my kids to go into the culinary industry, I always say, "No." It's a hard and demanding life. But if they want to follow that path even after watching my life up close and personal, I'd support them a hundred percent.

My stepdaughter, Jolie, has taken an interest in Ever. She often joins me in the kitchen when she's in Chicago. She's twelve and has her own chef's uniform, which she wears for service and she has assisted with everything from dishwashing to chopping and other food preparation tasks to plating the dishes. We're close, so her excitement about these rituals may just be because it's a way for us to spend more time together since I'm working so much. And she does love the positive attention that comes with me showing her how to learn those "behind the scenes" skills.

Still, this ritual connects me back to when my favorite way to spend a day was to accompany Bear at Grandpa Terpstra's tire shop, to spend time working together, one on one, just the two of us. I didn't have a passion for tire retreading, but I did love the environment, which made it easy for me to learn skills and a work ethic and a side of my dad I'm grateful to have known. And with Jolie, I love to see her curiosity and her enthusiasm about learning, about acclimating to the kitchen, about educating herself.

When I'm ready to retire from Ever, would it be the right thing for Jolie to take it over? The future remains to be seen. But for now, it's a pleasure to share the time with her in this way.

Back to my immediate family in Colorado.
From left to right: Baby Trisha, Bear, Jan, Robert Jr. (Tig), and Curtis.

Jan & Bear in back. Jill Terpstra (Jan's sister) to the back, right side.
From left to right in front: Robert Jr. (Tig), Trisha, and Curtis.

5-11-79

My dad and
my mom—Bear
and Jan Duffy.
This was not long
after they had
gotten together
in Colorado.

Duffy family-owned photo. 5/11/1979

Duffy family-owned photo.

Here's a young me...
Me at 5 years old in 1980
on a dirtbike in Colorado
at the old dirt track in the
desert that my dad and
brother Tig and my dad
would go out to—until
my dad's accident here.
You can see my dad
on his dirt bike in the
background.

Here's me back in high school with my girlfriend, Nikki—we were going to prom.

From left to right: Nikki, Curtis, Jan, and Bear.

This is one of my favorite photos of my parents that hangs as a framed photo on a wall in my home. Jan and Bear on Bear's motorcycle at a friend's biker party. This motorcycle was Bear's custom-made Harley on a 1947 Knucklehead frame.

Trio of Duffy kids. This was taken at a photo studio. Pretty cute little monsters.
From left to right: Trisha, Curtis, Robert Jr. (Tig). Circa 1980.
Duffy family photo.

This photo captures a pivotal moment—taken shortly after my brother Robert Jr. (Tig) and I literally landed on the doorstep
of my teenage mom, Jan in Colorado. From left to right: Robert Jr. (Tig), Jan, and that's me, rocking a stroller. Circa 1975.
Duffy family photo.

Jan Terpstra-Duffy on her wedding day.
September 12, 1975.

Rare photo of my father, Robert Duffy during his short stint in the Army after arriving in Colorado with his two baby sons—my brother Robert Jr. (Tig) and myself. This handsome young soldier would one day become a bearded, long-haired, tattooed and talented badass known to all as "Bear." Circa 1975.

Duffy family photo.

Duffy family photo.

My parents with us kids. Gotta love the sweaters my parents have on. From left to right: Jan, Curtis, Trisha, Robert Jr. (Tig), and Bear. NOTE: Bear is wearing a heavy-duty, silver and turquoise watch that he gifted me on my high school graduation—I still have that watch to this day.

Duffy family photo.

Duffy family photo.

Duffy family photo.

(Top) My dad…
The anti-cop… What's ironic
is that my dad was a cop for
a minute. This is a photo of
Bear during his cop days. I'm
sure my dad hated this job. I
went on ride-alongs with him
some nights…

Here I am
in the early 90's.
Love the hair!

Me with a 1994 Hot Food Cooking Competition winner certificate.
Photo credit: Kathy Zay.

Another photo from a 1994 cooking competition. This photo is special as my parents came to support me, though my mom had already divorced my dad and didn't want to be anywhere near my father. She showed up to support me regardless, and that means a lot.
Photo credit: Kathy Zay.

Teenage me sitting on dad's my dad's motorcycle on my high school graduation day. You can see my parents in the back.

Duffy family photo.

Duffy family photo.

Me at Muirfield Village Golf Club, circa 1995.

Me with Chef John Souza from Muirfield Village Golf Club.

Duffy family photo.

Me at a cooking competition, circa 1995.

Duffy family photo.

Me at Charlie Trotter's in Chicago, circa 2000.

Here's me at Grace restaurant. Circa 2013/2014.

Me and Michael Muser in front of a custom spice rack in the kitchen at Grace restaurant.
Duffy-owned photo.

A dish from Ever: Blueberry, chocolate, and hoja santa.
Photo credit: Michael Muser.

Here's some early sketches of the Ever restaurant logo before it was finalized.
Photo credit: Michael Muser.

Ever restaurant logo-sign affixed to outside wall near entrance.
Photo credit: Michael Muser.

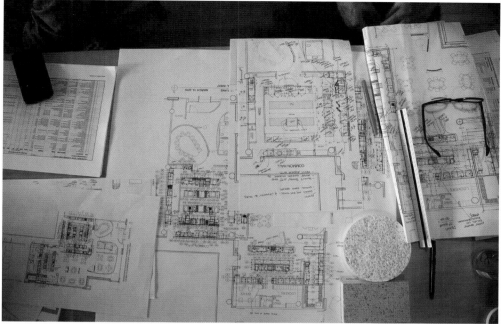

Original Ever building designs.

Photo credit: Michael Muser.

An early photo of Ever restaurant under construction.

Photo credit: Michael Muser.

Another dream-come-true: After cocktail lounge.

Chef de Cuisine Justin Selk holding a burger at Reve Burger.

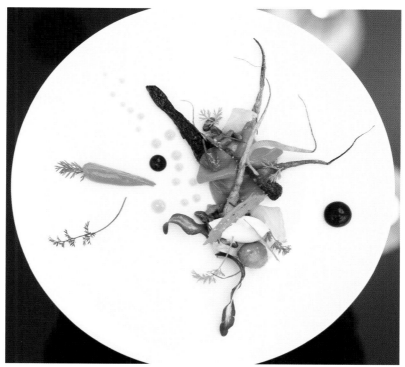

Carrot dish. Carrot, mascarpone, pistachios, and yuzu.

Fennel, hibiscus, passion fruit, and banana with rice pudding.

Here's one of my Curtis Duffy dishes at Ever: Tomato, brioche, fennel, and hyssop.
Photo credit: Michael Muser.

Here's one of my Curtis Duffy dishes at Ever: Oscietra caviar, apple, and nasturium.
Photo credit: Michael Muser.

Crab dish: Alaskan King
Crab, sudachi, cucumber,
floral cream, lemon balm.

Photo credit: Anthony Tahlier.

Here's me speaking at the Grand Chef's Gala (now renamed Jean Banchet Awards). Grace-era photo circa 2014.

Photo credit: Galdones.

My sweet girls and me—the proud papa—in the Grace restaurant kitchen. My girls are now taller than me!
From left to right: Eden, Curtis, Ava, circa 2015/2016.

Photo credit: Michael Muser.

Here's me working
in the kitchen at
Ever restaurant.

(Top) The great Farmer Lee Jones from the Chef's Garden on the opening day of Ever restaurant in 2020. I'm forever grateful for the realtionship I've had with Farmer Lee Jones all these years—he's always delivered the best produce items for my kitchen.

Here's me working in the kitchen at Ever restaurant.

Me with my good friend and collaborator—Jeremy Wagner—a full-time author and the co-writer of my memoir. I couldn't have told my story without his incredible writing skills and unwaivable support. Everyone thinks we look like we should be in a band together.
Photo credit: Stephanie Cabral.

Me with some of my dearest friends. From left to right: Me, my wife Jennifer, Kym Foglia, Jeremy Wagner, Tracy Vera, Joey Vera, Charlie Benante, and Carla Harvey.
Photo credit: Michael Muser.

Here's an early photo of me in my new chef's uniform just as we opened Ever in 2020.
Photo credit: Michael Muser.

My dream team and two pieces of my heart: Michael Muser and Amy Cordell celebrating Grace's 5-year anniversary.
Photo credit: Michael Muser.

Rare time off with my family in Miami. From left to right: Van, our dog Red, (Bowie is missing somewhere) me, Jolie, Ava, Eden, and my wife, Jennifer.

The happiest day of my life. Me and my wife Jennifer on our wedding day in Miami. April 13, 2019.

Here I am enjoying the vibe and calm of a day off in my kitchen at Ever restaurant. The beautiful, custom-made Bonnet stove is behind me—my Rolls Royce of ovens.
Photo credit: Stephanie Cabral.

Photo credit: Stephanie Cabral.

Photo credit: Michael Muser.

(Left) Here I am in the quiet, empty spaces of Ever. I love these quiet times here and I'm still blown away by the epic architecture and design we achieved at Ever. The entire restaurant, in every tiny way and detail is a legit work of art. It's all a part of that Ever experience—the "ambience," if you will.
(Right) Here's me working on a white asparagus dish in the kitchen.

Oscietra Grand Reserve Caviar
sweet potato, crème fraîche, OXALIS

King Crab
sudachi, cucumber, LEMON BALM

Coconut
makrut lime, chicken, CILANTRO

Ora King Salmon
mandarin, mustard, FENNEL

Duck
truffle, ricotta, KALE

Maitake
pasta, turnip, CHIVE

Wagyu
pistachio, apple, ANISE HYSSOP

Cranberry
olive oil, pastry cream, LEMON VERBENA

Banana
mango, rum, CHOCOLATE MINT

Tiny Sweets
Hazelnut, Yuzu

I create seasonal menus that change each season—spring, summer, fall, and winter. Here's my 2024 winter menu from Ever that offers a diverse range of dishes, straight from my imagination. These 10 dishes stand on their own, but paired with the right wines, they can elevate the dining experience. As you can see, I mix up both flora and fauna in my dishes—and in this winter menu, I start with a light dish, carry the guest through a range of palate-pleasing flavors, and end with a sweet dish at the end. And this time I also offered one of my favorite ingredients in the third course: Coconut! Photo credit: Tyler Affinito.

FORTY-THREE
HAPPILY EVER AFTER

Y ou want the Ever play-by-play?
You've got it …
September 2020: the Chicago Tribune awards Ever with
four stars.

October 2020: As Ever approaches its three-month anniversary, Illinois suspends indoor dining.

November 2020: Ever begins carryout service, with kitchen staff prepping dishes such as braised lamb and happy to be working.

December 2020: Muser and I open concept Rêve Burger to critical acclaim. It is also a money-making measure as Ever waits for Illinois to allow indoor dining again.

April 2021: Ever receives two Michelin stars with this note from the Michelin inspector:

Chef Curtis Duffy and Michael Muser have triumphantly returned, and now preside over a bespoke room where the chef's vision of fine dining enchants palates with complex flavors, stirring textures and visual fireworks.

2021: La Liste names Ever as one of the Best New Arrivals of the Year.

2021: Chicago Magazine names Ever as one of the Best New Restaurants.

November 2021: Ever places in Esquire's Best New Restaurants in America feature.

December 2021: At the Eater Chicago 2021 Awards honoring the best new restaurants in Chicago over the last two years, Ever and I are awarded with "Comeback of the Year."

April 2022: NBC5's "Chicago Today" hosts list Ever as one of the city's Top Restaurants.

2022: Ever receives two Michelin stars.

2022: The Chicago Tribune names Ever as one of the Best New Restaurants.

2022: Ever receives the AAA Five Diamond Rating.

June 2022: Despite my reluctance to appear on TV, I agree to guest on Netflix's *Iron Chef* reboot. In Episode 3, I go up against Iron Chef Dominique Crenn in a battle for the perfect pastry. Chef Crenn emerges as the winner.

July 2022: Rêve Burger shutters for good—but not before the Fulton Market spot is named one of "Chicago's 10 Best" by the Chicago Tribune.

October 2022: I open my first-ever cocktail bar, After, right next door to Ever in Fulton Market. After is considered the largest upscale bar to ever open in Chicago.

2023: Ever receives two Michelin stars.

2023: Ever receives the AAA Five Diamond Rating.

2024: The Robb Report ranks me among the 50 Most Powerful People in American Fine Dining.

2024: Ever receives two Michelin stars.

2025: La Liste lists Ever among the World's Top Restaurants.

FORTY-FOUR
LIVING THE "DREAM"

During COVID-19, my team at Ever and I created Rêve Burger—Rêve is "Ever" spelled backwards and also means "dream" in French—which was a means to an end.

Some referred to our creation of Rêve Burger as "Chef Duffy's hobby or indulgence, a pandemic side project away from the demands of Ever" —but it was so much more than that: We needed to develop some way to keep ourselves afloat during the City of Chicago indoor dining ban, and we had no idea when, if ever, that mandate would be lifted.

Without indoor dining, it wasn't possible for us to adapt our Ever cuisine in a way that made sense or would continue to encapsulate that experience, so we had to get creative. People knew our reputation for the highest quality in everything and we knew that during a distressing time, people would want familiar comfort food. So, we offered double cheeseburgers and fries and shakes.

We made them available for deliveries and curbside pickups, and they became an immediate hit. People went nuts for them.

When we came up with the concept for Rêve Burger, I knew one thing: we needed a different location. I couldn't have burger-patty smoke and grease filling my brand-new kitchen at Ever, and I wasn't going to flip burgers on our custom-built Bonnet stove, so logistics came into play.

Luck was on our side when I found an available, vacant building just cater-corner from Ever on West Fulton Street. Once we got that space, we were off and running. We launched Rêve Burger in December 2020 and it took off right away. We kept it going for a year and a half, long after the dining ban ended, because it had become so popular. But when the building we were using was slated to be torn down to make way for the construction of a new tower, we had to shut it down, and it was permanently closed on July 2, 2022.

Rêve Burger still lives on though, at the other establishment that Michael Muser and I created: After, our first cocktail lounge, located just one door east of Ever.

Ever. After. See what I did there?

The four-thousand-square-foot cocktail lounge was designed by Lawton Stanley Architects, who continue Ever's abstract, next-level, futuristic feel with a fourteen-seat curved bar, luxury chairs, and Venetian plaster throughout. After also has a private VIP space called the Observatory, which accommodates up to ten guests, as well as a private event room called Canvas for groups of eight to eighty for large events and buy-out packages.

Here, we offer a classy and extensive spirits and beverage menu featuring three special sections—a set of ten tweaked classics, ten non-alcoholic drinks, and ten selections to pair with dishes from a bites menu that includes skewered meats and vegetables cooked on a hibachi, and caviar sourced from San Gregorio de Polanco in Uruguay and presented with traditional garnishes. And of course there is Champagne to go with that, and perhaps, before or after, a flight of Scotch or gin.

And more about that food: Guests can come in for a full meal or a selection of small plates, but either way, the same attention to service and ambience comes through with the dinner fare.

Some popular menu items include:

Vietnamese Duck Wings enhanced with lime, fish sauce, and mint; Pork Belly Steamed Buns made with cucumber, sesame, and cilantro; Ibérico Tenderloin with polenta, maitake, and endive; Smoked Duck;

Glazed Scallop; Tortellini; Roasted Beets; Roasted Corn; Kampachi; Wagyu; Crème Brûlée; and, of course, that amazing Rêve Burger with American cheese, pickles, sauce, and Rêve fries.

It's a next-level, badass bites menu for a local cocktail lounge.

FORTY-FIVE
THE BEAR AND THE BEAR

I sure didn't see the popularity of the award-winning FX TV series, *The Bear*, coming.

The entire third season launched June 26, 2024 on Hulu. It rocketed to the Number One spot on Nielsen's streaming chart of original programs for the week of June 24—June 30 and it garnered, from what they tell me, some 1.2 billion viewing minutes.

Despite not being able to predict that, the show had always been on my radar, for several reasons.

The consultant for *The Bear*, Matt Danko—who's also the executive chef at the Emily Hotel—had worked with Muser and me over at Grace, and Grace had appeared in Season One flashbacks as the fictionalized location for Eleven Madison Park, Daniel Humm's three-Michelin-starred restaurant in New York. It had been a nice experience to reunite with Matt and it connected us early on to the show.

And once the series aired, the premise immediately took my attention, of course, because the central character, Carmen "Carmy" Berzatto —played by Jeremy Allen White, who's won multiple Emmy and Golden Globe Awards in this role—leaves his job as a chef at Eleven Madison Park and returns to Chicago to manage the kitchen at his brother's sandwich shop after his brother dies by suicide.

While these circumstances don't exactly parallel my own, I was, of course, interested to see how they would explore the emotional and real-world challenges that arise in the aftermath of suicide, and how they might depict those themes within the Chicago restaurant industry.

And then, in 2023, we were approached by *The Bear* crew to use Ever as the restaurant owned and run by chef Andrea Terry—played by the Academy Award-winning actress, Olivia Colman—which, in the series, is considered the world's best three-Michelin-starred restaurant. I can't even how tell you much Muser and I loved that the show actually *uses* "Ever" as the name of the restaurant in the series. Now, we don't have any say in the script; we're just renting the space to them, but we couldn't have asked for a better gift. We also found it funny that *The Bear* portrays Ever as this three-Michelin-starred restaurant, while right now as I write this in 2024, we still maintain two stars.

There's a joke in there somewhere.

Once things got rolling, in March, 2023, we closed Ever for a week for the filming. And then in April, we closed down After for a couple of days so that the same crew could wrap up Episode Four, in which After's kitchen became the set for a Copenhagen spot at which the show's bread-baker, Marcus—played by former Odd Future collective member Lionel Boyce—is mentored by a fictional pastry chef named Luca, who's played by Emmy-nominated British actor Will Poulter.

Amy Cordell appears in a handful of scenes as herself, which is terrific. Along those lines, I've been asked by people why they don't see me in the series as a main character. Well, I'm a chef, not an actor. To that end, I did insist on maintaining control over how the dishes are plated and what they'll look like in the show, and I worked with *The Bear's* culinary director, Courtney "Coco" Storer, to achieve that. And if you're looking closely, you'll see a nanosecond cameo of my face in an episode in the kitchen among the staff, and then, in Episode Seven ("Forks"), you can actually see my hands as I'm plating the dishes served at "Ever."

This imagery makes me think of how you'd see Waylon Jennings' hands playing the guitar to the theme song for every episode of *The Dukes of Hazzard*, and how Jennings had quipped in his lyrics, *"They keep a-showin' my hands and not my face on TV …"*

Speaking of that "Forks" episode, an interviewer with ABC-TV asked me about a scene that illustrates the role of an expeditor, who acts as the coordinator between the kitchen and the dining room in a manner that to me resembles air traffic control, using color codes to communicate the guests' requests and dietary restrictions. The scene was accurately depicted, and it showed how, once service gets going, the expeditor really does take full control of the kitchen

Another aspect of *The Bear* that resonated with me on a personal level was the trajectory of that character Richie—played by Ebon Moss-Bachrach, who's won two Emmy Awards in the role. He stages at "Ever," and you see him become inspired and motivated, full of drive and passionate about working inside a three-Michelin-starred restaurant. I mean, c'mon! That's me, decades ago. And seeing that reminds me of how much I love to spot that fire in so many young and hungry chefs, and how my aim is always to nurture that passion, because, as I often remind them: this job, this love, it's not some light switch.

Season Three of *The Bear* has done wonders for Ever's visibility. We now have tour buses pulling up to our sidewalk every week, filled with visitors who are taking pictures outside of our restaurant because it's where *The Bear* was filmed. The popularity of the TV series has also produced other interesting opportunities—some we've accepted, others not. For example, we've had offers from various people and companies who want to collaborate on a "Bear experience"—which means *they* want to *pay us* to work in my kitchen and polish forks, or to bring in groups who want a guided tour through every part of the restaurant and will pay for the experience.

It's both a bit insane—in a rock 'n' roll way—and also really cool. For all the aspects I explore to try to think outside the box, I never imagined something like this happening.

And on a very primal and poignant note, there is the series name, *"The Bear."* By now you know that was my father's name: BEAR.

The universe is talking, perhaps. There's something in all of that …

FORTY-SIX
YOU CAN'T CHOOSE YOUR FAMILY (UNFORTUNATELY)

Here There Be Tigers ...

One day, years ago when Grace was in full swing, my phone rang. I didn't recognize the number. Usually, I ignore unknown calls, but I decided to pick it up.

"Hello?"

A familiar voice greeted me through the receiver.

Robert Jr.? Tiger ... Tig ...

Christ, it had been ages.

Not that I was surprised about his timing. Since word had gotten out about the success of Grace, a number of estranged family members had come a-knockin'.

"Hey, Tig. How's the family?"

Tig didn't acknowledge the question. "I'm in between jobs and need a little cash. Behind on some bills."

I felt my teeth clench. *Of course, Tig wanted money.* They all did. Months before this call, Trisha had hit me up for a grand and never paid a cent back.

"What do you need?" I asked Tig.

"I could use a thousand bucks. Same as you did for Trish."

I wanted to explode. *Unbelievable.* But I cleared my throat and paused

319

as an idea formed. I said, "How about you send me your bills and I get them paid on a credit card? I don't have a lot of cash."

"What? With that big fancy restaurant you got up in Chicago? C'mon, Curt. Don't bullshit me now. Show a brother some love."

Brother?

That was a good one. I could remember having a brother, but not much brotherly love.

"I told you before—and our sister, too—I don't have money like that."

"That sucks, man." Tig sounded annoyed. "Gotta split."

He hung up on me.

I had hoped that our parents awful deaths would've brought us three Duffy kids closer together; we only had each other after that. That meant something to me, and I really tried to establish a real relationship with my siblings.

The first time I got hitched, I wanted to share my new wife Kim with my family. And I have to give credit to Kim for instilling in me the importance of family and urging me to reach out; her positive attitude and love for family moved me. So, together; we would call them all the time—my brother and my sister and my grandma and all of Jan's family in Colorado.

In return? Abso-fucking-lutely *nothing*.

These days, I'm fine with the status quo.

My brother is still alive, surprisingly. Less surprisingly, he's still drifting around the same town, hustling money with jack shit to show for it. I haven't seen him since my nephew—Trisha's second-oldest child—passed away several years ago in a car accident at only eighteen. Tig never picked up or returned my calls and I finally stopped trying to connect. I've had the same phone number for decades, but he never uses it.

Trisha eventually graduated nursing school and then later, she switched careers. From what I know, she now works as a deputy for the Franklin County Sheriff's Department. She's striving to do something more with her life. That makes me happy … and happy for her.

Even so, I'm always concerned about Trisha. For one, she's still in

Ohio, in the same town: Johnstown. I really wish she'd get the hell out of there. It's a difficult place and for our family, it holds a lot of negative vibes.

In addition to that, life has never been easy for her. Trisha had her first child at age fifteen, since then, she's had more—six kids total—and none of their fathers are in the picture, and it increases my admiration for how far she's come when I think about all she's been up against. I feel protective of my little sister, even more as each year goes by. I *always* want the best for her.

Trisha and I are on again/off again. We still have a lot of trust issues, obviously, but we seem to grow closer the older we get. I have a lot of love for her, but we still have things to sort out.

In 2015, I flew Trisha up to Chicago to hang for the Grace doc. She kept referring to me as her "culinary rockstar brother"—but she didn't eat at Grace that time. Unfortunately, when Trisha did finally come back to eat at Grace in 2017, I had just quit the restaurant. I didn't want her to know the truth about my falling out with Grace's owner, so I had to lie to her, telling her that I was working on an event somewhere else. In reality, I was down in Miami, trying to recover from the insanity that surrounded my departure. I still thanked her for coming, though, and arranged for her to have an epic dinner. I also made sure she was given a dozen roses at the restaurant. I had my team tell her that I was sorry to have missed her.

The fact that Trisha had made the effort to see me and dine on my cuisine meant the world to me. When Jennifer and I got married in 2019, Trisha came down to Miami for the wedding and it was wonderful to have her there.

In 2021, however, Trisha bitched me out about some interview I had done in 2013 in which she felt I portrayed her in a poor light. I tried to talk to her about it, but she just flat out cut me off and stopped talking to me, not replying to my texts or calls or Mother's Day greetings or birthday wishes.

However, Trisha came up and dined at Ever, for the first time, in 2022. We reconnected—but then hit that same fucking wall again. We've since mended fences and I hope we'll continue to be in each other's lives in a positive way.

In case you couldn't tell by now, my immediate Ohio family dynamic is, uh, *complicated*—to say the least.

I've tried to stay connected to Trisha's children, as well. Being an uncle has given me nieces and nephews of whom I'm fond, but unfortunately, I've yet to establish a meaningful relationship with any of them.

When I think of Trisha's kids, I also think of Robert Jr.'s kids. I've tried to connect with them, too. In fact, I had hoped to mentor one of his sons, who's in his twenties. I had seen something in this kid back when I was in the process of building Grace.

I'd gone back to Ohio to visit family and friends and when I connected with him, I thought, *I'm going to help this kid make something of himself.*

"You're not going to go *anywhere* if you stay here," I told him. "You're going to be stuck in the hamster wheel of this town, which offers no opportunities, and with these people around you sucking the life from you. When you're ready, I'm going to take you back to Chicago. You're going to come work for me. I got out; so can you."

What was really great was that my nephew *heard* me. He started saving money, working to move up to Chicago. I was going to give him that job, but the plan wasn't about just having him working in the big city, it was about inspiring him.

"You know what, I don't even want you to be a chef. I don't even want you to cook. I just want you to be around people who are passionate about doing something so you can absorb that and be inspired to discover your own dream. That's all I want for you because I believe in you."

That's what I told him from my heart.

When the appointed time came, I went down to get my nephew and bring him back with me. But when I arrived, he turned to me and said, "No … I'm not leaving, Uncle Curtis. I've decided that I'm going to stay here in Ohio with my dad."

I truly hope it works out for him. And if it doesn't, well, I'm always here for him.

In 2001, a year after I'd moved to Chicago, Robert Jr., got married.

I was surprised I'd gotten an invite to begin with—and surprised my brother was trying to make it a special day. Maybe Tig's new bride had something to do with that. Who knows? My brother hadn't been the type to subscribe to meaningful moments and gestures.

I made the trip back to Johnstown, Ohio, and arrived at the small church freshly showered and dressed up, game face on. I was there out of respect for my brother, but my expectations were low across the family board.

"Hey, Curt. Get over here." Tig waved me over and made some introductions. I shook hands and hugged a few family members. People asked me about Chicago and about being a chef. Small talk.

Then out of nowhere, Tig squeezed my shoulder from behind. "Hey Curt, you remember Sue, right?"

I turned around and faced my biological mother.

What the fuck is she doing here?

I was livid. My stomach roiled. This was only the *second* time I'd seen Sue since she'd dumped me off as a baby in Jan's arms—the *first* time I saw her in my teens is another story. I felt stiff as hell, the same way I'd felt the other time I saw Sue, back when I was a teenager.

I swallowed hard, not sure about what to do.

Do I shake her hand?

Hug her?

Walk out?

Sue smiled. "Hello, Curtis. You look very nice." She stepped forward and embraced me.

I don't want this, I thought.

As Sue hugged me, I looked over her shoulder and straight at Tig, who was giving me a knowing smile. Like, *Ha! Got you, brother.* I'd been in this scenario before—Tig had set me up this same way with Sue some years before this—that *first* time.

Once we parted and the awkward embrace was over, I tried to stop myself from shaking. I looked around to see if there was a corner I could disappear into and have a drink or two.

Before I could move, however, Tig was dragging me and others together for wedding photos.

The photographer directed groups of people to stand, huddle, smile.

I'm all for special days and memories, but the last thing I wanted was to stand alongside the woman—the *stranger*—who gave me up.

As the camera clicked and captured the moment for eternity, I wondered, *What would Jan think? What would Bear think, watching his shithead brother Bill and sister Penny pal around with the ex he hated?*

After the ceremony, I poked my head into the reception for a moment as I planned a stealthy escape. But before I could get out, Sue caught up to me.

I actually wanted to ask Sue about a lot of things—including her side of the Bear story—but that's a Pandora's box ill-suited for a wedding. So, I waited for her to open the conversation.

"I got something for you," she said, finally.

I frowned. "That's not necessary, Sue."

"No. No. You could use this." Sue dug around in her purse and pulled out some paper. "Here it is. Take it."

I stared at her hand and in it was cash and some clippings from a newspaper. "What's that?"

"It's twenty dollars—sorry I don't have more—but there's also some Walmart coupons. You can use the money and the coupons and get yourself something you like."

If only it were that cheap and simple to repair a life.

I never knew much about Sue.

I knew even less about her parents and family.

Although I adamantly refused to be part of Sue's life, I knew that Tig had been curious about her since the day Bear and Jan sat us down as kids. I knew that he had searched for her for years, and eventually, with whatever means he was able to employ in the days before search engines and social media, he somehow found her. I believe that he did it out of sincere curiosity—but also out of spite because he hated Jan so much. Whatever my brother's deal, though, I wanted nothing to do with it. As far as I was concerned, my biological mother didn't exist. Jan was my real mother. But despite my efforts to distance myself from Sue, my brother didn't respect my choice.

The more things change …

Now, about that *first* time I met Sue. One day after school, my brother showed up at the back door of a small restaurant I was working at.

"Hey, Curtis," he said. "I need you to come outside with me. I have an important friend I want you to meet."

"Tig, I haven't seen you in months and you pop up with this urgent meet-and-greet? I'm in the middle of working right now."

My brother wouldn't take no for an answer, so I walked outside to his car.

"Curt, I want you to meet your real mother. Our biological mother. This is Sue."

I was stunned, as you can imagine. I was seventeen years old and this lady, who's apparently my birth mother, is standing in front of me, next to Robert Jr.'s car. This was the *very first* time I was meeting her since she'd abandoned me at six months old.

I imagine the situation must have been weird for Sue as well—but only in the sense that she was meeting me for the first time since I'd been a newborn. It obviously wasn't a surprise encounter for her.

The moment I'm introduced to her, Sue doesn't extend a hand or try to hug me at all. No, instead, she tries to hand me money.

"I don't want your damn money," I blurted out. "That's not going to make up for the last seventeen years of my life!"

I turned around and walked away. In truth, I wanted to break my brother's neck for bushwhacking me like that. It was so uncool. More than anything, though, I felt distraught because I didn't know how I was going to tell Jan about the encounter. Yes, Robert Jr. had tricked me into meeting Sue. But that didn't matter. I was so worried it would hurt Jan's feelings.

Despite the physical abuse I'd suffered from my parents, I still held both my mom and dad in high regard and I know it had broken Jan's heart when Robert Jr. had rejected her love and she'd discovered that he'd developed a close relationship with Sue instead. After all, Jan had stepped in with her whole heart when she was only fifteen to raise us as her own.

I felt I had to tell Jan about this unexpected meeting right away. I didn't want to hide it. There wasn't any way I could have lived with myself if someone else had told Jan that I'd met Sue that day.

I could never hurt Jan the way my brother had. That was the number one reason I never wanted to have a relationship with my biological mother. To this day, I fear that if I had even the smallest, most benign relationship with Sue, it would be a major betrayal to Jan. I'm reluctant to even try and ask Sue the burning questions I've harbored for more than forty years because I feel that if Jan is watching me now from some spiritual afterlife, she'll still be hurt by me asking Sue about how she gave me up, about all the things my father told me—as if me seeking those answers would somehow make Jan feel she hadn't been enough of a mother. In reality, though, Jan has always been and always will be my only mother.

Still, Sue isn't completely removed from my life. Look, I'm pretty easy to stalk for anyone who feels compelled to do it. A Google search on "Chef Curtis Duffy" will bring up countless interviews, news bits, and more, and I never blocked Sue from getting a peek behind the curtain via social media.

Crazy as this sounds, I accepted Sue's friend request on Facebook, which probably sounds contradictory, but I don't look at it as a direct connection. I don't post a lot of personal things out there. In fact, I hardly use Facebook at all anymore—I have someone else managing it.

I admit, a few years ago, I visited Sue's Facebook page a few times but, other than satisfying an initial curiosity, I don't pay attention to her page and I haven't interacted with her there. I do remember that her profile said she was from Fredericktown, Ohio and that she lives in Zanesville, Ohio. I don't know much else about her other than her birthday and location. Her profile doesn't say what year she was born. I know that she was married. I also learned that she has a daughter by a totally different dude she was with many moons ago. Neither Sue nor my brother has ever once mentioned that I had another half-sister.

Sue has never reached out to me for anything on Facebook other than hitting me up with that one friend request. She's been respectful, keeping boundaries intact—perhaps knowing how I feel about her. I did see one interesting thing on her Facebook page: photos of my daughters. She'd lifted pictures of them from my page—along with other things that I've posted—and put those photos and things into her own Facebook albums. Of course, my daughters are Sue's biological granddaughters—and yet, she doesn't know them at all.

She also seemed focused on my success as a chef. She had posted photos and public accolades in the way someone does if they're obsessed with a celebrity. I get the impression that Sue cares more about me being her "superstar son" than as a biological child she gave up but now wishes to know in a meaningful way.

It's all really fucking weird.

That half-sister actually discovered me around the same time I learned about her. This half-sister used to hit me up relentlessly on social media platforms, but I wasn't ready to connect with her. I certainly wasn't wanting any involvement with Sue, so why would I want to be in contact with her daughter? Still, I get it. My half-sister is like me: a child of Sue, someone who didn't ask for this situation, someone who is sincerely curious about a newly discovered sibling. I appreciate and respect her feelings and inquisitive nature, but I've always felt, and still feel, that if I started a relationship with her, it was going to be too much for me. I'd be overwhelmed on an emotional level, on a mental level, on a "respect-for-Jan" level. So, I just wasn't interested.

And I'll go further.

Some of her attempts to reach me included odd comments that turned me off, things that I immediately thought were too similar to Sue's in the sense that she's not so much interested in getting to know me as her half-brother as she is in connecting to someone who appears to her to be successful, a celebrity, and—in her eyes—wealthy, who she's seen on Netflix. I didn't like the vibe.

Beyond my daughters and step-kids, my wife Jennifer, my sister Trisha, brother Robert Jr., and my parents, I just don't think about anyone else in my family tree. Other people are in my bloodline … but they're easy to forget, as far as I'm concerned.

As much as I'd be content to live my life without any connection with Sue, Tig—who I believe is still close with her—persists in trying to bring us together. He has told me numerous times that Sue *did* try to reach out to us. That's interesting news to me. Maybe things were hidden from us when we were younger. My dad harbored epic contempt for Sue from the time he was eighteen until the day he died, so it's possible any overtures she might have made when we were younger were hidden from us.

Surely, though, my brother told Sue about my parents deaths in 1994, so I wonder what kept her from trying to connect with me then. I don't remember a time when she tried to send me a personal email, or write me a letter, or ask anyone for my address or anything. I've never received one Facebook message from her. Not once wishing me a happy birthday, nothing.

So, when Robert Jr. pitches pro-Sue bullshit to me, I ignore it. If Sue wants to talk to me, she needs to make the effort to reach out to me on her own.

It's Jan's side of the family who remain important to me. I've taken numerous trips to see them in Colorado over the years and my Terpstra-related cousins have come to visit me. I feel it's vital to keep that connection, another way to keep Jan's memory alive for me.

One thing I love to remember about my mom is her laugh and how she always tried to lighten the mood—which was heavy and dark in our house, mostly because of my dad's bad attitude and iron fist. Jan was also hard as spikes, more so as years went by, but she tried to be the peacemaker in her own way. It was complicated. But when I think of Jan, what comes to me most often is her spirit and smile.

Bad Cop/Holy Roller ...

These days, I don't think Uncle Bill's a cop anymore.

Through Facebook, I discovered that he's now a religious church nut who belongs to a Christian biker club and his nickname is "Hitman." He's always been big, both him and my dad, and he was a third-or-fourth-degree black belt or some shit back in the day. From what I see, he's easily pushing 280 pounds now.

Bill wears biker vests with patches that say, "Prayer Warrior," "Road Captain," "Protector of the Word." His vests are also confusing: one features a Jewish Star of David and another is decorated with a metallic pin in the shape of spiked brass knuckles.

He's a walking contradiction, a Jesus-loving holy roller with a nickname that suggests he's paid to kill people. And yes, this is the same guy who nearly beat me to death when I was a child.

Did he choose this so-called "born-again faith" late in life because, as I've observed with some other born-agains, it helps him feel like he can hide behind Jesus for the bad shit he did? If so, he'll easily do bad shit again. I've seen this 'born-again' pattern; I know it.

Here on earth, you really have to focus on breaking that cycle of abuse. I'm talking about the same cycle with my father and his brother—yes, Bill—and *their* father before them had carried on, generation after generation taking the beatings and then doling out the beatings, right down the line.

FUCK THAT.

I was *never* like them at all—in my heart or in my actions.

I never felt the need to dominate and punish anyone, much less people I loved.

I broke that abuse cycle … in my own house, in my name, I fucking destroyed that wheel of generational trauma.

In the process I was burned, certainly, but I was learning to rise up and discovering that the best way to become *fireproof* was to extinguish the flames before they took hold.

FORTY-SEVEN
THE DEVIL GETS HIS DUE

M y life is good.
Time has passed.
Bygones and all that …

But sometimes, I smell brimstone and realize the Devil is still at work.

Whatever became of Dolos?

Dolos has resurfaced here and there. In November 2018, he replaced Grace with Yugen, an upscale contemporary Japanese restaurant located in the same spot on Randolph Street where Grace once resided. But by May 2021, Yugen had closed due to what had been reported as a nasty falling out between Dolos and the executive chef, Mari Katsumura, who had resigned.

And as I kept my finger on the pulse of Chicago's culinary and business scene, I'd learn that the best of Dolos's worst was yet to come.

On top of his restaurant failures at Randolph Street, Dolos ran into legal troubles with his other restaurant, Onward Chicago, a Rogers Park place that opened in 2018 on the ground floor of a Hampton Inn hotel. The property, situated at 6580 N. Sheridan Road, was owned by Loyola University and adjacent to its Chicago campus. Starting in September 2019—many months before the COVID-19 pandemic shut down Chicago businesses—Dolos apparently stopped paying the $10,000 per month rent. In May 2021, Loyola filed suit in Cook County Circuit Court to evict

Onward from its property and a second suit for more than $268,000 in back rent.

Dolos went to court complaining that he was given a raw deal—that Loyola *wanted* Dolos in this location because he was regarded as a "highly accomplished restaurateur" and a Loyola "alumnus and benefactor" who had the means to open a "fine dining restaurant" in the hotel building. Dolos went on to claim that he basically stepped up and "answered the call of Loyola, his alma mater" and that he supposedly invested $1.5 million of his own cash into Onward. Then with the onset of COVID-19 restrictions, Onward was forced to close.

Then, in September 2022 as the Loyola lawsuit drama continued in court, Dolos found himself in the crosshairs of Martin J. Walsh, the United States Secretary of Labor. The Department of Labor had launched an investigation, and then a lawsuit against Dolos and his company, Area Wide Realty Corporation—along with the Dolos-managed Area Wide Realty Corporation Cash Balance Pension Plan and Trust and Area Wide Realty Corporation Profit-Sharing Plan and Trust. Dolos was alleged to have misappropriated employee funds from his company's pension and profit-sharing plans.

A Federal judge approved an order directing Dolos to restore losses to his company's pension and profit-sharing plans after the DOL allegedly found funds were misappropriated. Moreover, Dolos also agreed to terminate the plans and distribute more than $400,000 to participants and beneficiaries within six months of the entry. Dolos was to deposit $12,500 into the Profit-Sharing Plan, waive the restoration of losses to his own plan accounts, and reallocate his account balance in the plans to restore participants' accounts to their December 31, 2018 balances.

As the Department of Labor's investigation and subsequent lawsuit showed, the action followed an investigation by the department's Employee Benefits Security Administration which revealed that in Spring 2011, Dolos allegedly transferred all funds from the Cicero-based company's employee benefit plans to personal annuity policies in his own name with his wife as the beneficiary. However, in 2012 and 2013, he filed annual reports for the employee benefit plans indicating the plans had assets. In 2015, Dolos allowed the fidelity bond to lapse for both plans.

In spring of 2016, Dolos deposited the amounts withdrawn in 2011 into accounts on behalf of each plan, but in 2017, he withdrew $79,649.50

from each plan and deposited the funds into a money market account in his and his wife's names.

In the consent order and judgment in the U.S. District Court for the Northern District of Illinois, Judge Martha M. Pacold ordered that Dolos be *permanently barred* from serving as a fiduciary in the future and further ordered him to pay a penalty of $15,845 for violating the Employee Retirement Income Security Act.

"This consent order ensures [Dolos] will not benefit from violating his employees' trust," said Employee Benefits Security Administration Acting Regional Director Kelli Hammerl in Chicago. "Fiduciaries must always work in the best interest of the fund. The U.S. Department of Labor's Employee Benefits Security Administration is committed to ensuring the integrity of employee benefit programs and holding those who violate the law accountable."

When I first heard the news, I wasn't surprised.

I view it as both karma and justice.

As Dolos flounders in a legal quagmire of his own making, I'm reminded of how he took all that Muser and I and our team had created and burned it to the ground—forcing *me* to burn it down— laughing at us as he watched everything go up in flames while hitting us with frivolous lawsuits to bankrupt me on top of it all.

But Dolos didn't destroy me.

And I've learned that the best way to become *fireproof* when dealing with that man is to not only continue to focus on ensuring success as my best revenge, but also to balance his toxic abuse by doing whatever I can to make the world a better place for as long as I'm blessed to be here.

If you take any inspiration from my story, let it be that.

FORTY-EIGHT
THE LAST SUPPER

What would I want for my last supper?

A beautiful roasted chicken, a nice bottle of tequila that I'd fall off the wagon for, my wife and family by my side. Some vegetables.

Dessert of crème brûlée or coconut flan or something rich and beautiful like that.

And give me some loud fucking music—*metal*. Some Slayer or Exodus or Danzig. Give me a hefty dollop of death metal. Maybe even a side of D.R.I.

My own ambience.

My own way.

∾

IF I COULD COOK for anyone today, living or dead, who would that be?

My parents.

I would, of course, love to have them experience the result of my drive, the hard work ethic that they saw me embrace at a young age. Because of the way I was brought up, wanting to overcome the challenges that came with being their son—wanting to make a good life, period—in a crazy way, my parents gave me the fire in my belly to aspire. Being able to cook them an epic meal would be a small way to say thank you to them for raising me, because it made me who I am today.

I get emotional when I imagine it.

I miss my parents greatly ...

I OFTEN SAY that I never forget where I came from ... I never forget what I've been through—especially with my parents and friends who left this world too early.

The thirtieth anniversary of my parents deaths was September 12, 2024. My first thought—and this will likely will not surprise you—was to host a gathering at Ever where I would invite everyone in the family to come together and celebrate Bear's and Jan's lives. But, as much as I cherish the importance of family, my own family is a complicated one, you know, and the more I thought about bringing everyone together, the more my concerns began to cast doubt on whether or not this would be a good way to honor them.

Who would come? Who would we want to come ... and not?

Would we be able to control that?

What behaviors would result as certain people's emotions were triggered?

Would anyone bring an agenda that would wrench the focus away from Jan and Bear?

Would I be worried the entire time about what I could and couldn't control?

I talked it over with Trisha and she shared my misgivings.

When that day came, I ended up working. I also took some time to reflect on my parents and explore ways I could take an active role in honoring their lives—I realize now, it's not just about what happened to them and what happened to me. To that end, my publisher—Dead Sky Publishing—and I will donate partial proceeds from this book to an organization in the suicide prevention community.

My experiences have given me the ability recognize others' passions, gifts, and challenges; to understand someone's dream, or recognize their nightmare, and to try to help them embrace it or leave it behind. I empathize with anyone who's struggling with loneliness, self-doubt, confusion, or feelings of failure. I admire anyone who's doing the hard work of facing their demons and taking steps to pull themselves over to the other side. And always, *always*, I care about anyone who's contemplating suicide, full stop.

CHEF CURTIS DUFFY AWARDS

#1 Most Exciting New Restaurant, CS Magazine (2012)
   Chef of the Year, Eater National Award (2013)
   Chef of the Year, Eater Chicago Award (2013)
   Restaurant of the Year, Eater National Award (2013)
   Four Star Rating, Phil Vettel of the Chicago Tribune (2013)
   Best New Restaurant, Chicago Magazine (2013)
   Best of the Best, Robb Report (2013)
   Best New Restaurant, Chicago Magazine (2013)
   Top Fifty Best New Restaurants, Bon Appetit (2013)
   Best New Restaurant Nomination, James Beard Awards (2013)
   Five Star Rating, Forbes Five Star Award (2014)
   Best Chef, Great Lakes Region Nominee, James Beard Awards, (2014)
   Five Diamond Rating, AAA Five Diamond Award (2014)
   Two Star Rating, Michelin Red Guide (2014)
   Chef of the Year, Jean Banchet Awards (2014)
   Restaurant of the Year, Jean Banchet Awards (2014)
   Best Restaurant Service, Jean Banchet Awards (2014)
   Best Chef de Cuisine, Jean Banchet Awards (2014)
   Best Sommelier, Jean Banchet Awards (2014)
   Top 10 Hottest Restaurants in the World, Zagat (2014)
   Chef of the Year, Chicago Tribune (2014)

Three Star Rating, Michelin Red Guide (2015)

Five Star Rating, Five Star Award, Forbes Travel Guide (2015)

Five Diamond Rating, AAA Five Diamond Award (2015)

Best Chef, Great Lakes Region Nominee, James Beard Awards, (2015)

Three Star Rating, Michelin Red Guide (2016)

Five Star Rating, Forbes Five Star Award (2016)

Five Diamond Rating, AAA Five Diamond Award (2016)

Best Chef, Great Lakes Region Winner, James Beard Awards, (2016)

Three Star Rating, Michelin Red Guide (2017)

Five Star Rating, Five Star Award, Forbes Travel Guide (2017)

Five Diamond Rating, AAA Five Diamond Award (2017)

Chicago Tribune, 4-star rating by Phil Vettel, (2020)

Four Star Rating, Phil Vettel of the Chicago Tribune (2021)

Two Star Rating, Michelin Red Guide (2021)

Esquire Magazine, Best New Restaurants in America, (2021)

Chicago Magazine, Best New Restaurants, (2021)

La Liste, Best New Arrivals of the Year, (2021)

Two Star Rating, Michelin Red Guide (2022)

AAA Five Diamond Rating, (2022)

Chicago Tribune, Best New Restaurants, (2022)

Rêve Burger named one of "Chicago's 10 Best" by the Chicago Tribune (2022)

Two Star Rating, Michelin Red Guide (2023)

Five Diamond Rating, AAA Five Diamond Award (2023)

The Robb Report, The 50 Most Powerful People in American Fine Dining (2024)

La Liste, World's Top Restaurants (2024)

Two Star Rating, Michelin Red Guide (2024)

La Liste, World's Top Restaurants (2025)

CURTIS'S ACKNOWLEDGEMENTS

I give my immeasurable thanks, high-fives, and immense love to the following people who've been a part of my journey in myriad ways … those who've believed in me or have made my life richer:

My wife, Jennifer Duffy—your love is my anchor and has been my constant source of strength, lifting me when I doubted myself and encouraging me to reach for heights I never thought possible.

Your passion is my fire—fueling me and igniting my drive and reminding me why I embarked on this journey in the first place.

Your unwavering care is my comfort and refuge, a reminder that no matter what challenges I face, I always have a home in your arms.

And your strength, both quiet and fierce, is my foundation, the invincible bedrock upon which all my dreams are built and inspires me every day to keep going, even when the road feels long.

You're the heart of my world and everything I hold dear and so much more … you're my partner, my greatest ally, my truest confidant, my greatest champion, my constant companion, and the love of my life.

Words will never fully exemplify the depth of my gratitude and love for you.

This book is as much yours as it is mine as you're a monumental part of my life story and have been along for the ride since this memoir first took shape. Your belief and support in my wanting to bare my soul in the pages of this book is a testament to the bond we share and the life we've built together.

Thank you for your patience, your sacrifices, your laughter, and your belief in me as I worked to see FIREPROOF through. With every word in my memoir, I carry you in my heart … with every page, I honor the love and passion that sustains our life together as you've been an important part of every chapter of my life through your embracing it all and sharing your thoughts with me.

I am endlessly grateful for you, and I will cherish and adore you always.

You've always been in my corner and have always reassured me and reminded me that I AM FIREPROOF!!!

I love you, my Love …

~

My daughters, Ava and Eden—you are my heart, my inspiration, and the reason I strive to be the best version of myself every day. This book is for you, a reminder of the love, strength, and endless possibilities that live within you. May you always know that you are capable of achieving anything your heart's desire, and that I will forever be here, cheering you on. Thank you for reminding me every day what it means to see the world with wonder and to love without limits. This is for you, my sweet girls—always and forever.

I love you, Dad.

My stepchildren Van and Jolie—you each hold a special place in my heart, and I am truly grateful for the love and joy you bring into my life. Watching you grow, learn, and navigate your own paths has been one of my greatest privileges. This book is for you, a small reminder of how much you are loved, appreciated, and cherished. Thank you for welcoming me into your lives with open hearts, for the laughter we share, and for being such a meaningful part of my life. I will always be here for you, supporting you with love, and all that I have to give.

I love you.

~

My dear friend, Jeremy Wagner—this book wouldn't have been possible without you. Your creativity, insight, and dedication have been the heart of this project. Working side by side, sharing ideas, and weaving our thoughts together has been an incredible experience for me.

Thank you for your unwavering support, your patience, and your belief in my story from the very start. Your friendship has made this journey not just successful, but deeply meaningful. This book is as much a reflection of our partnership as it is of my own journey. I look forward to all that we will continue to create and accomplish together. I'm so grateful for every word we've put into this memoir together.

You are my brother and I love you!

My dear friend, Kym Foglia-Wagner—your vision for greatness, has been both humbling and empowering. You've taught me to dream bigger, think deeper, and pursue excellence with a new purpose and passion.

Thank you for being my steadfast supporter.

Your belief in me has made all the difference, and I will forever be grateful for the impact you've had on my life.

I am forever grateful for your encouragement, your support, and your relentless confidence in me.

I love you!

My pups, Bowie and Red—thank you for the endless love, joy, and comfort you bring into our life every single day. Your wagging tails (Lack of), your excited greetings, and those soft, knowing eyes always make everything better. Whether we're playing, or just sharing a quiet moment, you remind me every day how beautiful life can be with you in our lives.

You are our constant source of happiness, and I am so grateful for the unconditional love and companionship you give us. Our hearts are fuller with you in it, and we'll always cherish the happiness you bring.

We love you!

Michael Muser—I extend my deepest gratitude to my longtime friend who's been through hell and back with me … you've been a constant source of inspiration.

Thank you for your endless encouragement and your ability to push me when I needed it. Working alongside you has not only been a professional privilege but also a personal one, and I'm incredibly grateful for everything we've achieved together.

Much love.

The badass Amy Cordell—I don't know what I'd do without you, all the loyal staff and teams and "get shit done" people who've been in the trenches with me from Buxton Inn, Muirfield Village Golf Club, Tartan Fields, Charlie Trotter's, Trio, Avenues (The Peninsula Hotel), Alinea, Grace, Ever and After.

To Jason Chan—Thank you for your unwavering support, wisdom, and generosity of spirit. Your belief in me has been a source of strength, shaping me in ways that words cannot fully express. Beyond knowledge, you have taught me compassion, resilience, and the beauty of lifelong learning. Your guidance has instilled in me great discipline and a deep passion for martial arts—lessons that will stay with me always. Thank you for your daily encouragement and inspiration. I am forever grateful for your presence in my life.

You are my brother, I love you!

My sister Trisha, my brother Robert (Tig), Ruth Snider, Kathy Zay, Guillermo and Marie Perez, Niurka Perez, Javier, Aisha and Max Perez, Guillermo (Rodman) Perez, Steve Wands and Kristy Baptist and Anna Kubik at Dead Sky Publishing for the constant belief and support, Eddie Yoshimura (Shihan), Pat White, Wayne Gregory, Jeff Weber, Kai Lerman, Jamie Kluz, Regan and Katie Koivisto, Farmer Lee Jones and The Chef's Garden, Ken Wilcox, Nick Kokonas, Maria Zec, Matt Danko, Phil Vettel, Kevin Boehm, John Saunders, Charlie Trotter, Matthias Merges, Homaro "Omar" Cantu, Grant Achatz, Daniel Boulud, Thomas Keller, Helen Rogan, Shawn Macomber, Joe Matthews at IPG, Charlie Benante, Carla Harvey, Billy Corgan, Chloe Mandel, Glenn Danzig, Paul Stanley, Trent

Reznor, Courtney "Coco" Storer and Christopher Storer and *The Bear*, Pequod's Pizza, Mike Gebert, Jay Verma, Tim and Janet Simonec, Scott and Jessica Crawford, Steven and Kristin Greene, Danny Valdez, Evelyn Boguslawski, Ryan Hilley, Cynthia Ochterbeck, Nicholas Romero, Sean O'Callaghan, Nick Frahm, Octavio Estrada, Lucas Trahan, Richie Farina, Phillip Foss, Carrie Nahabedian, Aaron Gersonde, Giuseppe Tentori, Dave LeFavre, Duane Clark, Gary Adcock, Tiffany Hollis and Dashing Diner, Tony and Amber Kuehner, Mike Miczek and Dark Matter Coffee, John and Diane Souza, Frankie Nasso, Aphotic Media, Eric Pritchard, Corey Soria and Shannon, Brandon Wright, Andrea DeWerd and Amanda Livingston at The Future of Agency, Alexis Adlouni and Jill Cromwell Wang at Cromwell Creative, Greg and Stefan at MXML Creative, Katherine Turman, Stephanie Cabral, Justin Selk, David Connell, all the various Yachtley Crew misfits I've traveled with, the Michelin Guide, Jean Banchet and the Jean Banchet Awards, James Beard and the James Beard Foundation, the Auguste Escoffier School of Culinary Arts, Meals on Wheels, Share Our Strength, PAWS Foundation, the Boys and Girls Club, the Cystic Fibrosis Foundation, all of the foundations for Suicide Prevention, and anyone else that I may have forgotten, my apologies—you know who you are!

JEREMY'S ACKNOWLEDGEMENTS

There's many people who have been a part of the journey I embarked on when I began writing Curtis Duffy's FIREPROOF memoir— all whom I'm so grateful for thanks—like all the fine editors, believers, early readers, teams, and friends who've gotten us here in one way shape or form:

Thank you, Curtis Duffy. Writing your memoir has been one of the most incredible and emotional experiences of my life. I'm honored that you put your faith and trust in me to do this right—and we did it OUR way. This journey we took together in writing this memoir has moved me and inspired me in profound ways … every page holds an extremely special and meaningful place in my heart. And the memoir aside, you always continue to inspire me on a daily basis with your incredible strength, ambition, big heart, wisdom, and focus on excellence—excellence in both what you create and in how you live your life. You've taught me so much and I embrace it all with immense gratitude.

You're my brother for life and I love you.

To my wife Kym … you own my heart. The deep and overflowing love and passion my heart has for you cannot be fully described—for me to articulate my love for you can't be done through words and language as those alone fail to fully elucidate what you mean to me. It's impossible to epitomize and convey how much you mean to me and how crazy in love with you I am. With that, I'll use what I have—my affection and my heartfelt words—to tell you that I'm so fortunate and grateful to have had you come into my world because you're the absolute love of my life forever. You're also my best friend, my rock, the most amazing and beautiful soul I've ever known—and you're all mine. Also, throughout the process of writing FIREPROOF, you've been my biggest supporter and positive force throughout this entire experience. And you've always believed in Curtis and me this entire time … and you've done more for Curtis and me than anyone on this planet.

I'll never find the words that will define what you mean to me and my heart, but the best I can do is tell you that I love you for eternity, my love.

To Steve Wands, you're the best partner a guy could have and I don't know what I'd do without you. Your dedication and passion for DSP and everything you do for the company and our authors/creators is appreciated beyond measure. I'm so very grateful you rolled into my life and built this empire with me. You forever rock and rule, Boo!

I give a very special thanks to Tony Bosco who, in 2015, first suggested that we dine at Curtis Duffy's epic restaurant, GRACE, in Chicago—which we did along with my wife Kym and others. That first dinner at GRACE changed my life in so many ways. I experienced cuisine and wine pairings on a level that that defies explanation. Curtis Duffy's "Four Pillars" were on point that night: the service, the cuisine, the wine, the ambience … ALL of that was beyond stellar, it blew me away and the experience remains with me to this day. Because of dining at GRACE that first time, I met Curtis Duffy and he became one of my best friends and now we have both created FIREPROOF. Again, it all started with you, Tony, and for that, I'm forever grateful.

Far beyond grateful to my first editor for FIREPROOF who got this epic story on track—the great Helen Rogan. To my my other editors and friends—Katherine Turman, Shawn Macomber, and Julia Borcherts—who all helped me sharpen FIREPROOF into a killer memoir while also keeping me sane. All my love to Tyler Affinito & Zoe Foglia & Megan

Yundt. My mentor and forever brother, Peter Blauner—and the amazing Peg Tyre who introduced me to Helen Rogan, Stephanie Cabral, Joe Matthews and Tim McCall and everyone at IPG, Cevin Bryerman at Publishers Weekly, Trevor Fletcher at Criteria Recording Studios, Kristy Baptist (my dear friend and "Cold Husk") and Anna Kubik at Dead Sky Publishing, Joel McIver, Del James, Charlie Benante, Carla Harvey, Gabino Iglesias, Jennifer Duffy, Michael Muser, Amy Cordell, my dear pal Frankie Nasso, Richard Pine and Inkwell Management, Andrea DeWerd and Amanda Livingston at The Future of Agency, Alexis Adlouni and Jill Cromwell Wang at Cromwell Collective, Greg Morrison and Stefan Clark at MXML Creative, and my family and friends.

A WORD ON FIREPROOF—AND FIRE FOR WRITERS

As all of you readers have made it this far, I wanted to give you a "bonus track" here and share with you how this memoir came to be as I'm often asked how FIREPROOF: Memoir of a Chef started with Curtis Duffy and me ...

Curtis Duffy is one of my best friends ... a true brother, trusted confidant, and family to my wife Kym and me along with his wife Jennifer and all of their kids. We instantly bonded over metal and rock music, biker culture, and more.

The week following my first meeting of Curtis and dining at Grace, I watched the documentary on the making of that restaurant and the tidbits on Curtis's life gave a glimpse into his turbulent childhood and his parents deaths. I was soon fascinated by his life story.

A couple of years later as Curtis and I grew really close, he called me one day and asked if he could meet with me at my Miami Beach house as he wanted to discuss something important. I immediately said, "Yes. Get your ass over here!"

It was on that day Curtis asked me to write his memoir, FIREPROOF: Memoir of a Chef.

Now, I've primarily been a novelist, but I've had my share of non-fiction writing/journalist gigs over the years—and I'm always open to spreading my wings as a writer and will write different things; be it memoirs, scripts, documentary films, bios, etc.

But what remains paramount to me is that I will NOT write anything I'm NOT into. I only write my brand of fiction—which is usually dark AF —and with non-fiction, I only write about people/things that I'm interested in. And these subjects aren't pretty. I have the luxury of writing what I want, I don't write for the money—I do it for the passion for the craft and for what blows my hair back.

Anyway, some years back when Curtis asked me to if I'd write his memoir, I first asked him, "Why me?" and also asked, "Why you wanna do your memoir, bro? You're young! Memoirs should be written when you're older ... like, when you're Keith Richards age."

Well, it was then that Curtis said that he loved my writing (specifically my first two novels) and he only trusted ME to tell his story the right way.

THAT meant more to me than anything right out of the box.

Curtis had said that despite the first documentary film about him and all the various interviews he'd done over the years, no one ever really got his life story right—it was much deeper, darker, sensitive and inspiring than what had been put out there ...

He was right about all of that.

So after Curtis had given me some intimate details no one else publicly knew about his childhood, or his culinary journey, or the bikers and outlaws, the kitchen heroes and the many monsters, the good, the bad, the ugly—and the beautiful—I was totally sold!

I couldn't wait to write FIREPROOF: Memoir of a Chef!

That said, I had told Curtis that if I was going to write his memoir, he had to be BRUTALLY HONEST with me—even if it hurt like a motherfucker—and he had to trust my way of telling his story while keeping his vision and his voice intact.

It's this collaboration that made the magic happen.

I hate boring memoirs that have no grit or candor—and I sure AF wasn't going to write anything that wasn't exciting, compelling, and would hide some brutal truths.

Curtis got it ... he agreed immediately to what I asked of him if I were to partner with him on this incredible journey. We were from then on not just the bestest of friends, we were bonded by a special connection and a pact to deliver an unforgettable, one-of-a-kind memoir the likes of which no one has ever read … that was the mission.

I think I did around 60 hours of audio interviews with Curtis … it was very emotional … we cried a LOT, we also laughed our asses off a LOT during the process—and if you've read it and got this far, you know why.

Once I finished interviewing Curtis, I had all the audio transcribed and turned into a Himalayan mountain of story that I had to sort out. The amazing editor Helen Rogan came along and helped me sort that mountain of material so that I had "the book" in order—and then I took it from there.

Funny thing about the process of FIREPROOF, every time I thought I was done, I wasn't! FIREPROOF starts when Curtis is born in the 70's … but as I was going along and getting to 2021/2022, Curtis suddenly had a new restaurant—EVER—which he opened during COVID-19 … then he opened a burger place, then a cocktail lounge, AFTER … and then something came along that also changed the dynamic of Curtis's story: the TV series, *THE BEAR*.

The hits kept coming and I kept writing …

Curtis and I achieved what we set out to do … we stuck to our guns, kept Curtis's voice and integrity intact, told the truth, kept his world up-to-speed on the page, and we've now given the world Curtis's true-life-story.

Wanna call it a memoir? A chef memoir? Or a hardcore culinary road out of hell? Give it a name or a tag … we sure did, and we call this, "FIREPROOF: Memoir of a Chef." It's ALL those tags and more. This book IS 1000% Curtis Duffy—and he's made of aramid fibers, baby!

I hope you all enjoyed it. And Curtis, thanks again … I love you brother!

Also, a note to aspiring writers:

Throughout this process, Curtis and I had to deal with many non-believers, naysayers, bullies, know-it-alls, and general asshats who tried telling Curtis and me how THEY think we should do a memoir and said we fucked up by not doing things THEIR way—including the few literary agents and acquisition editors who signed us up with great zeal and enthusiasm and promises but ended up wasting our time and ghosting us because we refused to dilute our vision.

I hope that all of you doubters and windbags are reading this and seeing that all of your varying and negative opinions and shitty attitudes meant nothing in the end—and you can all politely fuck off.

Curtis and I never compromised and we preserved our integrity and vision for FIREPROOF: Memoir of a Chef throughout this entire process … we wrote the memoir we wanted to write and succeeded in seeing it through.

That said, I urge ALL writers and creators to NEVER water-down or compromise your work because some self-proclaimed "expert" who doesn't like your style thinks they know what's best for you … and if given the chance, I guarantee they'll turn your book into something that is generic, dishonest, and not acceptable to your voice and vision.

You'll know the type when you see them … they're always negative … and instead of encouraging, they'll make you feel unworthy of their time and take away your fire and your voice.

In my experience, every negative "expert" has their own opinion on what would make your book a success in THEIR voice—and as I've learned, all these "experts" will also say that that any other "experts" who've advised you are ALL wrong—only THEIR individual opinions about your work matters.

It's extremely important to note that there ARE great editors, agents, first readers, and others who you can learn from, so don't take my tone as me being all "anti-publishing-pros" because I'm not at all. Really, my point and perspective is that I'm just "anti-asshole" and have zero tolerance for anyone telling you what you can or can't do with your art.

Be open-minded to "healthy suggestions" on making your work BETTER. Listen to helpful, experienced, and nurturing editors as they're a lot like professional music producers in a recording studio—they're gonna make an album even more amazing with their skills.

When it comes to editors, I've been fortunate to have worked with some of the best: Ed Stackler, Helen Rogan, Shawn Macomber, Katherine Turman, Julia Borcherts, and others. They've taught me so much about the craft, they care, they patiently share their wisdom, I'm always eagerly learning, and they've made my books better.

I'm not a know-it-all writer who dismisses editors. My work is never flawless even after numerous revisions. So when when of these amazing editors I trust tells me to "jump," I ask, "how high?!"

Those are the types of pros you want on your side and they won't take away your voice … they'll actually make your voice louder as you excel at the craft.

Relevant to being open to editorial suggestions, every writer should not be a "know it all" either … you have to take critiques and editorial suggestions on the chin and have a positive attitude—you'll know the best editorial people when they come into your world; constructive editors, developmental editors, copy-editors, and even talented agents.

That said, I urge you to always listen to your heart and trust in yourself … cancel out gatekeepers and all the negative noise and dig your heels in and never settle for anything that trades your principles and voice for someone who wants to take that away … always let YOUR VOICE shine as it should, and NEVER drink the Kool-Aid when someone tells you that your work isn't what THEY think is acceptable.

Write and create what YOU want to write and create … write because you're passionate about the craft and your story—not because you want to appease a polarizing agent or editor … or because you hope for a huge payday. Prove the other know-it-alls wrong when you publish a story or book that is 1000% what YOU intended it to be.

— Jeremy Wagner, March 2025

ABOUT CURTIS DUFFY

World-renowned, James Beard Award-winning, Michelin-starred chef, **Curtis Duffy**, was raised in Ohio. Duffy moved to Chicago to work for legendary chef, Charlie Trotter before becoming *chef de cuisine* at Alinea. As head chef at Avenues, Duffy earned two Michelin stars. Duffy later opened Grace restaurant, earning three Michelin stars four years in a row. Duffy since opened Michelin-starred restaurant, Ever, and After lounge.

Duffy has appeared on *Top Chef*, *Iron Chef*, and his dishes and Ever restaurant have been featured heavily in Hulu's hit series, *The Bear*.

Duffy volunteers for Chicago's Banchet Awards, the Grand Chef's Gala, and sits on the Auguste Escoffier School of Culinary Arts advisory board, where a $25,000 scholarship in his name is awarded.

Duffy lives between Chicago and Miami with his wife, Jennifer Duffy and their children. *Fireproof: Memoir of a Chef* is his first book.

@curtisduffy

www.curtisduffy.com

ABOUT JEREMY WAGNER

Jeremy Wagner is a guitarist, songwriter, and bestselling author. His debut novel *The Armageddon Chord* is the recipient of the Hiram Award and Barnes & Noble Top 10 paperback bestseller. His novel *Rabid Heart* was nominated for a Splatterpunk Award for Best Horror Novel, received an Independent Publisher's IPPY Award for both Best Horror e-Book, and was a Next Generation Book Award finalist for Best Horror Novel.

Wagner released two books in 2025: *Fireproof: Memoir of a Chef* with Chef Curtis Duffy and the dark-crime novel *Wretch*.

Living between Chicago and Miami with his wife Kym, Wagner writes books and screenplays full time and has released several albums with his bands, Broken Hope and Earthburner.

@jeremyxwagner

www.jeremyxwagner.com

THE AUTHORS SUPPORT THE FOLLOWING AGENCIES:

988 Suicide and Crisis Lifeline
Dial **988** on your phone

WINGS Program, Inc.
*Providing housing, integrated services, education and advocacy to end domestic violence.
www.wingsprogram.com

American Foundation for Suicide Prevention
*The American Foundation for Suicide Prevention (AFSP) is a voluntary health organization that gives those affected by suicide a nationwide community empowered by research, education and advocacy to take action against this leading cause of death.
www.afsp.org

The Trevor Project
*The leading suicide prevention organization for lesbian, gay, bisexual, transgender, queer & questioning (LGBTQ) young people).
www.thetrevorproject.org